BRITISH IMPERIAL
AIR POWER

PURDUE STUDIES IN AERONAUTICS AND ASTRONAUTICS

James R. Hansen, Series Editor

Purdue Studies in Aeronautics and Astronautics builds on Purdue's leadership in aeronautic and astronautic engineering, as well as the historic accomplishments of many of its luminary alums. Works in the series will explore cutting-edge topics in aeronautics and astronautics enterprises, tell unique stories from the history of flight and space travel, and contemplate the future of human space exploration and colonization.

(●)

RECENT BOOKS IN THE SERIES

A Reluctant Icon: Letters to Neil Armstrong
by James R. Hansen

John Houbolt: The Unsung Hero of the Apollo Moon Landings
by William F. Causey

Dear Neil Armstrong: Letters to the First Man from All Mankind
by James R. Hansen

Piercing the Horizon: The Story of Visionary NASA Chief Tom Paine
by Sunny Tsiao

Calculated Risk: The Supersonic Life and Times of Gus Grissom
by George Leopold

Spacewalker: My Journey in Space and Faith as NASA's Record-Setting Frequent Flyer
by Jerry L. Ross

BRITISH IMPERIAL AIR POWER

The Royal Air Forces and the Defense
of Australia and New Zealand
Between the World Wars

Alex M Spencer

Purdue University Press
West Lafayette, Indiana

---

*The funding and support of the author by the Smithsonian Institution
made the research and writing of this book possible.*

Copyright 2020 by Smithsonian Institution. All rights reserved.
Printed in the United States of America.

Cataloging-in-Publication data is on file with the Library of Congress.
Paperback ISBN: 978-1-55753-940-3
epub ISBN: 978-1-55753-942-7
epdf ISBN: 978-1-55753-941-0

Cover image: Courtesy of the National Library of New Zealand.

*To my wife, Mary: her love and support was invaluable
and helped sustain me throughout the production of this book*

CONTENTS

INTRODUCTION 1

CHAPTER 1
The First Imperial Air Defense Schemes, 1918–1919 11

CHAPTER 2
The Formation of the Royal Australian Air Force
and the First Reassessments of Pacific Defenses, 1920–1921 37

CHAPTER 3
The Empire's Air Defense: The Geddes Cuts of 1922,
and the 1923 Imperial Conference and Their Influence
on the Empire's Air Defense, 1922–1923 53

CHAPTER 4
The Royal Air Force and Postwar Air Transport
Defense Planning and the Airmail Scheme, 1919–1939 73

CHAPTER 5
Airships and the Empire:
Defense, Schemes, and Disaster, 1919–1930 93

CHAPTER 6
Air Defense and the Labour Party: Singapore Naval Base
and the 1926 Imperial Conference, 1924–1926   117

CHAPTER 7
Imperial Air Mobility, the Salmond Report,
and Air Marshal Trenchard's Last Salvo, 1927–1929   137

CHAPTER 8
Depression and Disarmament, 1929–1933   163

CHAPTER 9
The International Crises and Imperial Rearmament, 1934–1936   183

CHAPTER 10
The Final Preparations, 1937–1940   213

EPILOGUE   241

Notes   255
Bibliography   291
Index   299
About the Author   309

INTRODUCTION

At approximately 10 o'clock on the morning of February 19, 1942, the Imperial Japanese Navy and Army Air Force opened a coordinated attack on Darwin, Australia. More than 188 aircraft launched from four aircraft carriers and fifty-five land-based bombers destroyed shipping and the harbor's transport and military infrastructure. Nearly an hour later, a subsequent raid by Japanese army bombers attacked the Royal Australian Air Force base at Parap, destroying numerous aircraft and base facilities. From February 1942 through November 1943, the Japanese conducted sixty-four more air attacks on Darwin. In addition, the Japanese carried out similar strikes on Townsville, Katherine, Windham, Derby, Broome, and Port Hedland. Even though Australia and New Zealand joined the war in 1939, their respective air forces were ill prepared at the outbreak of war with Japan because the majority of their military assets had been sent to the Middle East in support of British operations.

The study of the development of the air defense of Great Britain's Pacific Dominions demonstrates the difficulty of applying the emerging military aviation technology to the defense of the global British Empire during the interwar years. It also provides insight into the changing nature of the political relationship between the Dominions and Britain within the British imperial structure. At the end of World War I, both Australia and New Zealand secured independent control of their respective armed forces through their sacrifices made on the battlefields in the Middle East and Western Front and declining confidence in British military leadership. Similar to the other nations that participated in the war, the population of these two Dominions in the 1920s developed a strong aversion to war, not wishing to repeat the sacrifices made by their soldiers, sailors, and airmen on someone else's behalf. The economic dislocation experienced by the Dominions, created by the war and the Depression, meant little money was available to fund their respective air forces.[1] As a result, the empire's air services spent the entire interwar period attempting to create a comprehensive strategy in the face of these handicaps.

For many aviation advocates during the interwar period, the airplane represented a panacea to the imperial defense needs. They always prefaced their arguments with the word "potential." The airplane could potentially replace the navy; it could potentially provide substantial savings in defense expenditure; it could potentially move rapidly to threatened regions; and it could potentially defend the coast from attack or invasion. For all of these claims, there was no supporting empirical data. In short, aviation advocates offered the air force as a third option for the empire's defense, in an attempt to replace the Royal Navy and British Army.

At first glance, it is easy to accuse Britain and its Dominions of willful neglect of their armed forces during the interwar years. As early as 1934, however, Britain's military and political leadership understood the threat to peace and stability that Germany, Italy, and Japan represented, but the empire faced a difficult strategic problem in having a military force structure inadequate to defend the vast worldwide imperial possessions and the inability to pay for the needed expansion. The General Staff, to the best of their ability, began to implement the necessary steps required to expand their military forces to meet these threats and particularly directed funds to expand their respective air forces. Although the leadership was much criticized in the postwar period, their diligence paid dividends as early as 1940, when Britain's aircraft industry outpaced German aircraft production, and by 1944, the air forces of the British Empire experienced an expansion well beyond the perceived needs contemplated by the military and political leadership during the interwar period. Many of the policies adopted and implemented by the RAF, RAAF, and RNZAF during the interwar years made this expansion possible.

The Royal Australian Air Force (RAAF) experienced a fourfold increase from seventeen operational squadrons in 1939 to seventy-one in 1944. This included operational squadrons in Britain comprised of four heavy bomber, three medium/attack bomber, seven fighter, and one flying boat squadrons; in the Middle East there were two medium/attack bomber and two fighter squadrons; and in the Pacific the RAAF fielded a force of fifty-five squadrons that included fourteen fighter, fifteen attack/medium bomber, eleven transport and liaison, eight seaplane, and seven heavy bomber squadrons.[2] In addition, more than 4,000 Australian pilots, air crew members, and mechanics served in Royal Air Force (RAF) units throughout the war.

Likewise, the smaller Royal New Zealand Air Force (RNZAF) sustained a similar expansion from four prewar squadrons to thirty-three squadrons by 1944. By the end of the war, New Zealand had based eight squadrons overseas, including seven in Britain, consisting of two fighter, three attack/medium bomber, one heavy bomber, and one flying boat squadrons, as well as one fighter squadron stationed in West Africa. Twenty-six RNZAF squadrons served in the Pacific theater and included thirteen fighter, six attack/medium bomber, two flying boat, two torpedo, two liaison/transport, and one dive-bomber squadrons that complemented American Army Air Forces, marine, and navy units throughout the entire Solomon Islands campaign.[3] In addition, New Zealand provided more than 10,363 trained personnel for service in the Royal Air Force.[4]

The raids on Darwin and the dramatic expansion of the Pacific Dominions' air forces reflect the strategic decisions made during the interwar period concerning those nations' aerial defense. With the advantage of hindsight, the Japanese air attacks on Australia confirmed the judgment of the British chiefs of the Imperial General Staff that the greatest threat to the continent would be raids and that Japan's air power was incapable of a knockout blow. In addition, the chiefs' views were confirmed when the Japanese decided not to invade Australia in early 1942.[5]

By the beginning of the World War II, there were essentially two Australian and New Zealand air forces that emerged from the interwar period. One consisted of the units and personnel that served in Britain as part of the Royal Air Force and that fulfilled the Dominions' imperial commitments and prewar strategic assumptions. These units were trained, equipped, patterned after, and served alongside other RAF units. These Australian and New Zealand air force units represented the most significant contribution of men and materiel by the two Dominions in Western Europe during the war. Following the North African campaign, no Australian ground unit fought in Europe and only one New Zealand division served in the Italian campaign.

Australia and New Zealand's second air force were those RAAF and RNZAF units serving in the Pacific. These units represented the majority of the Dominions' air power and the changing nature of their relationship with Britain. Both nations developed and kept a high percentage of their units in the Pacific for self-defense rather than providing them for the greater "imperial" need. Moreover, the makeup of these units totally disregarded the prewar assumption of imperial uniformity. The RAAF units were an eclectic mix of British, Australian-built British and American designs, and American aircraft. In the case of New Zealand by the end of the war, all of its twenty-six squadrons were equipped exclusively with American aircraft. The rapid expansion of both air forces would not have been possible without the aircraft provided by the United States. The war underscored the Dominions' transition from the British to the American sphere of influence.

During the interwar period the Royal Air Force had to fight to maintain its independence. Likewise, the RAAF and RNZAF, because of political, economic, and technological circumstances, were largely "paper" air forces. In their effort to maintain their very existence, these imperial air forces presented themselves as a viable and economical third option in the defense of Britain's global empire.

The inspiration of this work comes out of my interest in the Royal Navy during the interwar period. The terrible loss of HMS *Prince of Wales* and *Repulse* to waves of Japanese torpedo bombers on December 10, 1941, and the surrender of 84,000 British and Commonwealth troops brought on many books about the failed "Fleet to Singapore" strategy conceived by Fleet Admiral John Jellicoe in 1919. The plan called for the construction of a major naval facility located at Singapore to service and house the bulk of the Royal Navy if a crisis developed in the Pacific against the Japanese. Ian McGibbon's *Bluewater Rationale* and Ian Hamill's *The Strategic Illusion*, major works, both illustrate the importance of Singapore serving as a defensive hub to protect Britain's eastern empire, particularly Australia and New Zealand. The Royal Air Force, equipped with inadequate aircraft that were few in number, tended to receive less treatment by historians. This changed in recent times with the publication of Christopher Shores and Brian Cull's thorough volume, *Bloody Shambles: The Drift to War to the Fall of Singapore*, and Graham Clayton's more focused study, *Last Stand in Singapore: The Story of 488 Squadron RNZAF*. One aspect of historical research on the RAF in the fall of Singapore points blame for the collapse at Air Marshal Sir Robert Brooke-Popham, Commander-in-Chief Far East. Appointed to the position in October 1941, he was on the job for less than four months before war broke out in the Pacific. Brooke-Popham's role is only recently receiving a reevaluation in Peter Dye's *The Man Who Took the Rap: Sir Robert Brooke-Popham and the Fall of Singapore*. After reading these studies and others, I began to wonder if the RAF was making similar efforts concerning the defense of the Pacific empire. The answer was yes in an almost forgotten survey by Group Captain Arthur Bettington. Like Jellicoe, Bettington toured the Pacific Dominions in the immediate post–World War I period and made recommendations concerning the future of aerial defenses of the Dominions. So I became more interested in the Royal Air Force during the interwar period and wanted to trace its defense planning for the empire.

The vast majority of works on the RAF of the interwar period tend to emphasize British strategic bombing doctrine as conceived by Air Marshal Sir Hugh Trenchard. They trace a direct path to the massive formations of Halifax and Lancaster heavy bombers that laid waste to German cities. Four of the earliest works are Hilary St. George Saunders's *Per Ardua: The Rise of British Air Power, 1911–1939*; H. Montgomery Hyde's *British Air Policy between the Wars, 1919–1939*; Neville Jones's *The Beginnings of Strategic Air Power: A History of the British Bomber Force, 1923–1939*; and Barry Powers's *Strategy without Slide-Rule: British Air Strategy, 1914–1939*. In more recent times are Malcom Smith's *British Air Strategy between the Wars, 1919–1939* and Tami Davis Biddle's *Rhetoric and Reality in Air Warfare: The Evolution of British and American Ideas about Strategic Bombing, 1914–1945*. All of these histories focus on the role that the RAF would play in European air space and do not address the position the RAF was attempting to forge in imperial defense. If strategic bombing was a keystone to RAF planning during the interwar period, why did Bomber Command have such horrible aircraft at the beginning of World War II? The bomber force would not see its first four-engine heavy bomber in the Short Stirling until the summer of 1940 at the height of the Battle of Britain. During the interwar period the RAF attempted to establish itself as a coequal in imperial defense beside the Royal Navy and British Army. Yes, Trenchard wrote about the need for a strategic bombing force, a duty in war unique to the RAF and a way to justify its continued independence. Trenchard was also a political realist and looked for any activity during the interwar period to keep the force autonomous from the army and navy. This has brought a number of interesting studies that examine the use of the RAF in the role of colonial control and policing. The most noted of these works include David Omissi's *Airpower and Colonial Control: The Royal Air Force 1919–1939* and Barry Renfrew's *Wings of Empire: The Forgotten Wars of the Royal Air Force, 1919–1939*.

To discover how air power developed in the Pacific, one must turn to historians from Australia and New Zealand for the answer. The opening chapters of the two official histories of the RAAF and RNZAF in World War II in Douglas Gillison's *Australia in the War of 1939–1945, Series 3, Air, vol. I, Royal Australian Air Force, 1939–1942* and Sqd. Ldr. J. M. S. Ross's *New Zealand in the Second World War 1939–1945: The Royal New Zealand* outline the activities of the origins, founding, and interwar activities of their respective Dominion's air forces. C. D. Coulthard-Clark's *The Third Brother: The Royal Australian Air Force 1921–1939* is an excellent and comprehensive study of the RAAF between the wars. John McCarthy's *Australia and Imperial Defense: A Study in Air and Sea Power, 1918–1939* and W. David McIntyre's *New Zealand Prepares for War: Defence Policy, 1919–39* are both wide-ranging examinations of the defense policies of Australia and New Zealand and both demonstrate the importance of these forces in the defense of their region of the Pacific.

Now that a full century has passed since the end of World War I, this work, *British Imperial Air Power: The Royal Air Forces and the Defense of Australia and New Zealand Between the World Wars*, hopes to provide a fresh and comprehensive examination of the role that air power would play in the Pacific.

I alone am responsible for this manuscript but no work is the sole product of its author. During the course of its research and writing, I relied on numerous individuals for assistance and it could not be completed without them. The author thanks those most responsible in support of this work. The following chairs of the Aeronautics Division at the Smithsonian Institution's National Air and Space Museum, Tom Crouch, Dominick Pisano, Peter L. Jakab, F. Robert van der Linden, Russell Lee, and Jeremy Kinney for providing the time, financial assistance, and opportunity to conduct research at various archives throughout the world. To Nicholas Partridge who helped shepherd the book's contract to completion with Purdue University Press. Without their support, this work would not have been possible. I would particularly like to thank F. Robert van der Linden who read numerous drafts and was always a sounding board for my thoughts as I developed the chapters of my book. To Dr. Hines Hall at Auburn University whose help and guidance was critical to my academic career.

The author also thanks the professional archival and library staffs from those in the front line managing the reference desk to the individuals deep in the stacks pulling records at the National Air and Space Museum, Smithsonian Institution; the National Archives, Kew; the National Archives of Australia at Canberra and Melbourne; and the Archives of New Zealand, Wellington; without them the historian's task is impossible. I wish that I could name all of you individually in recognition of the truly valuable work that you do. In addition, I would like to thank the staff members from the following museums: the Australian War Memorial, the Royal Air Force Museum, the Royal Australian and Royal New Zealand Air Force Museums, the Yamato Museum, the National Portrait Gallery, London, and the National Library of New Zealand who provided all of the illustrations for this work.

In addition, Dr. Ron Wilkerson who was the first teacher to encourage my interest in history and whose enthusiasm for history was inspiring; and the unselfish guidance of Dr. Brian Farrell of the National University of Singapore who helped me unlock the files during my very first research trip to the National Archives at Kew.

I would also like to thank my family, my sister Cynthia, and my brother Todd for their support and encouragement that kept me grounded during the course of my studies. My ultimate thanks go to my father, Stephen, and mother, Hildegard, whose love, support, and guidance sustain my every endeavor.

CHAPTER 1

THE FIRST IMPERIAL AIR DEFENSE SCHEMES, 1918–1919

> *It will be appreciated that the complexity of the problem is increased by the fact that in the case of the Royal Air Force there is no pre-war experience to which reference can be made.*[1]
> —Lord William Douglas Weir

At the end of World War I, Britain's leaders had to reconsider the traditional pillars of imperial foreign policy: a balance of power on the European continent, free and clear trade routes to imperial possessions and the Dominions, and superiority of the Royal Navy on the seas. Germany's defeat, along with the revolution in Russia, created a power vacuum in Europe. Decimated by four years of war, the European powers could not fill this void, though some tried. The rising influence of the United States and imperial Japan tipped the balance of power away from Britain in the Pacific, although Britain may well have lost its influence before the war in its efforts to counter the growing threat of the Imperial German Fleet in European waters.

To add to the British circumstances, Britain's global territorial responsibilities actually expanded in the war's aftermath. By the end of 1918, a military expedition to assist the White Russians against the Bolsheviks, control of new Middle Eastern mandates, and the suppression of nationalist movements throughout the empire placed additional military burdens on Britain. Labor unrest, mutinies, and the Irish uprising further complicated Britain's postwar military circumstances at home. Winston Churchill summed up the situation when he stated, "I cannot too strongly press on the Government the danger, the extreme danger, of His Majesty's Army being spread all over the world, strong nowhere and weak everywhere."[2] The huge national debt, created by the war, limited many military options that had been available in the past. Chief of the Air Staff Sir Hugh Trenchard echoed Churchill's warnings from the air force's perspective:

> The necessity for economy remains unchanged, but the peaceful conditions hoped for have been far from realized. So great a portion of the world has been pervaded by the spirit of unrest, and so largely have the commitments of the Empire been increased by the results of the war . . . [3]

The Dominions further compounded Britain's foreign and military policy difficulties. During the war, the Dominions' prime ministers demanded and were promised inclusion in policy decisions that potentially affected their respective states. At the same time, Australia and New Zealand pursued courses of action that ran counter to traditional British interests, such as claiming mandate responsibility over regional Pacific islands that were of no interest in London. This placed the British Empire in direct competition with Japan. While the Dominions demanded greater independence with regard to their emerging foreign policies, they insisted that Great Britain remain committed to their defense.

With Germany defeated and Russia enmeshed in civil war, British leaders found a new threat to the empire: Britain's Pacific ally, Japan. The Anglo-Japanese Naval Alliance, signed in January 1902, allowed the Royal Navy to remain concentrated in European waters to counter the growth of the Imperial German Navy. In addition, the agreement helped to defend against any threat to British and Japanese interests in the Pacific from Russian expansion. During the war, the agreement proved its value when Japanese warships provided escorts to the troopships filled with Australians and New Zealanders on their way to the Middle Eastern and Western fronts and even suffered some losses in the Mediterranean. However, in the postwar environment, could the agreement remain intact? Many thought not.

In assessing the postwar world, Trenchard remarked about the Japanese:

> It is not improbable after the storm in Europe, the centre of pressure of unrest will move eastwards and that the future will find it located in China and Japan. There would appear, therefore, to be grounds for an increase of our naval strength in the Pacific and pari passu for the building up of a suitable air force.
>
> These considerations have already been weighted in Australia and New Zealand, and both dominions have intimated their desire for air services.[4]

Australian prime minister William "Billy" Hughes did not help Britain's relationship with Japan. While making his way to Europe in June 1918, he made a speech in New York City in which he proposed a new vision for the future of Pacific security:

> In order to ensure the existence of Australia as a commonwealth of federal states of free people, the Australians must be

provided with a strong guarantee against invasion, and such a guarantee might be found in an Australian Monroe doctrine in the South Pacific.

To ensure the safety of Australian territory, it is important that control over the islands on the eastern and northern coasts of Australia should either be taken over by Australia herself, or entrusted to some brave and civilized State. It is the United States to which the Australians look for assistance in the matter.[5]

Hughes's comments were as unpopular in Britain as they were in Japan. For the first time Australians looked to a power other than Britain for their security. Hughes imagined an American Pacific Monroe Doctrine backed up by American naval and military power or at the very least the creation of a "hands off the Australian Pacific" policy. This position staked out by Hughes in New York continued to be his steadfast posture at the Versailles Peace Conference. During the war, Australia and Japan expanded their spheres of influence in the Pacific. The Australians, who felt threatened by the German presence in New Guinea, took control of the island early in the war. In addition, a joint Australian and New Zealand force captured Samoa. Meanwhile, the Japanese, taking advantage of the German weakness, moved south and occupied the Marshall and Caroline island groups.

These actions disrupted the peace discussions at Versailles in January 1919. When Prime Minister Hughes arrived in Paris, he fully intended to maintain Australian sovereignty over New Guinea. He believed that all of the northern islands were essential for Australian security. Hughes's claims to the islands and "Pacific Monroe Doctrine" directly clashed with President Wilson's "just peace" based on his Fourteen Points and position that no nation should benefit from victory. Concerning Australian claims in the Pacific, Hughes's reaction was recorded in the minutes of the Imperial War Cabinet meeting that took place on December 30,

1918. Hughes opposed Wilson's position of independence for the former German colonies and argued that Wilson did not understand how essential these islands were for Australia's own security.[6]

In January 1919, the meetings at Versailles addressed the topic of Germany's Pacific colonies. At a meeting of the Council of Ten, Hughes stated his uncompromising position:

> Strategically the Pacific Islands encompass Australia like a fortress . . . this is a string of islands suitable for coaling and submarine bases, from which Australia could be attacked. If there were at the very door of Australia a potential or actual enemy, Australia could not feel safe. The islands are as necessary to Australia as water to a city. If they were in the hands of a superior, there would be no peace for Australia.[7]

Hughes's concerns did not impress President Wilson who believed that the old notions of national security would not be applicable in the postwar world and that Hughes's position was "based on a fundamental lack of faith in the League of Nations."[8] On this point, Hughes agreed with President Wilson, for Hughes placed little faith in the league's ability to control "bad neighbors."[9] Because of Wilson's position, Hughes likely viewed the U.S. support in Pacific security as unreliable and returned to the position that Australian security was still best served within the British imperial system.

The stance taken by Hughes at Versailles placed British prime minister David Lloyd George in a difficult position between attempting to sustain imperial unity by supporting Australian territorial claims and at the same time maintaining a constructive relationship with Wilson. South African prime minister Ian Smuts proposed a compromise. Smuts designed the mandate system, which placed the former German colonies into three categories based on their social and economic development and geographical location. The Smuts compromise became Article 22 of the League of Nations Compact. Under a Class "C" mandate classification, the administration of New Guinea became Australia's responsibility:

> Owing to the sparseness of their population, their small size, or their remoteness from centers of civilisation, or their geographical continuity to the territory of the Mandatory, and other circumstances, can best be administered under the laws of the Mandatory as an integral portion of its territory.[10]

The only power remaining in the Pacific that threatened peace, from the Dominions' perspective, was Japan. Whereas Australia and New Zealand considered their own actions as defensive, they viewed Japanese annexation of the Marshall and Caroline Islands as aggressive expansionism. New Zealand's defense minister, Sir James Allen, believed that the British Empire would "regret" letting the Japanese remain in control of the two island groups.[11]

In a cable, Monroe Furguson, governor general of Australia, also expressed concerns that Japanese expansionism was a threat to the newly formed League of Nations and the agreements made at Versailles. In Furguson's opinion, the Japanese expansion into the central Pacific was challenging decisions made at Versailles because "she is a powerful nation having at her disposal great military resources [and] cannot be allowed to flout the solemn decision of the Conference."[12]

With the emerging diplomatic tension between the British and Japanese empires exacerbated by Australia's political leadership, Britain's military began to evaluate how to defend the Pacific. Early in 1919, former First Sea Lord Admiral John Jellicoe left on an imperial cruise with instructions to determine the naval defense of the empire. At the same time, the leadership of the Royal Air Force began to examine their service's future role in peacetime defense of the empire. The process of the transition to peacetime operations would be more difficult for the Royal Air Force compared to the army or navy. Created during the war by combining the Royal Flying Corps and Royal Naval Air Service, the RAF had no peacetime tradition such as providing security in some remote outpost of the empire or showing the flag during a diplomatic cruise. The new service faced a hostile army and navy wanting to break apart the RAF and reclaim their respective air branches that were taken from them during the war. The air force's leadership looked to the emerging antagonism with the Japanese as a basis to formulate its future responsibilities in defense of the empire.

The president of the Air Council, Lord Weir, asserted in December 1918 that the Royal Air Force would take an important part in imperial defense. Weir argued that aviation had proved its value during the war but its future potential was unclear because the current state of aircraft development was still in its "infancy." For Weir, air power in time would become an equal partner in imperial defense alongside the army and the navy, and "it will be necessary to provide an Air Force of such strength as will amply meet the needs of the Empire."[13]

Less than a month following the signing of the Armistice on November 11, 1918, Trenchard, newly appointed chief of the Air Staff, issued a memorandum outlining the RAF's vision of postwar defense:

> The Imperial aspects of the question [of air defense] cannot be overrated and must be considered equally with those pertaining to purely national requirements; the foundations of the air power of the British Empire must be well and truly laid.[14]

From the scale and scope of the memorandum, it appears that the Air Staff was clearly working on the imperial air defense issues well before the war's end. Trenchard's memorandum delineated how the

RAF would participate in and potentially come to dominate the defense responsibilities for the empire. The Air Staff examined how to utilize the air force in small and large conflicts while maintaining its independence from the navy and army. It outlined specific force structures and dispositions throughout the empire and argued that the Dominions' air services would need to play a direct and vital role in the future air defense of the empire.

The flying distances were truly daunting, especially for the limited capabilities of the aircraft of the day. Trenchard recognized that the state of aviation technology limited the effectiveness of air power and force projection, "owing to the comparatively short radius of action of contemporary aircraft."[15] The Air Ministry plotted a route from London to Australia that required 59 stops—one every 200 miles—and covered the 11,500 miles to Darwin. Nevertheless, this did not deter Trenchard's belief in the future potential of air power: "we possess a rapid and economical instrument by which to ensure peace and good government in our outer Empire."[16]

A vital element of the overall air defense of the empire from the perspective of the Royal Air Force was the participation of each of the Dominions in any scheme that would emerge in the postwar period. Trenchard wrote that both Pacific Dominions were interested in establishing air forces as a part of their own security against a threat from Japan.[17]

The Air Ministry also felt that the Dominions' air forces would need to have aircraft and training similar to the RAF. This would allow the two forces, even though separated by vast geographic distances, easily to mesh at any crisis spot.

Lord Weir in a memorandum to the War Cabinet emphasized the point that imperial defense would become ever more dependent upon Dominion participation, and he felt that in the future the airplane would be a critical element in that defense. Trenchard also believed that the RAF could not move forward in any imperial air defense scheme until the Dominions made some decision about the size and form of their own air forces.[18] Trenchard's position regarding Dominion participation was different from the commanders of the Royal Navy. He looked upon the Dominions as full partners in aerial defense rather than providing adjunct forces:

> The Dominions should be approached with a view to assistance in reconstituting the air staff into an Imperial Air Staff on the lines of the Imperial General Staff.
>
> While it is not desired in any way to accentuate Eastern political complexities, the pressure of unrest in this sphere must be faced. In the past the fears of Australia resulted in the formation of the nucleus of the Australian Navy, and Australia has already inaugurated her own Air Service which her distance from the Mother Country renders all important.[19]

Trenchard envisioned an Imperial Air Force with all the imperial members acting in unison. Such an agreement with the Dominions could extend the empire's air defense capabilities while limiting the financial burden for Britain and the Royal Air Force. Trenchard argued that:

> Too much stress cannot be laid on the importance of unity and the necessity for organising these aerial resources on similar lines . . . both sides must make every effort to strengthen until a state of perfect and efficient cooperation exists between the various components of the British Empire.
>
> The first essential is that methods of training and organisation and types of machines and equipment should be standardised. Each Dominion would require a Central School at which flying, navigation, aerial gunnery and bomb dropping, cooperation with land and sea forces, meteorology and

photography would be taught on similar lines. As types of machines improve replacements should be made on a proportionate scale, and interchange of personnel should take place so that training and operation methods, improvements due to innovation, etc., may be co-ordinated throughout the whole of the Imperial Air Force. Thus, if necessity arises, reinforcements can be transferred from one quarter of the globe to another, and on arrival at their destination will fit automatically into their appointed places and carry out their appointed duties.[20]

The need for imperial unity was a consistent theme from the leaders within the Air Ministry. Once again, Frederick Sykes, assistant air minister, emphasized this point in a speech before a luncheon of the London Chamber of Commerce. Sykes believed that "air forces have become and will remain a leading consideration in questions of national and Imperial defence. The day is indeed not far distant when aircraft will rank equally . . . with other and older forms of war material."[21]

The Air Ministry wasted no time contacting the Australians about the extent of their participation in an Imperial Air Force. On January 14, 1919, Major Clive L. Baillieu, the Air Ministry's Australian liaison officer, wrote to Australian Imperial Force Headquarters and requested that Australia provide information or plans regarding the air force strength relating to naval and army needs, personnel numbers and training methods, equipment needs, standardization of training and equipment, and commercial aviation plans in order to provide a reserve of pilots and mechanics.[22]

The concept of imperial aviation unity was not new. The origins of Australian military aviation dated back to 1915 when the Commonwealth government formed the Australian Flying Corps to cooperate with imperial troops operating in the Middle East. By the end of the war, they had a force of more than 280 pilots and 3,000 support personnel. In the postwar world, the Australian government saw the value of an aerial striking force and continued funding of an air force.

Australian leaders did not question the need to participate in the empire's defense, but they did question the scale and scope of their participation and continually reassessed the degree of support they could provide. There was going to be an Australian Air Service as a component of imperial defense. The debates surrounding the role and formation of an Australian Air Force were similar to those of the Royal Air Force's role taking place in Britain.

Because the strategic need to attack an enemy's industrial and communication capacity by air did not exist in the South Pacific, the Australian air power advocates were in a much weaker position relative to the Australian Army and Royal Australian Navy. The air service would be required to act in a subordinate role to the other services. Their aircraft would operate tactically, providing air cover for ground or naval forces on the defensive and striking enemy shipping or ground troops on the offensive.

Before the British asked the question regarding Australian involvement in air defense, the Australians were considering their capability and the strength of their air arm. In a meeting of the Australian Council of Defence in early November 1918, the central discussion on the agenda was the future form of an Australian Air Service. The chief of the Australian General Staff, Major General John G. Legge, "thought that there would be less extravagance if Australia had a[n] [air] branch under the control of the Navy and Military."[23] In the immediate postwar period, the question of controlling Australia's air forces remained the central debate in the Council of Defence:

> The provision of a nucleus of an Air Force [needed] to meet certain fundamental needs of the Navy and the Army. This can be done for an annual expenditure of £1,100,000.

The Air Force recommended is auxiliary to the Navy and the Army and is not an independent Force. It provides merely for the minimum needs of existing defence services. Bearing in mind the economic condition of the country and the fact that time is pressing, the Council considers that the provision of these minimum needs should be undertaken first but, consistent with this provision, the development of aviation should proceed—for instance by the encouragement of commercial aviation.

In the opinion of the Council, this minimum expenditure will give Australia a "sporting chance" of holding out till British command of the Pacific can be established. With any less expenditure there would be no chance to security to Australia in the event of War [with Japan].[24]

During these formative months following the war, the members of the Council of Defence agreed that it was important that Australia have significant air forces but they would not accept the creation of a separate air force for the Commonwealth. For Australia's military leadership the principal defense of the Dominion was still dependent upon the army and the navy. Because there was no strategic justification for a separate air force, aircraft would have an important role to play but would remain subordinate or auxiliary to the ground and sea forces. In addition, Australia's leadership was not confident that air power alone could "assure" the national defense.[25]

Australia's navy and army leaders decided to split the Dominion's air assets between the two services and share training facilities. They felt that the army would ultimately require seven fighter squadrons, six reconnaissance squadrons, and two heavy bomber squadrons. The navy would need one torpedo squadron, one shipborne aircraft squadron, and eleven flying boat squadrons.[26] These twenty-eight squadrons, they predicted, would be the minimum requirement to give Australia a "sporting chance." Ultimately, these squadrons were viewed only as air auxiliaries to the naval and military forces.

In the postwar economic environment, the proposed annual expenditure of £1,100,000 was an extravagant if not absurd amount for the Australians. Economic realities would soon force them to halve this amount of money for an air force. It was reported in April 1919 that

> A scheme of aerial defence, which has been drafted by the Commonwealth Government, contemplates the establishment of various aviation schools with squadrons of Aeroplanes and seaplanes, together with an airship section, the personnel of the scheme numbering 1,400. There will be an initial expenditure of £500,000, and an annual expenditure of the same amount.[27]

Undeterred by the reduction of the military funding, the Council of Defence created a uniquely Australian solution to the problem. They envisioned the creation of a dual force consisting of a permanent air force and an aviation militia or the "Citizen Air Force."

> It is proposed to establish both permanent and Citizen Force Units. Permanent units will be required for Naval centres, for isolated squadrons, and for training squadrons. It is proposed that 2 Reconnoitering Squadrons, 1 Flying-boat Squadron, to be formed next year will be on the Citizen Force basis. The difficulty of a Citizen Force, in the future, will be the time required for continuous training for a pilot which takes about one year.
>
> Air Units will be organised as part of an Australian Air Corps. This Corps will be formed in two wings, one for the Navy and one for the Army. The Corps will be controlled

separately from the Navy or Army by the Minister of Defence. An Air Council composed of sailors and soldiers detailed from the Naval and Military Boards will advise upon principle; the administrative control of the Air Corps will be in the hands of an Air Board, subordinate to the Air Council, and composed of flying officers.[28]

The value of the Citizen Air Force would be continually examined throughout the interwar period. The formation of the Volunteer Reserve in Britain originated from this Australian idea.

Britain's military leadership did not forget New Zealand. They recognized that this Dominion's fate was closely linked to that of Australia. In 1919, Trenchard stated:

> The possibility of unrest in the East affects New Zealand equally with Australia. The length of her coast line makes her peculiarly vulnerable to attack and her distance from the Mother Country makes it necessary for her to be able to hold her own until the arrival of available reinforcements.[29]

Early in 1919, New Zealand's defense minister, Sir James Allen, requested that the Royal Air Force send an adviser to New Zealand to provide recommendations for the Dominion's postwar air defense and aviation policy. The RAF sent Group Captain Arthur Vere Bettington to assess New Zealand's state of affairs. Bettington issued a lengthy report to Allen in July that echoed many of the positions in Trenchard's memoranda on "Air Power Requirements of Empire." But like many of these early postwar planning documents, Bettington's recommendations were not realistic and went far beyond the scale and scope that New Zealand's political leaders or budgets were prepared to handle.

Figure 1.1. Lt. Col. Arthur Bettington (right) with New Zealand aviation pioneer Sir Henry Wigram (left) at the Sockburn Aerodrome, New Zealand in 1919. Following World War I, Bettington toured Australia and New Zealand to determine the two Dominions' aerial defense requirements. His subsequent report and recommendations laid the foundation of imperial interwar aerial defense strategy. (Photograph courtesy of Air Force Museum of New Zealand)

With the war over in Europe, Bettington argued that international instability would continue because of the vacuum left in Europe by the defeat of the Central Powers. Bettington reiterated Trenchard's position that Japan might threaten peace in the Pacific:

> It is impossible to reconcile the aspirations of all the nations. Signs of this are already visible with certain Eastern nations who have openly claimed equal rights. The Japanese may be persistent in its demands for equality . . . for this reason, also as a result of the elimination in the near future of the Central

European Empires as warlike groups, the centre of unrest in the world may now be assumed to have moved from Western Europe to the Pacific.[30]

Bettington warned that the potential antagonism between the British Empire and Japan would place New Zealand in the middle of any conflict between the two imperial powers. No longer could they enjoy the protection afforded by vast distance from the traditional sources of conflict in Europe:

> While it is not desired to appear unduly pessimistic or to pose as a scaremonger, the Eastern political complexities and unrest should be squarely faced. The geographical position of this Dominion renders an efficient defence force a greater necessity than in the past. . . . The distance from the Mother Country is so great that considerable time must elapse before assistance could be expected from that quarter. The nearest point from which help might arrive is over 1200 miles away and even then it is by no means unlikely that Australia might find herself threatened at the same time and not in a position to give aid.[31]

Bettington repeated the common theme among the air power advocates that an air force would be an important third option for imperial defense alongside the Royal Navy and British Army. Bettington summarized this point:

> Highly trained Air Forces are now essential components of all efficient defensive and fighting forces, as aviation provides a new and distinct striking force of temendous [sic] potentiality. . . . A Nation thinking in three dimensions will lead and defeat a nation thinking in two, both in time of peace and war.[32]

Bettington underscored Trenchard's proposal that New Zealand should participate in the Imperial Air Force. In addition, there was an important connection between civil and military aviation if New Zealand were to participate in imperial affairs. Bettington also stressed that New Zealand's air force should be prepared to render assistance to any part of the empire.

So that New Zealand's aerial policy became a reality, Bettington strongly recommended that the Dominion should take immediate steps to build an air force compatible with that of the British and Australian air forces by standardizing their training, equipment, and procedures.[33]

New Zealand's meager industrial capacity made the Dominion dependent upon Britain for its aviation equipment and infrastructure. New Zealand would need to purchase all of this material from Britain to maintain compatibility with its imperial partners, Bettington reported:

> It may be assumed that for some years to come at least, New Zealand will not be in a position to manufacture anything more than the actual aeroplane or seaplane and will have to rely on imported engines, guns, bombs, wireless sets, navigational and other aircraft instruments, etc. As the close co-ordination of aircraft equipment of the British Empire is of such vital importance, it is proposed that in the first instance the complete machines and engines with all their component parts and armament be purchased in England, in consultation with the Air Ministry, due regard being given to the standardisation, as far as practicable, with the policy of Australia and the rest of the Empire.[34]

In retrospect, Bettington's proposal for New Zealand's aerial force structure seems modest—seeking seven squadrons that included one fighter, one day and night bombing, one scout, one torpedo, and two flying boat squadrons, two air bases, and one training depot.[35] Bettington argued that this force structure was the minimum required to defend the strategic points on New Zealand's North and South Islands.[36*]

Reasonable as the proposals seemed, New Zealand's leaders were not prepared to adopt Bettington's scheme. Following a review of the plan by New Zealand's cabinet, Minister of Defence Allen informed him that it was "impracticable" for the Dominion to spend the funds called for to implement the civil and military aviation scheme that he outlined.[37]

In response to Allen's admission that New Zealand could not afford extensive aerial expenditures, Bettington sent him a number of suggestions that further limited these defense burdens. He proposed to Allen a reduction in his recommendation by three or four squadrons, hoping that this proposition might address the fiscal concerns of the cabinet. Once again, he received a negative reply.

By the end of August 1919, Bettington counseled New Zealand's cabinet that the Dominion still needed to participate in the imperial partnership. He asked that the cabinet consider appointing an air liaison officer to track developments in commercial and military aviation and establish or subsidize an aviation school on the North Island near Auckland and on the South Island near Christchurch. Finally, he recommended that veteran New Zealanders with aviation training should be kept on a reserve list and trained annually on the latest developments.[38]

---

*Beddington considered the following as the "chief nerve" centers and the most likely to be attacked:
    a. Wellington and the Cook Strait
    b. Auckland
    c. Christchurch and Lyttelton
    d. The northernmost part of New Zealand including Awanui
    e. Invercargill and Awarua
    f. The coal fields of Westport and Graymouth
    g. Dunedin and Port Chalmers
To defend these strategic points, he proposed New Zealand establish first-class air bases at Wellington, Auckland, Christchurch, and Dunedin.

For Bettington, these three steps were the minimum actions that New Zealand could take to maintain a credible aerial presence.

To this end, New Zealand's government agreed. To create a reserve of aviators and aviation mechanics, the government devised a scheme to provide financial subsidies to the Sockburn and Kohimarama flying schools. During the war, both schools had provided preliminary training for New Zealanders who later served in the Royal Air Force. It became these two schools' responsibility to train an active reserve of 200 pilots, to provide periodic flight training and lectures, and to train a cadre of aircraft mechanics. In the end, New Zealand's government was only prepared to spend £25,000 annually on any form of aviation, civil or military.[39]

Early in 1919, while the Australians and New Zealanders considered their own air defense plans, aerial strategists in London devised an idea that they hoped would address the fiscal concerns of the Dominions relating to the creation of their aerial defense and striking force and ensure that they would begin working toward the unified Imperial Air Force: British leaders initiated the transfer or gift of 100 surplus aircraft to each Dominion. The origin of the aircraft gift was Trenchard's idea. Under-Secretary of State for Air Gen. John Edward Bernard Seely took the idea to the Imperial War Cabinet. For Seely, a gift of aircraft to the Dominions provided "an opportunity of giving assistance to Dominions which will be valued by them and which should be of great use in the general interest of the defence of the Empire by Air."[40]

On May 29, 1919, the War Cabinet approved Seely's proposal and decided to offer each Dominion government 100 surplus aircraft out of the thousands of serviceable aircraft left over at the end of the war. The War Cabinet decided that this gift would be available to any Dominion or colonial government that required aircraft and that as much publicity as possible should be generated on behalf of the government.[41]

On June 4, 1919, cables went out to the Dominions and Colonies informing their respective cabinets that the Air Ministry was proposing to send each of them aircraft to become the core of their respective air forces. The gift of aircraft to the Dominions was well timed. Without monetary resources or established aircraft facilities and with limited military equipment at home, the transfer of aircraft would allow the Dominions to form the nucleus of their own air arms.

The Australians were most eager to obtain the aircraft offered by Britain. On June 21, 1919, Brig. Gen. Thomas A. Blamey submitted the initial request for four squadrons to "form the nucleus of the Australian Air Force."[42] The British Air Staff recommended that this Australian force should consist of twenty-four Sopwith Snipes, twenty-four Bristol Fighters, eighteen de Havilland D.H. 9s, and ten Vickers Vimy bombers, one of the larger aircraft in the Royal Air Force's inventory. For the Australians, the gift amounted to more than £624,000.[43] In addition, the British Air Staff made additional suggestions regarding the importance of the Australians operating similar equipment as the British.

On July 9, 1919, in a letter from Lt. Col. H. Macquire, the RAF's liaison officer to the Australian government, to Australian defense minister Sir George Pearce, Macquire made additional suggestions regarding equipment to be sent to Australia:

> With reference to the proposed gift of 100 Aeroplanes by H.M. Government and the equipment of 4 Squadrons of the Australian Air Force, I forward the following proposals.
>
> That the following types and numbers of machines should be asked for:
>
> 35 AVROS. Training
>
> 30 S.E. 5 Viper engines in lieu of Snipes asked for.
>
> 35 D.H.9a, in lieu of Squadron D.H.9a with Rolls engines asked for.[44]

Figure 1.2. Royal Aircraft Factory S.E.5a #A2-1 at Yanakie, Victoria. This aircraft was one of 35 S.E.5as given to the RAAF by the British government as part of the 1920 Imperial Gift. The RAAF's leadership requested the S.E.5a over the Sopwith Snipe because the aircraft was more stable and easier to fly. (Photograph courtesy of the Australian War Memorial)

The Avro 504 would become the principal training aircraft for the infant Australian Air Service. The replacement of the Sopwith Snipe with the S.E.5a indicates Macquire's preference for a safer and more stable aircraft.

For Australia, the 100-airplane gift was only the beginning of its air force. Prime Minister Hughes envisioned the creation of an Australian aircraft-manufacturing sector whereby the 100 aircraft nucleus would be supplemented over time by more than 200 aircraft built exclusively in the Dominion. On July 4, 1919, Hughes wrote Prime Minister Lloyd George:

> In reference to your request that I should outline my views as to the manufacture of AEROPLANES in Australia and its relation to the Air Defence of Australia: My view is that the best policy would be for the Commonwealth Government to

arrange for some British firm of repute to commence manufacture in Australia. To this end, I would recommend that arrangements should be with such a firm, and that we should stipulate for the right to take over the works on equitable terms at any time, and also to have the right of control of such works during war.[45]

In an August 4, 1919, cable to Defence Minister Pearce, Hughes approved Australia's acceptance of the aircraft gift from Britain along with his desire that construction of aircraft should take place in Australia.[46] However, few things are truly free; Australia had to cover the £25,000 to £30,000 freight expense to transport the aircraft to the Commonwealth.[47]

The plan to supplement the aircraft gift with Australian-built aircraft illustrated Australia's paramount desire to assert its independence. The Committee of Defence established an Aircraft Construction Committee to guide the creation of an Australian aircraft industry. In its first report, the newly formed body recognized the importance and limitations for Australia in the sphere of manufacturing. The Australian government decided that they should produce dual-purpose aircraft such as the de Havilland D.H.4, capable of both bombing and aerial fighting. It was also important that the materials used to construct these aircraft should be from local sources. Though the committee making these recommendations agreed on the use of British equipment, a small fissure emerged. The Australian Air Board, established in 1920 to control and administer the air force according to the policies established by the Air Council, advised for the "adoption of American 'Liberty' engines in preference to a British type considering simplicity of manufacture."[48] This was the first time, but not the last, Australians went outside the imperial system for aircraft equipment. In 1938, a more serious rift would take place over the adoption of American equipment.

The gift of 100 aircraft from the British government was not received in New Zealand with the same enthusiasm as it was in Australia. When the British submitted their offer to New Zealand, Colonel Bettington was writing his plan to develop military aviation in New Zealand. In a June 5, 1919, letter to Sir James Allen, Bettington urged that the Dominion accept the British government's offer, "as keen competition for the available supplies was likely."[49]

On August 27, 1919, Defence Minister Allen informed Bettington that New Zealand did not have the means to service a hundred machines and that the offer would have to be declined.[50] Allen's rejection of the British offer was greeted with surprise and disbelief in Britain. Stanley Spooner, founder and editor of *Flight*, commented:

> Sir J. Allen, the New Zealand Minister of Defence, says that the British offer of Aeroplanes is "undoubtedly valuable," representing about £500,000, but its acceptance depends upon the policy of New Zealand, which is not yet determined. The *Wellington Post*, commenting upon this statement, says that the offer of Aeroplanes should remind New Zealand equally of British generosity and of her own responsibilities. Admitted, in partnership with the Empire, to the League of Nations, the Dominions should rise to the full status of manhood and accept the gifts as a trust for the purposes for which they are offered and undertake the fundamental obligation of self-defence.
>
> What does the Minister of Defence mean exactly when he says that the policy of New Zealand has not been determined and that upon this determination depends the acceptance or rejection of the Mother Country's gift? Does he mean to convey that it is possible New Zealand, which has borne such a gallant part in the War, will rest content under the shadow of the League of Nations and take no part in preparing to defend

herself or the Empire? It is impossible to say, but we do think some more adequate explanation is called for of why it should be necessary to publicly hint at the refusal of the free gift of aircraft which ought to form an essential part of the Dominions' contribution to Empire defence. As to the determination of policy, it again seems to us that it is really about time the constituents of Empire had formulated their policy sufficiently to be able to say whether or not aerial defence is to form a part of the programme.[51]

Bettington told the New Zealanders that he thought the government would be ill advised not to accept at least some of the aeroplanes offered, and that a certain number of these could be used in the periodical training given to his suggested Reserve force.[52] Facing pressure from the editorial writers and the British government, in September 1919, Allen accepted thirty-eight gift aircraft, twenty Avro 504 trainers, nine de Havilland D.H.9as, nine S.E.5a fighters, and six large flying patrol boats.[53] The British government accepted the New Zealanders' request to limit the number of aircraft in the original offer. Owing to the delay in its acceptance, only a reduced number of machines arrived in New Zealand in 1921: twenty Avro 504s, nine D.H.9s, two D.H.4s, and two Bristol Fighters.[54]

The early postwar plans and gift of aircraft to Australia and New Zealand had no realistic or immediate effect on the defense of the Dominions in 1919. There was no air threat. The vast distances that the British faced to move aircraft to the South Pacific were just as daunting to any potential enemy. Nevertheless, these plans and the gift served a useful purpose. Defense planners began to examine the use of air power to defend the eastern empire. The idea of a ready reserve or cadre of pilots and mechanics in the Dominions would later transform itself into the Empire Air Training Scheme, which trained tens of thousands of pilots and aircrew for service in World War II. Moreover, the plans laid the foundation for an aviation industry. Finally, the schemes encouraged the importance of an "imperial" standard for pilot training, aerial tactics, and equipment. The ideas outlined by the early planners remained constant themes in air defense throughout the interwar years.

CHAPTER 2

THE FORMATION OF THE ROYAL AUSTRALIAN AIR FORCE AND THE FIRST REASSESSMENTS OF PACIFIC DEFENSES, 1920–1921

> *Has the problem of Imperial Defence outgrown the limits of our resources? That would certainly appear the case if it is only approached on the old lines of thought. A fresh inspiration is required; may not this be found in mechanical warfare? The Air Force is an example of a mechanical and scientific service: if then, its possibilities be fully explored, we may be far on the way to solve the problem of economical defence.*[1]
>
> —*Air Staff*

Many domestic and foreign policy decisions made by the British government complicated the number of options available to the leadership of the Royal Air Force (RAF) as they formulated the postwar role of air power. With regard to threats to the Pacific Dominions, only the United States and Japan could challenge Britain's position. British strategists considered war with the United States as unthinkable. In contrast, the possibility of a war with Japan, while certainly undesirable, was not unthinkable. Thus, postwar imperial discussions and international agreements centered on curtailing the possibility of war with Japan but also on countering the possible Japanese threat.

In an examination of the current condition of imperial air defenses in the Far East in early 1921, the British Air Staff determined that key factors were the Australian air assets and how these units would contribute to both imperial and Australian security. The Air Staff detailed the status of the seven Australian combat squadrons defending the ports of Melbourne and Sydney and optimistically reported that with these squadrons, "Australia has already made great progress in the maintenance of an Air Force."[2] The Air Staff also cautioned that:

> The problem of the defence of this country appears to consist largely in the defence of the district lying N. and S. of a line drawn from Brisbane to Adelaide. W. and N. of this line the country is sparsely inhabited, little developed and deficient in road and railway facilities. No Pacific Power desirous of effecting a raid across thousands of miles of sea could contemplate landing in these undeveloped territories to roam unmolested, but effecting nothing, until the British Fleet arrived to challenge their command of the sea.[3]

In the Air Staff's opinion, Australia's vastness and isolation was its greatest defense advantage. Even though there were few air units, they were required only at three or four strategic locations. Thus, the Air Staff assumed that the Japanese would attack the ports of Brisbane, Sydney, Melbourne, or Adelaide. The British planners felt that the Australians needed minimal additions to their current force structure to shore up the Dominion's air defenses. The British Air Staff concluded that a seaplane patrol and a torpedo squadron were required in Brisbane and Sydney. Another vital component of Australia's air defense would be self-sufficiency in the form of an independent domestic aviation industry. The Air Staff hoped that Australia could ultimately manufacture much of their needed aircraft and support equipment.[4] It would not be until the mid-1930s that the establishment of an Australian aircraft industry began to take shape along the lines anticipated at this time.

Australia continued to lead the other Dominions in matters of air defense. On March 31, 1921, the Australian government formed the Royal Australian Air Force (RAAF) as a separate service under the control of a new Air Board and an Air Council. The Air Board had direct responsibility over the operations of the RAAF and consisted of officers with flying experience.[5] To ensure continued cooperation with the army and navy, an Air Council also had representation from the other services. Ultimately, a centralized Defence Committee replaced the Air Board.[6]

The newly created air force centralized most of its operations outside Melbourne. Here the Air Force Headquarters would operate out of the Victoria Barracks with a newly formed No. 1 Flying Training School and the No. 1 Aircraft Depot located at the Point Cook Air Field. Another key component of the RAAF's organization was the establishment of an Air Liaison Office at the Air Ministry in London. This office was to keep track of the RAF's technical, training, and operational development, and ensure that RAAF procedures paralleled those of the RAF.[7]

Australia's Air Council recognized that postwar budgets would be sparse and that the infant RAAF had no hope of maintaining itself with state-of-the-art aircraft. Thus, the council directed these limited resources to personnel development and aviation infrastructure:

> Whatever organisation is maintained in Australia it should be so designed as to allow of possible expansion in the future and

must not provide for peace requirements alone.

During the immediate future the bulk of the available funds will be best spent in training personnel and providing an efficient ground organisation such as land, buildings, workshops, etc., the cost of which is not recurring, rather than in re-equipping units with most modern types of aircraft so long as those now in our possession meet the need of training and so long as the present likelihood of peace continues.[8]

Figure 2.1. Air Marshal Richard "Dicky" Williams. On March 31, 1921, the Royal Australian Air Force (RAAF) was formed as a separate service. Instrumental in the formation of the RAAF, AM Williams became its first chief of the Air Staff. Williams served for sixteen years as CAS until his removal in 1938. (Photograph courtesy of the Australian War Memorial)

By this policy, Australian military planners hoped to gain a more effective organization within the limited available budget. The Defence Council reported that the air force would remain essentially a paper force but with the goal of maintaining an efficient organization and a small but well-trained cadre of pilots, observers, and mechanics.[9] With this "skeleton" organization, the Australian Air Council thought that it could provide for the current and future needs of their air defense for approximately £250,000 per annum while allowing for the rapid expansion of the RAAF in the event of a military crisis.[10]

The British Air Staff also examined the status of New Zealand's air defenses, which were simply nonexistent. The New Zealanders had turned down the earlier gift of aircraft and demonstrated little interest in obtaining any military aircraft in the future. The Air Staff noted the Dominion's key defense advantage was its vast distance from any threat. "The [defense] problem of New Zealand is very similar to that of Australia, and the distance to be covered is much the same."[11]

The Air Staff was particularly concerned about the lack of any combat air units and argued for New Zealand to deploy at least four squadrons. A seaplane and torpedo squadron located respectively on both the North and South Islands could form the nucleus of the Dominion's air defenses.[12] The New Zealanders did not entirely abandon the idea of an aerial defense for the Dominion, but like the Australians, the government of William Ferguson Massey did not want to spend the country's limited budget on military requirements. Brigadier-General George S. Richardson, general officer in charge of administration, stated that in his opinion "New Zealand could not afford to maintain Military and Naval Aviation Services."[13] Once again, combining civil and military aviation was the answer for the New Zealanders. F. W. Furkert, engineer-in-chief of the Public Works Department, thought the "Government should support Civil Aviation and not undertake Naval and Military Aviation as an organisation."[14] Commander T. A. Williams, the Air Board's naval adviser, also concurred with Mr. Furkert's position. By August 1921, the recently created New Zealand Air Board, chaired by Major General Sir Edward W. C. Chaytor, the commander of all New Zealand's military forces, agreed to encourage civil flying by providing government subsidies to the privately owned Sockburn and Kohimarama flying schools. In addition, the New Zealand Air Board agreed to encourage new aviation enterprises by not placing excessive regulatory provisions on private enterprise.[15]

By the summer of 1921, the Air Staff in London was becoming concerned about the lack of development of the Dominions' air forces and their military aviation capabilities. The Air Staff believed that a synchronized aerial effort was essential for the empire's aerial defense.[16] Planners at the Air Ministry studied the position of imperial air assets and their application. The Air Staff established a four-tier concept for imperial air defense, including defense against air attack, prevention from overseas invasion and coastal defense, protection of maritime commerce, and finally, the role of the air force in support of naval and ground forces. Concerning air attack, the Air Staff recognized that the actual danger to the Pacific Dominions was minimal and felt that "Only small aerial fighting forces will be required."[17] This contradicted the public claims of the "Air Power" advocates such as the American general William ("Billy") Mitchell and their assertions that airplanes could defeat a naval force. The Air Staff recognized that in its present state the airplane was a minimal threat to an enemy battleship.

> The Air Service can best be employed in attacks on the enemy's aircraft-carrying vessels. This entails concentration on the torpedo aeroplane and flying boats of long range operation from shore bases. Considerable development is required before air forces become a menace to the heavily protected capital ship, but aircraft carriers in their present stage of design can be attacked with good prospects of success with bombs and torpedoes.[18]

In aerial attacks against enemy shipping, the Air Staff believed that aircraft were most effective against lightly armed and armored support vessels. Here an air force would be most useful by interdicting an enemy's trade and sea communications as well as preventing the transport and disembarkation of invasion forces.

By advocating a maritime interdiction policy, the Air Staff challenged the traditional role of the Royal Navy in imperial defense. They contended that aircraft could protect the sea-lanes from surface and submarine raiders more efficiently and economically than with surface ships:

> Aircraft, properly distributed along maritime communications and operating from shore bases in conjunction with certain naval elements, should do much to ensure the safety of commerce within the limits of their radius of action. Maritime Dominions such as Australia and New Zealand will have a special interest in securing their coastal traffic in this manner and may assist in covering the local approaches to the main maritime routes against enemy attack.[19]

These early proposals regarding maritime operations encroached upon the Royal Navy's responsibilities and soon became a serious point of contention between the air force and navy. The debate over maritime defense responsibilities eventually ignited an ugly public battle between the two services. The British Air Staff argued that the air force, as the most mobile of all of the nation's military services, was the most utilitarian defense force for the vast expanse of the empire. On this point, the Air Staff was wrong, because the infrastructure necessary for this mobility did not exist and the short range and light payload capability of the aircraft of the period limited their maritime and other missions. The Air Staff anticipated a future when technological improvements to aircraft could overcome these existing obstacles. Although the infrastructure did not exist at this time, the Air Ministry planned to direct money toward airfield construction in future budget cycles to enable aircraft to operate throughout the empire. It is clear that the Air Staff's schemes were not practical at this time.

The Air Staff viewed imperial air defense as a cooperative effort with the Dominions. To facilitate this cooperation, the RAF's role was to assist the Dominions with the training and development of pilots and mechanics, research new aviation technologies, and establish standardized equipment and tactics.[20] In addition, the Air Staff felt that the Dominions could contribute to a certain extent to aeronautical research but needed to avoid duplication of any research that took place in Britain. Arguing that the Dominions would best serve imperial research efforts by examining problems unique to their particular conditions, the Air Staff thought that investigation of the effects of the local climate on materials, especially fabrics, dopes, glue, and wood, would be most beneficial.[21]

At the 1921 Imperial Conference, a number of decisions had long-term repercussions for imperial defense. The central topic concerning security in the Pacific was the renewal of the 1902 Anglo-Japanese Alliance. Although the future of this treaty directly affected the Royal Navy, the Air Staff looked at the changing defense environment as, at the very least, an opportunity to ensure their future independence or possibly to expand their imperial defense responsibilities and thus prevent the reduction of their budget. The Anglo-Japanese treaty had effectively reduced the Royal Navy's defense obligations in the Pacific for twenty years. The question of renewing the treaty created a heated debate among the empire's leaders at the 1921 conference.

Dominion leaders took great interest in its extension or cancellation. Cracks in imperial unity revealed the Dominions were developing independent foreign policies that focused on their particular or unique needs. Prime Minister David Lloyd George in his opening statements described the future of the Anglo-Japanese Alliance as "one of the most urgent and important of the foreign questions."[22] The leaders of the Pacific Dominions felt strongly that their region would become the next region for international crisis. Prime Minister Hughes declared, "The war and the Panama Canal has [sic] shifted the World's stage from the Mediterranean and Atlantic to the Pacific."[23] New Zealand's prime minister, William Ferguson Massey, simply stated, "The next naval war will be fought in the Pacific."[24] Japan's annexation of the Marshall and Caroline island groups and its control over Shantung pointed toward encroachment into the British sphere of influence.[25] In addition, the Japanese began to monopolize transportation and limited Western trade in their sphere of the Chinese market, which ran counter to the American "Open Door" policy and the British concept of "Equal Opportunity."[26] Some feared that cancelling the Anglo-Japanese Alliance would further divide the two powers.

Canadians were concerned that continuation of the treaty would place Britain at odds with the United States. Following the war, Canadian economic and political interests moved closer to the United States and away from the imperial system. Prior to the Imperial Conference, the Canadian governor general, Sir Victor Christian William Cavendish, cabled then Colonial Secretary Winston Churchill about the continuation of the naval agreement.

> The question of the Anglo-Japanese Alliance, I assume will be decided at the June meetings of Prime Ministers. . . . It may be useful to let you know our views now.
>
> We feel that every possible effort should be made to find some alternative policy to that of renewal.
>
> We think we should terminate the Alliance and endeavour at once to bring about a Conference of Pacific Powers. Such a course would enable us to end the alliance with good grace.[27]

In response to Cavendish's concerns, Churchill assumed that the Pacific prime ministers, Hughes and Massey, would agree with the Canadian view. Churchill cabled, "Australia and New Zealand have very strong racial objections to the Japanese, and would be disposed to throw in their lot with the United States against Japan."²⁸ The Australians and New Zealanders did not agree with the treaty's cancellation and in fact became the treaty's strongest advocates. In his opening remarks at the conference, Hughes stated:

> Australia is very strongly in favour of renewal of the Treaty. . . . Should we not be in a better position to exercise greater influence over the Eastern policy as an Ally of that great Eastern Power, than as her enemy? . . . To renew this Treaty is to impose on her some of those restraints inseparable from Treaties with other civilised nations like ourselves. We will do well for the world's peace—we will do well for China—we will do well for the Commonwealth of British nations to renew this Treaty. We want peace.²⁹

New Zealand prime minister Massey, like Hughes, supported renewal of the treaty. He opened his comments about the importance of the treaty to New Zealanders and praised the Japanese for fulfilling their treaty obligations by protecting their troop transports during the war. Massey was far less fervent in his comments about renewal than Hughes was, but for Massey renewal was just as critical to New Zealand's future security.

> I took my Parliament into my fullest confidence so far as the proposed Japanese Treaty was concerned and I told them that in my opinion with whatever modifications may be necessary, I was quite prepared to support its renewal. It is only right to admit that, in saying that, I am guided to a certain extent by what took place during the war period.³⁰

The renewal issue generated strong acrimony between the imperial premiers. Hughes and Massey were in favor of renewal; Jan Smuts of South Africa and Arthur Meighen of Canada argued for its cancellation.

Smuts thought that imperial policy should align more closely to that of the United States and avoid a potential armaments race with the Americans.[31] David Lloyd George feared termination would antagonize the Japanese and its continuation would anger the United States; both were unacceptable options. The United States' invitation to negotiate the limitation of great power naval arms helped defuse the crisis. The conference members postponed a final decision regarding the treaty's renewal until after the Washington Naval Conference.

When President Warren Harding extended invitations to the world's naval powers in the summer of 1921, he went beyond the topic of naval disarmament and included on the agenda issues relating to the Pacific and Far East. During his opening remarks American secretary of state Charles Evans Hughes surprised the conference attendees and suggested that the naval powers scrap millions of tons of naval armaments and institute a ten-year "holiday" of new capital ship construction. The now famous 5:5:3 capital ship tonnage ratio between Great Britain, the United States, and Japan became the most recognized agreement at the conference.

Initially, the British set aside the subject of Pacific security while the conferees dealt with the sweeping American proposals regarding naval disarmament. Yet, a regional settlement in the Pacific was one of the foremost concerns that split the British imperial delegation. On the opening day of the conference, the British representative and former Conservative prime minister, Arthur Balfour, cabled Lloyd George with a five-point plan that he felt could settle any present or future disputes among the Americans, Japanese, and British. Balfour hoped to settle Pacific issues with a Four Power Pact between Britain, France, Japan, and the United States to maintain the status quo in the Pacific; end the Anglo-Japanese agreement without creating animosity with Japan; leave open future options for a defensive treaty with Japan against Germany or Russia; settle Pacific matters to the satisfaction of Australia and New Zealand;

and finally, ease American worries that Britain would back Japan in any conflict between the two powers.³² These five points prepared by Balfour became the framework of the Four Power Pact of December 13. With the addition of France, the Pacific powers in Article II of the pact agreed to the peaceful settlement of disputes by conferences and to respect the status of each nation's territorial and mandate claims.³³ The Four Power Pact ended the Anglo-Japanese naval alliance.

The end of the alliance did not reassure the Pacific Dominions. New Zealand's representative at Washington, Sir John Salmond, reluctantly admitted that the treaty represented "the only satisfactory method of overcoming the difficulties involved in [ending] the existence of the Anglo-Japanese Alliance."³⁴ A year following the Washington Conference, Australia's new prime minister, Stanley Bruce, stated that the decision taken "certainly did not solve the problem of the future safety of Australia."³⁵ As the leaders of the Pacific Dominions feared, the cancellation of the Anglo-Japanese Alliance angered and frustrated the Japanese delegation at Washington. Lieutenant-General Kunishige Tanaka, a member of that delegation, wrote of the events:

> In short, the conference proved to be an attempt to oppress the non-Anglo Saxon races by the two English speaking countries, Britain and the United States. Britain helped the US both directly and indirectly, taking a hostile attitude towards Japan, her ally in the Anglo-Japanese Alliance and finally succeeded in abandoning the alliance, on conditions favourable to themselves. It was a great victory for them brought about by crafty British Diplomacy.³⁶

The Aviation Sub-Committee discussed matters relating to aerial disarmament at the conference. The apparently more significant naval agreements and Pacific Four Power Pact overshadowed the conclusions reached by the aviation committee. Air Vice Marshal Sir John F. A. Higgins represented the British Empire delegation in the conference's Aviation Sub-Committee. Before the meetings, the Air Staff relayed explicit instructions to Higgins from Chief of the Air Staff Trenchard not to make any compromises concerning air defense. In a ciphered telegram sent on December 3, 1921, the Air Staff stressed that Higgins not give in to limiting the strength of the air force. It was not diplomatically possible to limit any attack against Britain; the British Isles were highly susceptible to damage from aerial bombing and single-seat fighters were an essential defensive rather than offensive weapon.[37] It appears from the conclusions of the Aviation Sub-Committee that Trenchard's position relayed by Higgins held sway.

Unlike the talks that surrounded naval arms, any attempts to limit air arms completely failed. The subcommittee forwarded an idealistic view of the potential peaceful application of aircraft.

> This Committee understands that the purpose of this Conference is to promote peace and to remove the causes of warfare. It must be understood distinctly that if the Conference decided to limit the development of commercial aircraft in order to retard the development of air power, the immediate result will be the retarded development of means of transportation and communication which will itself, if unrestricted, largely act to bring about the same result, the removal of some of the causes of warfare. To limit the science of aeronautics in its present stage is to shut the door on progress.[38]

Among the numerous avenues for aerial arms considered at Washington were limiting the number of aircraft, aircraft horsepower, an aircraft's lift capacity, the number of air force personnel, and restricting budgets. All were deemed impracticable.[39] Foreign Minister Lord Balfour confirmed this in a dispatch to Prime Minister Lloyd George: "You are already fully impressed with the disparity in the air forces available.... We recognise reluctantly the practical difficulties in enforcing a limitation in air armaments."[40] In addition, the committee understood that it was nearly impossible to limit aircraft or establish national air strength ratios like negotiations accomplished with capital ships at Washington. The ability to mass produce aircraft rapidly enabled a nation to expand its air force quickly, whereas a capital ship took years to build.[41] Once again, the Aviation Sub-Committee came to the incorrect conclusion. It took the remainder of the interwar period to construct the hundreds of airfields needed to link the empire, and the mass production of aircraft required factories and skilled workers that would require years to put in place. Finally, the proper training of new pilots and crews for these aircraft took at least one full year.

Another aspect of the committee's discussions was the potential application of commercial aircraft for military purposes. The members concurred that: "All aircraft will be of some military value no matter what restrictions may be placed upon their character. Some can probably be converted with but few changes into military aircraft."[42] Restrictions on commercial aircraft could retard economic development and the progress of commercial aviation.

Finally, there was unwillingness by the participating nations at Washington to limit the size of their air forces because of their imperial liabilities:

> The potentialities of air forces in policing and garrisoning semi-civilized or uncivilized countries are as yet only partially realized. The number of aircraft required for such duties will vary with the size and nature of the territories to be patrolled and with the value placed on their services by different nations.[43]

It was easier for the powers to agree to limitations on their navies because those were used against one another and not against lesser powers or colonial entities. During the conference, the Royal Air Force began numerous aerial policing operations throughout the empire, especially in the Middle East. In September, the Air Staff reported to the cabinet about the RAF's daily engagements in Iraq and Afghanistan.[44] In the immediate future, the airplane proved to be an inexpensive tool for internal security, and the imperial powers were unwilling to set limits on its use. Trenchard felt that imperial defense was now entering a new era and argued vigorously about the utility of aircraft in that future role:

> we should surely endeavour to recast our system of defence, and rely to a far greater extent than hitherto upon a service [the Royal Air Force], which by virtue of its range and mobility and the nature of its armament is able to utilise machines in substitution for, and not as a mere addition to, man power.[45]

Trenchard's arguments centered on the economical utility of aircraft in defense were appropriate. By the end of 1921, Britain's economy was in shambles, and he hoped that an economic argument would prove more persuasive. Some manufacturing sectors such as shipping suffered a 38 to 40 percent unemployment rate.[46] In response, Lloyd George's government instituted severe budget cuts across all sectors of expenditure. To determine the specifics of these cuts, the government established the Committee of National Expenditure under the chairmanship of Sir Eric Geddes. The £87 million in budget reductions submitted by the committee became known as the "Geddes Axe."[47]

During the two years that followed the 1919 Imperial Conference, there was a temporary change in the focus of British imperial defense policy away from Europe and toward the Pacific. The leadership of the Royal Air Force saw the newly created Royal Australian Air Force as more than a partner in imperial air defense. For the RAF leaders, it was essential that these imperial air forces maintain similar equipment, training, and air doctrine. Unlike the Royal Navy, the air forces demonstrated an inclination to cede local and even regional defense responsibility and command over to the pertinent Dominion. The navy viewed imperial defense as its global responsibility and considered the naval forces of the Dominions as a supplement to the Royal Navy, remaining under the authority of the local British station commander.

In foreign policy, the growing independence of the Dominions made international negotiations more difficult for the Foreign Office in the immediate postwar period. The renewal of the Anglo-Japanese Alliance demonstrated the split between the British government and the Dominions. In addition, the Dominions desired representation independent of the "British Imperial" delegation during the negotiations at Washington. Cracks in imperial unity began to emerge when the Dominions' leaders advocated their foreign policy and defense needs based on their particular regional concerns rather than on global imperial interests. The news from Washington hailed the major powers' readiness to reduce their battle fleets as a major achievement to secure a lasting peace. In comparison, the news that there was no agreement concerning air power seemed insignificant. For a brief moment, the leadership of the Royal Air Force felt that the service's future was secure, because there had been no force reduction imposed by the Washington Conference and they were confident their increased duties in imperial defenses would sustain adequate funding levels. This optimism was short lived.

CHAPTER 3

THE EMPIRE'S AIR DEFENSE: THE GEDDES CUTS OF 1922, AND THE 1923 IMPERIAL CONFERENCE AND THEIR INFLUENCE ON THE EMPIRE'S AIR DEFENSE, 1922–1923

It has been said that with the advent of the Air Arm, Great Britain has ceased to be an island; it is at least certain that the defence of the Empire will rest to an increasing extent as time goes on, on the efficiency and adequacy of the Royal Air Force. In time of peace it is impossible to maintain a standing Air Force comparable to that which would be required in time of war.[1]

—*Winston S. Churchill*

The future prospects for the Royal Air Force (RAF) appeared to be secure for a brief moment. The failed effort of the air disarmament discussions at the Washington Conference and the increased role of the RAF in imperial policing provided a sense of optimism for its leadership. In fact, a future for an independent air force was far from certain;

the service now faced deep budget cuts instigated by the "Geddes Axe" and the interservice rivalries almost eliminated the four-year-old service. These two threats to the Royal Air Force had a significant bearing on its near and long-term operations and defense planning. By the 1923 Imperial Conference, the drama created by these domestic pressures seemed settled and there was hope that a more orderly process for defense planning could proceed.

By 1921, the postwar recession in Britain was entrenched. Faced with chronic unemployment combined with inflationary pressures, the Treasury, under the leadership of the new chancellor of the exchequer, Sir Robert Horne, fought these dilemmas with the traditional tool of cutting government expenditures. When Prime Minister Lloyd George determined that Horne's £75 million in cuts were not enough, he established the Committee of Expenditure headed by Sir Eric Geddes to find another £100 million in reductions. In the 1920s version of a "Peace Dividend," the preponderance of these cuts came from the military services. The most far-reaching transformation that the Committee of Expenditure proposed was amalgamation of the Admiralty, War Office, and the Air Ministry into a single Ministry of Defence. All three services strongly lobbied against these efforts. A single ministry was not realized until 1964. Unfortunately for the Air Ministry, the committee continued to eye the department for elimination and proposed the return of its functions to the Admiralty and War Office. On October 14, 1921, the committee asked of the Air Ministry:

> The Committee consider[ed] that the advantages and disadvantages of a separate Air Ministry should be fully explored. Is it not a fact that the policy of having an entirely separate organisation and Minister for Air Services has not been followed by any other Nations?[2]

The Air Ministry quickly responded to the committee's proposal, claiming that the other services "underrate and misunderstand the potentialities of the air service as an independent arm."³ The Air Ministry continued by asserting the value of a separate air force in terms the committee understood: "This tendency manifests itself firstly in underrating the probable course and effect of air operation in warfare of the future, and secondly in an inability to recognize the possibilities of economical substitution of air power for sea or land power."⁴ The RAF's budget was £15 million compared to £43 million for the army and £112 million for the Royal Navy.⁵ Before the advent of Geddes's committee, the air force made self-imposed budget reductions in anticipation of a postwar cutback. Further cuts to the RAF's funds now seemed to accomplish little toward the targeted £100 million reduction goal of the Geddes Committee. Even though the Air Ministry made important points, the Geddes Committee was anxious to cut every extraneous pound found in every departmental budget. The committee ignored the Air Ministry's arguments and imposed further cuts. In retrospect and considering the desperation to find budget cuts, it is surprising that the Air Ministry remained a functioning entity.

The Geddes Committee had eventually to abandon the idea of a single Ministry of Defence. All three services had ardent supporters who argued that unification was impracticable in the early 1920s. A central tenet proposed by the committee asked the services to assume that Britain would not fight a major war for the next ten years. With the advantage of hindsight, this assumption proved to be an accurate prediction of European events. For the Royal Air Force this "Ten Year Rule" made significant reductions to the service's 1922–1923 Air Estimates.

The Committee of Expenditure proposed that the Royal Air Force slash its £15 million 1920–1921 budget by £5.92 million, or nearly 40 percent. The committee obtained these savings by eliminating £2.5

million allocated to eight and a half active service squadrons; £1 million directed for the purchase of new aircraft and equipment, £1 million for the purchase or maintenance upkeep of RAF facilities, and the remaining £1.42 million decreases in administration, research, supplies, and civil aviation.[6] The Air Council, the government's senior advisory body on aviation matters, felt that the committee arrived at the savings based on erroneous calculations.[7] The council estimated that only £2.8 million in savings could be achieved through the elimination of the programs identified by the committee.[8] In addition, there was growing concern within the Air Council that the RAF attained more responsibilities throughout the empire just as it was facing additional budget reductions.[9]

At the end of 1921, a cabinet subcommittee formed under the chairmanship of Winston Churchill reviewed the Geddes cuts and reported on their final disposition in the 1922–1923 estimates. Churchill's subcommittee gave each department one last opportunity to defend themselves against the proposed cuts. From January 21 to January 23, 1922,

Figure 3.1. Sir Eric Campbell Geddes. Under a budget commission charged to reduce Britain's postwar government expenditures dramatically, the Geddes budget "axe" nearly eliminated the Royal Air Force and returned its squadrons back to the control of the Royal Navy and the British Army. The RAF's leadership saved the service by appealing to the Geddes Commission charter and arguing that aircraft could defend the empire less expensively than the navy or army. (Photograph courtesy of the National Portrait Gallery, London)

the committee members met with Air Minister Sir Frederick Guest and Sir Hugh Trenchard over how these reductions would impinge on the Air Ministry and Royal Air Force's operations. Though Churchill did not agree to the £5.92 million decreases proposed by Geddes, he did warn the meeting's participants that the country's financial situation required a several million pound reduction to the Air Estimates and they would have to seek additional economies over the next several years.[10]

Trenchard expressed his concern that the Royal Air Force had only 700 operational aircraft and that "the Air Force was now living on the war stocks of machines, which would be exhausted, assuming normal wastage, in 1924–1925."[11] Air Minister Guest warned that the proposed air force reductions could curtail the services' overseas operations, warning that "these commitments had been agreed upon by the Government and it was impossible to affect any economics in this direction unless the Government was prepared to change the policy which had already been decided upon."[12]

As the former secretary of state for air, Churchill was sympathetic to Guest's situation. He expressed concern that the majority of the operational squadrons were stationed overseas, leaving no protection over Britain. In addition, Churchill appreciated the RAF's operational cost savings by relieving the other services in the Middle East.[13] In the final report written by Churchill's subcommittee, the group noted the self-imposed economies by the Royal Air Force.

> We are strongly impressed, as were the Geddes Committee, by the sense of economy and of thrifty administration possessed by the Chief of the Air Staff. We cannot feel that there is any large opening for further pruning. The result might well be to destroy the efficiency of the whole force and waste to a large extent such funds as were allocated to it.[14]

This sympathy did not go far, however, and Churchill's group called for the secretary of state for air to submit further proposals for an additional reduction of £750,000 in the estimates for 1922/1923 to produce net estimates of £10,250,000. If these cuts were achieved, the subcommittee noted, "we are satisfied that it will represent the absolute maximum of economy possible at the present time."[15]

In the final version of the "Report of National Expenditure," the Royal Air Force received high praise from the committee for its self-imposed economies but still incurred significant monetary reductions. The committee also encouraged the further application of aircraft for imperial defense. The committee based its favor of the air force on their perceived economies afforded by aviation in imperial defense matters: "The question of aerial versus naval or military command in operations in the future will doubtless cause difficulties; but economies to an increasing extent ought to result in the older arms from the advent of the Air Force."[16] The report also determined that by exclusively using the RAF, the cost of military operations in the Middle East could reduce the 1922–1923 estimates by £14 million from the £27 million spent in the 1921–1922 estimates.[17] The Geddes Committee concluded, "It can no longer be denied that by the intelligent application of air power, it is possible to utilise machinery in substitution for, and not as a mere addition to man-power."[18] Although the majority of Parliament and the cabinet rejected the concept of a Ministry of Defence, the Committee of Expenditure maintained its position of a single Ministry of Defence:

> Full economy in the fighting services cannot be realised under existing conditions. There is overlapping and duplication throughout. . . . the three Forces must be brought together by the creation of a co-ordinating authority responsible for seeing that each Force plays its part, and is allotted appropriate responsibility for carrying out various functions.[19]

It is also probable that the Committee of Expenditure favored a unified defense structure under a Ministry of Defence because the current arrangement pitted the three services against one another. Desperate to protect their dwindling budgets in Parliament, the report only exacerbated the sniping among the services.

Although the Royal Air Force was the junior service, its leadership maneuvered its political position like veterans. The Air Council was either unable or unwilling to reduce the number of RAF squadrons stationed overseas because they were all involved in active or recurrent operations. To reach Geddes's eight-and-a-half squadron cut, the members of the Air Council identified that the majority of the squadrons should be the ones designated for naval and army cooperation. Specifically, the Air Council called for the abolition of five and one half naval cooperation squadrons, two army cooperation squadrons, and one overseas squadron stationed in Egypt.[20] This action would leave only one squadron of aircraft assigned specifically to work with each of the respective services. The Air Council recognized that "[we] do not anticipate that the Admiralty or War Office will willingly accept these proposals."[21] Admiral of the Fleet Sir David Beatty noted:

> The proposal practically amounts to abolishing Aircraft as a Naval weapon, and would effectively prevent any possibility of substituting aircraft for surface craft in the solution of Naval problems, besides greatly reducing the efficiency of all other naval weapons, the use of which depends to a great extent on Air co-operation.[22]

In addition to the pending cuts, the Air Council members also attempted to undermine the other services by demonstrating how air power could substitute for the other services, a conclusion in which the Geddes Committee concurred. In January 1922, Field Marshal Henry

Wilson, chief of the Imperial General Staff, wrote to the secretary of state for war, Sir Laming Worthington-Evans, noting his annoyance with the Geddes Committee's proposal to replace his cavalry units with aircraft: "It appears to be the advent of the Air Force which has influenced them in this direction."[23] Field Marshal Wilson then continued:

> To assert that the place of cavalry can entirely be taken by aircraft in the work of close reconnaissance protection and support is a complete fallacy. Aircraft in its present state of development is only effective against an enemy presenting a tangible and extensive target or for bombing women and children.[24]

The actions of the Air Ministry placed the Admiralty in a difficult position concerning the use of aircraft in naval defense. In a memorandum to the cabinet in early 1922, Admiral Beatty outlined the dangers that the Air Ministry actions would have on the future aviation activities of the fleet. Beatty recognized that the "air weapon has become an integral part of the fleet" both tactically and strategically.[25] The Air Ministry's planned elimination of naval cooperation squadrons confirmed Beatty's concern that the naval air contingent was dependent upon the good will of a separate government ministry. In addition, he argued that the navy required a comparatively small air contingent but with experience in both air and naval matters.[26]

The Air Ministry's action of cutting the army and naval cooperation squadrons along with the Geddes budget reductions initiated a bitter fight among the three services. By January 1922, the Admiralty sided with the War Office and called for the abolition of the Air Ministry for financial as well as strategic reasons. On February 4, 1922, Secretary of State for War Sir Laming Worthington-Evans argued for the return of some Air Ministry functions to the War Office:

I believe not only that this transfer would result in the saving as far as the Army is concerned, of anything up to £1½m a year but that real progress in military aviation will be greater if the friction inevitable between the older and newer services is removed by an undivided responsibility and single control.[27]

Likewise, the Admiralty concurred with the army's position regarding the potential monetary savings by returning naval aviation to their control. In addition, the Admiralty also recognized that the cuts to naval aviation proposed by the Geddes Committee and the Royal Air Force essentially eliminated the existence of naval aviation in Britain.[28] The leadership of the Royal Navy felt that naval aviation would not develop adequately until they had their own air service administered within the Admiralty rather than in the Air Ministry.[29]

Faced by a unified attack from the two senior services, Capt. Edgar Ludlow-Hewitt, who would later rise to lead Bomber Command at the outbreak of World War II, helped to craft the Air Ministry's response to the army and navy's arguments. In a series of notes in January 1922, Ludlow-Hewitt argued that the two services looked upon the Air Force as a supplementary force and that "they have little conception of the independent power of the Air Force to affect the result of a war."[30] In addition, the two services needed to realize that the air force was now an essential and independent military arm:

> The immense possibilities of air development in the future, when fully understood, will render any suggestion of splitting the Air up between the Navy and the Army no more logical and no less absurd than a suggestion to split up the Army between the Navy and the Air Force.[31]

Leaders of the Royal Navy understood perfectly well the growing military value of aircraft. Why else was the service so adamant about reconstituting the Royal Naval Air Service? The navy wanted to have their own air component because they clearly recognized that naval air requirements would not be an Air Force priority. The antiquated quality of the Fleet Air Arm's equipment at the beginning of World War II confirmed the navy's concerns and the Air Ministry and air force's disinterest in developing naval aircraft during the interwar period.

Secretary of State for Air Frederick Guest wrote to the cabinet that the hostility that was now emerging between the services was against the public's interest.[32] Guest worried that even though the Royal Air Force could provide cost-effective security, the drastic cuts to the service's budget would retard technical development and ultimately diminish national security.[33] Guest was also concerned about the public's perception of the war of words between the Royal Navy and the RAF. He noted to the cabinet, "I do not know that this perpetual controversy is good for either of the services or that it leads to anything but discord."[34]

Interestingly, in the evaluation of the Geddes reductions, Churchill's subcommittee expressed concern about their effect upon imperial air defense both in Europe and in the Pacific. In Europe, the committee observed that the British Isles were "practically without means of defence against a Continental attack from the air."[35] The committee also commented at length about the weakness of Britain's forces in the Pacific, where British possessions were defenseless against any aggressive move by Japan. Churchill's report made a prophetic prediction regarding a war with Japan:

> Obviously we cannot hold Hong Kong in the event of a war with Japan. Unless Singapore is adequately protected before it is attacked, we cannot hold Singapore. . . . If Singapore fell in the first two or three months of a war the whole Pacific would fall

under the complete supremacy of Japan and many years might elapse before either Britain or the United States could re-enter that ocean in effective strength. India, Burma, the Straits Settlements, Australia, New Zealand are all at the present time within the scope of potential Japanese superior action.[36]

Churchill's continual references to Singapore and Japanese aggression influenced the British postwar Pacific defense doctrine. In February 1919, Admiral of the Fleet John R. Jellicoe departed on an imperial cruise with instructions to evaluate the future needs of imperial naval defense. Jellicoe recommended in his four-volume report the construction of a major fleet base at Singapore. By transferring a large proportion of the Royal Navy strength to this strategic location, the navy could then protect the approaches to India, Australia, and New Zealand. Jellicoe's conclusions received a positive reaction from both Australians and New Zealanders because the plan focused on Pacific defense. For the remainder of the interwar period, the Royal Air Force would repeatedly attempt to include themselves in this strategy. The Pacific Dominions had to confront the contradiction in British defense policy between limited military budgets and armament reductions and the British commitment to Pacific defense.

These contradictions became apparent to the Australians, who realized that with the budget reductions in Britain, they would become more responsible for their own defense. In the early months of 1922, Prime Minister Hughes called for a reevaluation of the Dominion's defense needs and capabilities. It became the declared policy of the Australian government to establish air defense bases in each of the country's states pending the availability of funding.[37]

In April 1922, under directions from the prime minister, and in reaction to international circumstances and political events in Britain, the recently formed Royal Australian Air Force Headquarters issued its first policy statement in reference to the Dominion's air defense. Australia's immediate air defense policy would be based on three main principles: that the Washington Conference reduced but did not eliminate the possibility of war; the Australian Parliament would strictly limit future defense funding; and the service's future budget was likely not to exceed its current £328,000 annual budget.[38] With these three restrictions placed upon the RAAF, the air force ceased to exist as a significant military arm. In response to these pressures, the RAAF Headquarters decided to concentrate its efforts on training personnel and constructing aviation infrastructure rather than buying new equipment that would be subject to obsolescence.[39] Considering the pace of technical developments of aircraft during the interwar period and the limited budget provided to the air force, this was a reasoned approach.

In the immediate future, the RAAF Headquarters personnel would be responsible for keeping up with technical progress in aviation, studying existing and developing new tactics, and, unlike the British model, developing close cooperation with the other armed services. In addition, training a cadre of both pilots and mechanics was crucial for the creation of an air force that would be required to expand rapidly in the advent of a national emergency. This cadre would include individuals who were involved in civil aviation. Finally, the air force leadership saw their small air force as a point defense tool, envisioning a chain of airfields constructed throughout the country. These prepositioned airfields would facilitate the allocation and concentration of Australia's limited number of aircraft to any threatened region of the continent.[40] The 1922–1923 budget priority was the purchase of land to construct an aircraft maintenance depot outside of Melbourne. This depot was intended as the primary maintenance facility for the air units based at Point Cook by conducting major aircraft refits and overhauls. The primitive infrastructure at Point Cook made these types of repairs more difficult. In addition, the RAAF acquired land for a new airbase outside Sydney. For the RAAF, "it is conceivable that the East Coast of Australia and Sydney in particular may, in case of emergency, be nearer than Melbourne to the scene of operations."[41] Sydney was a rational choice because it was Australia's most strategic port, and the leadership of both the navy and the air force believed that "there is no doubt that protection from enemy aircraft will be necessary."[42] An airbase at Sydney also provided strategic advantages over Melbourne because it was five hundred miles closer to the expected areas of future operations on the sparsely populated northern coast of Australia.

In 1922, there were no powers that could possible threaten Australia or New Zealand from the air, land, or sea. The accepted view at that time was that Japan could only conduct small raids or commerce attacks. Land- and carrier-based aircraft were too primitive and were not capable of producing serious harm. The air strategy adopted by the RAAF in 1922 recognized this and designed a practical long-term policy. Moreover, the service's leaders did not appear to be as concerned as the Royal Air Force's leadership about their independent status. The primary justification made by the British air power advocates for an independent air force was the need for a strategic bomber force to attack enemy production and transportation infrastructure independent from land or naval actions. In addition, the air force was the nation's primary defense against enemy bomber aircraft.[43] The military realities of the Pacific tempered the RAAF's ambitions for independence. Simply put, there were no strategic targets within a realistic range of Australia. Australia's air force leaders clearly viewed the force's operations as tactical—directly in support of navy and army operations. The primary justification for the RAAF's independence was to ensure that the force could develop in a coordinated manner with the Royal Air Force.

Because of the needs of Australia's army and navy, the RAAF concentrated on infrastructure improvements. The bases needed for air defense would be in place for the day when aircraft could threaten the

Dominion or would serve as staging areas to operate aircraft from more forward locations. This foresight proved most valuable during World War II when these bases were already available for Australian and American air operations in the Southwest Pacific in 1942 and 1943.[44]

By the summer of 1922, many raised objections to the Geddes Axe in the British Parliament. For several months, *Flight*, the voice for aviation in Britain, printed the transcripts of the floor debates. On June 2, 1922, Sir William Joynson-Hicks, a conservative MP who was an ardent aviation supporter, asked Prime Minister Lloyd George what the government's policy was about its "air position." Major-General John Bernard Seely, the former undersecretary of state for air, wondered what "steps to ensure that our safety in the air shall receive full consideration relative to our other defensive services?"[45] By September, the magazine reported that the few aircraft in the air force's inventory were down to reconditioned war surplus aircraft and only a few experimental types.[46] In response to these lines of questioning by Parliament's air advocates, Lloyd George asked for their patience and indicated that he was waiting for a report from the Committee of Imperial Defence that outlined Britain's and the empire's air security. By October, these concerns for the Royal Air Force were lost in the confusion brought about by the collapse of Lloyd George's government.

The crisis in Anatolia created by the Greek-Turkish war now came to a head. The Turkish forces commanded by Mustapha Kemal threatened the British garrison stationed at the village of Chanak and the neutrality of the Dardanelles Straits. If the British were to maintain this position, they would require the support and military resources of the entire empire. While the New Zealanders raised 12,000 troops for the operation, the Australians, Canadians, and South Africans were not prepared blindly to follow Britain.[47] When Lloyd George failed to secure the Dominions' military support, the garrison's position became untenable.[48] The Chanak Crisis was the last in a series of political blunders by Lloyd George that finally convinced the Conservatives to abandon his coalition government. In addition, the crisis also demonstrated that there were cracks developing in imperial unity. The Dominions, with the memory of the disaster of Gallipoli fresh in their memory, were unwilling to support Britain in another Turkish adventure.

When the Conservative government of Andrew Bonar Law took power in October 1922, the new secretary of state for air, Sir Samuel Hoare, attempted to correct the erosion of the air force created by the Geddes cuts. In an address before the 1923 Air Conference, a meeting of Britain's foremost aviation corporate and government leaders, Hoare spoke about the Royal Air Force's declining strength. In his opinion, large military expenditures placed an "intolerable burden upon trade and industry," but were necessary because "the world was still a dangerous place."[49] Hoare contended, "Whether we like it or not the greater part of the national expenditure upon air must, for the present, go to our military commitments of home and Imperial defence."[50]

By March 1923, the new Conservative government responded to the erosion of the Royal Air Force's budget created by the Geddes Axe. The Air Estimates for that year saw a £1,116,000 increase from the previous year. In addition, the government designated £3,870,000 exclusively for the purchase of new aircraft.[51] With the new increases, the Committee of Imperial Defence Sub-Committee of National and Imperial Defence, members Lord Peel, secretary of state for India, Sir Samuel Hoare, and Leo Amery, First Lord of the Admiralty, met that summer to discuss the agenda of imperial defense matters for the 1923 Imperial Conference. The growing insurgency throughout the Middle East became the subcommittee's primary defense concern. In this regard, the group believed that for the immediate future the bulk of the Royal Air Force's strength would remain in Egypt, Palestine, Iraq, and along the Indian/Afghan border.[52] The subcommittee believed that Dominion air forces should complement the Royal Air Force in the unlikely event of a war with a major power breaking out. Sir Samuel

Hoare suggested that "one of the best means of helping the Dominions would be by exchange of personnel."[53] In Leo Amery's opinion, they needed to have the Dominions agree to organize their forces in parallel with the Royal Air Force.[54] When the imperial ministers met in London in September and October of 1923, the conference adopted this outlook put forward by Lord Peel's subcommittee.

On October 4, 1923, the conference attendees issued a detailed memorandum on the future of imperial air defense. The conditions agreed to by the conference focused on ways to provide mutual benefits for personnel matters and equipment. The foremost concern was for each Dominion to create an efficient peacetime air force organization and staff structure so that each force could mutually assist all imperial members in an emergency. They concluded:

> If organisations have to be improvised, staffs created, aircraft and equipment provided and plans matured after the outbreak of war, the value of air co-operation, however willingly and enthusiastically given, will be greatly lessened.[55]

To make certain that the air services of the empire meshed with each other, the conference agreed that similar training of personnel in areas of command, piloting, and mechanics was essential. The members of the conference recognized that training expenses could "be out of all proportion" to the sizes of the air force that each Dominion might eventually maintain, so they agreed to establish a technical trade school for the empire.[56] A new scheme outlined the training of permanent and short service officers. It became each Dominion's responsibility to select appropriate candidates for training at the Royal Air Force War College at Cranwell. Following the successful completion of their training, the graduates then served four years in Royal Air Force units. This system benefited both the RAF and the Dominions' air forces.

The personnel exchange outlined at the 1923 Imperial Conference intended to support all members within the imperial system. The conference's foremost interest was to ensure that the air force personnel from Britain and the Dominions shared a common doctrine to "facilitate their mutual co-operation."[57] The Royal Air Force gained a large pool of junior officers at no expense because their pay was the responsibility of their Dominion of origin. In return, the Dominions would benefit because their pilots would gain four years of operational experience at the expense of the Royal Air Force without the need to purchase and maintain large numbers of aircraft.[58] The system envisioned for the support services at the Imperial Conference proved to be impractical because of the expense of sending and housing the large number of students overseas. In Australia, they attempted to solve this problem by insisting that any individual wishing to join the RAAF as an aviation mechanic had to possess previous technical training.[59] The results were less than satisfactory; anyone with these trade skills had a better opportunity in the private sector.

Another key agreement regarded the standardization of aircraft and aircraft production. Recognizing that aviation would become an ever more important component in the future defense of the empire, the conference concluded that the present dependence upon the obsolescent war surplus aircraft needed to be corrected.[60] There was also a growing concern that all aircraft production was taking place only in Britain. In the opinion of those attending the conference, if there was a serious threat to one of the Dominions, "this state of affairs might have grave results."[61] There was a fear that the supply of aircraft to the Dominions could be cut if they became isolated. To correct this potential threat, the conference agreed to encourage the development of aircraft production in each Dominion or at least establish a "nucleus industry" capable of expansion in times of emergency.[62]

Figure 3.2. A *Punch* cartoon by Bernard Partridge commenting on the 1923 Imperial Conference depicting a lion overseeing a bunch of unruly cubs representing the Dominions. The discussions at the conference regarding aerial defense were as unruly as depicted in the cartoon. (Photograph courtesy of the National Archives of Australia)

Finally, the 1923 Imperial Conference insisted upon the need to standardize completely the types of aircraft and aircraft parts, believing standardization would lower production costs and ease pilot training and transition delays, resulting in a "great military advantage."[63] The push for standardization also included nomenclature, aerodynamic and engine research, aircraft armament, and electronic equipment.[64] Even though this appeared to be a good idea, in actuality it proved impractical. Tactics and equipment designed for Europe were unsuitable for the geographic distances and climate in the Pacific. Strategists relegated the Southwest Pacific to a secondary theater of operations and it did not receive a steady flow of military materiel. This had significant consequences during World War II and the majority of the equipment supplied to the Pacific Dominions came from the United States, not from Great Britain.

By the end of 1923, there was growing alarm within the British Air Ministry concerning the total absence of any aviation arm in New Zealand. Earlier in the year, on June 14, New Zealand formed the New Zealand Permanent Air Force (NZPAF) and its auxiliary or territorial element, the New Zealand Air Force (NZAF). The NZPAF consisted of only fifteen aircraft that included two Bristol fighters, two deHavilland D.H.4s and four D.H.9s, and seven antiquated Avro 504 trainers, and the NZAF had no aircraft but 104 reserve officers.[65] On November 7, 1923, the deputy chief of the Air Staff, Air Commodore John N. Steel, chaired a conference with members of the Air Staff and New Zealand's representative, Rear Admiral Alan Hotham, to determine how best to correct the problem. In addition, the conference attendees identified the best method for the Royal Air Force and the New Zealand air force to cooperate with each other in the event of a war or smaller conflict. Rear Admiral Hotham recognized that "the present state of aviation in New Zealand was almost negligible."[66] From Air Commodore Steel's viewpoint, New Zealand needed to take some small steps to create a nucleus for an air arm.[67] Hotham was skeptical that New Zealand really required a separate air force because such a force would be an adjunct to a ground or naval force. In addition, a standing air force was impractical for New Zealand because the Dominion organized all of its military formations "on a militia basis."

New Zealand's reluctance to establish an air force began to frustrate the British Air Ministry. Trenchard himself became involved and offered to assist the Dominion with the development of an air force by assigning a permanent RAF officer to advise the New Zealanders on air matters.[68] Unfortunately for Trenchard, the Dominion's leadership was unwilling to make expensive commitments in cash or personnel to form an extensive air defense component. In a terse reply to the offer, Secretary of the Air Ministry Walter F. Nicholson informed Trenchard: "Admiral Alan Hotham expressed the view that it was premature to consider extensive schemes of co-operation as regards personnel since the flying service in that Dominion [NZ] was still in its infancy."[69] Essentially, New Zealand's air force was stillborn. Several years would pass before the country made any progress regarding air defense.

By the Imperial Conference of 1923, it was clear that the Geddes Axe cut too deeply into the operating budget of the Royal Air Force. In retrospect, Geddes's no war for ten years assumption was surprisingly accurate. Without the advantage of hindsight, there was a growing concern within the Conservative government that the cuts went too far and that some reversals were required. There was also a growing consensus that the strength of the RAF was lacking, particularly to Britain's closest neighbor, France. New calls from the Air Ministry for air parity emerged but realizing them would have to wait. Political change came in Britain with the advent of Ramsay MacDonald's first Labour government, which did not support rearmament.

CHAPTER 4

THE ROYAL AIR FORCE AND POSTWAR AIR TRANSPORT DEFENSE PLANNING AND THE AIRMAIL SCHEME, 1919–1939

> *The future of Aviation—the future, perhaps, of the Air Force—will come, I hope, from the need of peaceful commerce rather than the tragic necessities of war.*[1]
>
> —Lord Weir

During the waning months of World War I, the leadership of the Royal Air Force (RAF) searched for a postwar role, uncertain that it would survive the budget cuts that were certain to come. In response to this concern, the Air Ministry decided that one way the RAF could play a meaningful part was to help develop the British Empire's commercial airways. From 1918 until the formation of Imperial Airways in early 1924, the air force personnel mapped air routes throughout the empire, flew the mails, and carried passengers. These commercial operations were more than routes and timetables; leaders within the Air Ministry and in private industry saw this as an opportunity to subsidize the infant aircraft industry. They also believed that the RAF's involvement in commercial endeavors would improve the air defense of the empire. The newly created air routes could serve as a means to move both air and ground units quickly from one trouble spot in the empire to another. They also hoped that flying commercially would provide and maintain a ready reserve of experienced pilots and ground mechanics in cases of national emergency. Unfortunately, as a military organization, the RAF was ill suited to operate as a commercial venture and eventually commercial endeavors clashed with military needs.

On May 22, 1917, Lord Cowdray, president of the Air Board, formed the Civil Aerial Transport Committee under the leadership of Lord Northcliffe, the owner of the *Times* and director of propaganda in Lloyd George's cabinet. This new committee's thirty-five members came from each Dominion and the pertinent government departments including the Air Ministry, the Admiralty, the Board of Trade, the Home Office, the Foreign Office, Post, and Colonial Offices. The committee was charged with three duties: first, to develop the means to expand and regulate civil and commercial aviation after the war; second, find ways to employ and train pilots and aircraft mechanics; and finally, convert the anticipated thousands of surplus military aircraft into civilian use.[2] The committee's recommendations became the origin of the Royal Air Force's postwar commercial activities.

The Civil Aerial Transport Committee first needed to establish how and by whom Great Britain's civil aviation sector should be regulated. The majority of the committee believed that British commercial air activities should remain under the control of the Air Ministry.[3] Frank Pick, the committee's vice-chairman and the head of the London Passenger Transport Board, was the lone dissenter: "I can only suggest that warlike considerations equally led to the decision to place the control of civil aerial transport with the Air Ministry, whose prime function must be warlike, and the conduct of war." Pick continued:

> On the analogy of railways, shipping, canals, tramways, etc., the Board of Trade . . . would be the fitting department of the Government to be concerned with the commercial and civil aspects of aeronautics.
>
> The Air Ministry would continue to be responsible for all those aspects of aeronautics, other than commercial.[4]

Pick recognized that there was a clear distinction between the military and commercial uses of aircraft. The majority of the committee's members disagreed. In fact, the committee's majority concluded that military and commercial aviation needs paralleled one another. This belief became clear in their initial plans for imperial air routes. The committee recognized the ambitious task to link the empire by air:

> This end will have been achieved when a system of properly planned and predetermined air routes have been instituted, with their aerodromes and other requirements, satisfying both military and commercial needs, between which there is no real conflict. On these routes, there should be civil aerial services wherever there is a reasonable demand for the facilities of aerial traffic and irrespective of the test of financial success.[5]

Clearly, the committee questioned the financial viability of an imperial aerial transport system that was a massive financial undertaking. The capital expenditure to purchase land and construct airfields was beyond the capabilities of any private aviation company. Again, the committee turned to the military to solve this situation and contemplated that existing and future military airfields should be made available to private and commercial aircraft.[6]

The committee hypothesized that air power would be critical to the future imperial defense. Thus, it was the responsibility of the government to sustain a viable aviation industry through direct and indirect subsidies:

> Aerial power will be as necessary for the protection of Great Britain and the existence of the Empire in the future, as naval power has been in the past. The Committee are accordingly of [the] opinion that it will be necessary, after the conclusion of the War, to take such measures as will maintain the power of production in this country, with its attendant power of design and progressive experiment. Without continuity, it would be impossible to have the organisation immediately available when required.[7]

Sir Hugh Trenchard concurred with their conclusions: "The future of commercial aviation must largely depend on the Royal Air Force for provisions of the necessary pilots and technical workers."[8] For Trenchard, imperial air defense would depend upon a sound air transportation system and industrial base. In his opinion, the demand for aircraft generated by the private sector would keep aircraft production lines operating. The private sector's needs would also encourage new and innovative aircraft designs and would lead to higher performance in military machines.[9] In addition to maintaining a viable aircraft industry, an additional benefit from commercial operations would be a ready reserve of aircraft in a national emergency. Trenchard likewise thought that commercial aircraft could be readily transformed from civilian to military configuration. Finally, he hoped that a vibrant commercial sector would augment the RAF by providing a reserve of trained pilots and mechanics that would allow for the air force's rapid expansion in times of national emergency.[10] In December 1918, President of the Air Council Weir examined the future relationship of military and commercial aviation. In his memorandum to the cabinet, Weir recognized that at that time, commercial aviation was nonexistent but that encouraging its development would provide enormous social and economic benefits for "civilisation."[11]

Figure 4.1. The president of the Air Council, Lord William Weir, and his secretary. In December 1918, he outlined the critical need to link military and commercial aviation for the defense of the empire. (Photograph courtesy of the Royal Air Force Museum)

Early in 1919, the RAF began to implement the transport schemes outlined by the Civil Aerial Transport Committee. On January 10, 1919, two squadrons organized daily scheduled flights between England and Paris in support of the British diplomatic mission to the Versailles Peace Conference, carrying dispatches and diplomats to and from the conference. For the next ten months, these RAF aircraft conducted more than 749 flights, transported 1,008 bags of mail, and carried 934 passengers.[12] In addition, the RAF had success with experimental airmail service with regularly scheduled deliveries to Marquise, Valenciennes, and Namur. On March 1, 1919, 8 Squadron and 120 Squadron inaugurated a second airmail route to the continent by providing regular service between Folkestone and Cologne.

In mid-January 1919, a major realignment took place with the formation of the Air Ministry and Winston Churchill replaced Weir as the air minister. Churchill's dual appointment as air minister and secretary of state for war was not without controversy. Many in the British aviation community feared that Churchill's appointment was the first step in dismantling the RAF and redistributing its units back to the army and navy.[13] These fears were unfounded. On February 12, the government added the aviation civil branch to the organizational structure within the Air Ministry and Churchill's portfolio's responsibilities and thereby addressed Frank Pick's earlier concern that the Air Ministry was exclusively interested in military affairs. Major-General Sir Frederick Sykes became the first undersecretary for civil aviation and Trenchard returned to the command of the RAF. One key aspect of Sykes's program was to begin establishing the air route system in concert with the RAF that would connect Britain with the Dominions. Sykes initiated a series of long-distance demonstration flights to prove the feasibility of air travel. In addition, Sykes's department began planning and constructing interlinked chains of airfields throughout the empire.[14] To further advance Sykes's agenda, in March Parliament passed the Aerial Navigation Bill.

This bill was the first legislation approved in Britain since 1913 that concerned civil aviation. It was a temporary measure that once again opened flying throughout the British Isles to civilian entities that ceased operations during the war. It also allowed the Air Ministry to regulate civilian aeronautics without the constant intervention from Parliament. Before the bill's passage, flying in the country was restricted to military aircraft. In addition, the bill permitted foreign air carriers to transport goods and mail into and out of Britain.[15] Sykes argued that it would be impossible to permit any form of civilian flying throughout Britain without the passage of the bill.[16]

With experience gained from the short flights to the continent, Britain's leaders now recognized the value of such air services throughout the empire. The first goal was to launch an air route to Egypt. Planners saw Cairo as the critical hub for any imperial air service, just as the Suez Canal was critical to British shipping interests. With an air hub established in Cairo, the Air Ministry envisioned air routes radiating south to Cape Town and eastward into Iraq, India, and ultimately to Australia and New Zealand.[17]

The leaders of Australia and New Zealand viewed an imperial air route as a vital imperial communication and defense link. To encourage the development of the Pacific air route, Australian prime minister Hughes offered a £10,000 prize in April 1919 to the first aerial flight to transit from London to Australia. Captain Ross Smith, a pilot with 1 Squadron of the Australian Flying Corps, was working on such a plan for months before Hughes offered the prize. Smith mapped the entire air route across India, Burma, and through the Southwest Pacific to a final landing site at Adelaide. Smith's preparatory work was the origin of the air route to Australia. Encouraged by Alcott and Brown's June crossing of the Atlantic in the Vickers Vimy, Smith stated that his own twin-engine "[Vickers'] unfailing reliability during ensuing long-distance flights inspired in me great confidence and opened my eyes to the possibilities of modern aeroplanes and their application to commercial uses."[18] From November 12, 1919, to March 3, 1920, Smith and his brother Keith completed this 14,000-mile flight and won the prize offered by Hughes. In addition to the prize money, the Prince of Wales awarded both brothers the Knight Commander of the Order of the British Empire on June 23, 1920.[19] The Australians' flight proved that it was possible to fly the great distance from Europe to Australia; however, the Vickers was not as mechanically dependable as Smith had hoped and weather conspired against the crew, making the journey longer than the normal steamship service. The flight demonstrated that imperial air travel was not yet practical and did not produce immediate or lasting dividends.

In December 1919, the Air Ministry dispatched three RAF teams to Africa to lay out an air route from Cairo to the Cape. The first team mapped the route from Cairo to Sudan; team two charted the

Figure 4.2. The Vickers Vimy flown by Sir Ross MacPherson Smith and his brother Sir Keith Smith. The two Australian brothers completed the first flight from the United Kingdom to Australia from November 12 to December 10, 1919, in 136 hours of flying time. The flight won the £10,000 prize offered by Australian prime minister Billy Hughes and demonstrated the potential of commercial and military air mobility within the British Empire. (Photograph courtesy of the Smithsonian National Air and Space Museum)

region from Sudan to Rhodesia; and team three plotted the route from Rhodesia to Cape Town.[20] These teams also began site preparation for new airfields with the use of native levies. All work by these teams proved to be for naught. Overcome by equipment failure, lack of supplies, and disease, these aerial expeditions failed miserably.

Nevertheless, in early 1920, it appeared that imperial air service was off to an auspicious start. Smith's flight to Australia neared its completion and the work of the three RAF teams dispatched to Africa seemed to be progressing. By the end of the year, it became clear that commercial aviation could not survive without substantial financial support from the government. Facing huge war debts and other expenses, the government issued austere budgets and was not prepared to subsidize the private companies to the extent required to establish a viable air transport system.

In April 1920, Lord Weir sent a report to Churchill, arguing for government subsidies to the British aviation industry for commercial and strategic reasons: "The existence of a healthy civil aerial transport industry would tend to ensure the supply of material to the Royal Air Force and reduce the cost."[21] Interestingly, Trenchard was opposed to the direct subsidy scheme proposed by Weir: "Apart from the general objection to any system of subsidies, I doubt if they would fulfill their object. . . . I fail to see how such subsidies will increase demand in any way."[22] From Trenchard's perspective, the best use of the government's limited funds would assist both the commercial carriers as well as the RAF through the construction of airfields and navigational infrastructure.[23]

In an attempt to influence change in the public and private sentiment in aviation, the Air Ministry convened the first Air Congress at London's Guildhall in October 1920. Representatives from the government and private industry met to discuss the current state of civil and military aeronautics in Britain and how to best proceed into the future. By the last quarter of the year it became clear that Britain's failing aeronautical industries would need government support to keep the country's aircraft production lines open as well as to maintain commercial flight operations. In his opening statement, Sykes pleaded for these subsidies and he believed that government financial backing was the only way that British aviation would survive. For Sykes, aviation was different from the nation's other transportation industries. He elaborated on the reasons why civil aviation needed continued financial support because the industry had no point of reference or history to conduct its operations. In Sykes's view, a system of subsidies would enable Britain's emerging airlines to conduct operations and gain more experience.[24]

Sykes feared that the loss of a sound aircraft-manufacturing base would have consequences for the future security of the empire. He also pointed out the problems that Great Britain faced in establishing a workable air route system from the home islands to the rest of the empire:

> We have to consider commercial aviation, not only from the Continental, but from the Imperial point of view. Here we have the long distances favourable to aircraft, though England unfortunately is detached by a wide stretch, either of ocean or foreign territory, from the nearest Dominion or possession. In the one case the range is too great for aeroplanes; in the other they are dependent on foreign landing grounds. The key-routes in the Imperial system are those from England to Egypt and Egypt to India.[25]

Sykes realized that Britain alone could not handle the burden of establishing an empire-wide air transport system. The Dominions and Colonies had to develop their own aviation systems to link the empire together. In addition, he repeated that the lack of a sound commercial airways system would have harmful effects on the RAF:

> Without such encouragement the air transport industry, which is yet in its infancy, may wilt . . . but we will have to face the almost complete disintegration of the expert designing and construction staffs built up during the war and the potential loss to the Royal Air Force.[26]

In responding to Sykes's paper, conservative MP William Joynson-Hicks felt that he placed too much emphasis on the commercial-military connection in the development of an imperial air scheme. He stressed the points made by Frank Pick in 1918:

> The first point that occurs to me is as to the relationship between military and civil aviation. . . . I am convinced that before long, in the course of a few years, when civil aviation has taken its full part in the transport of the country, it will tend to diverge from military aviation. There must be in the near future a complete divergence, because, to begin with, the type of machine needed for civil aviation.[27]

Major-General Sir Sefton Brancker, chairman of the Daimler Air Line, supported Joynson-Hicks's position that Britain's commercial aviation sector would be better served if it were removed from the Air Ministry:

> Supposing that aerial transport had been placed under the Ministry of Transport a year or two ago, we might even now have been in a very different position as regards aerial transport and Government assistance, because it would be under a Minister whose direct whose responsibility was transport.[28]

Brancker quickly changed this position when he became responsible for commercial aviation, replacing Frederick Sykes as director-general of civil aviation in 1922.

By the time of the Air Congress, private ventures were clearly suffering from their inability to turn a profit carrying passengers and mails. These companies faced subsidized foreign competition as well as direct competition with the RAF, to which the Air Ministry gave the sole responsibility to carry government officials and dispatches. Samuel Instone, president of Instone Air Lines, presented a bleak picture of the situation: "After our experience, I should like to come to the financial side of commercial aviation. I am bold enough to say, after the experience of 12 months, that commercial aviation to-day is a financial failure."[29] By the third day of the conference, discussions turned to military aviation. The RAF's and Royal Navy's representatives, Trenchard and Rear-Admiral Sir A. E. M. Chatfield, continued to state that military aviation needed a sound commercial aviation system to succeed. Trenchard affirmed that:

> One is forced to the conclusion that the Royal Air Force, for a first-class war, must be dependent on outside aid, and what outside aid is possible except civil aviation? [Much] the same way that the Navy relies on the mercantile marine but to a far greater extent.[30]

The Royal Navy's position in these discussions was rather limited. At this time, the navy's leadership was still fighting to have its air assets returned to it. Admiral Chatfield was an advocate of naval aviation, and like others who preceded him, continued to link the interests of commercial to military aviation:

> The Navy is vitally interested in aviation, and I would fully endorse all that has been said about the importance of civil and commercial aviation. There is no doubt that the country which can first make commercial and civil aviation a real live thing will open up itself the possibilities of becoming a great air power. . . . It is an undoubted fact that it is upon civil aviators that we shall have to rely in war time.[31]

Chatfield was also concerned that the navy would lose its last aviation responsibility—airships.

Meanwhile, Sir Sefton Brancker again continued to harp on the theme of reserves for the air force:

> First and foremost it is obvious that if we cannot keep a large standing Air Force, we must have a reserve, and a large and

efficient reserve, which is well trained and easily obtained in a crisis. Obviously again the healthiest and most efficient, and at the same time the most economical, form of reserves is a flourishing aerial transport industry.[32]

Sir John Forbes-Sempill's concluding remarks summarized the feelings of all attending the conference: "Anyone not already convinced of the absolute necessity of keeping Civil Aviation alive . . . would be well to note that it is emphatically stated that the efficiency of the Royal Air Force in time of war is absolutely dependent on Civil Aviation."[33] Although all of the participants and the Air Congress and Lord Weir's group agreed that a strong commercial air transportation system was required, they were unable to design any substantive schemes to resolve the deteriorating situation.

By the beginning of 1921, the state of British commercial aviation was in complete disarray. Any hopes created by the 1920 Air Congress disappeared. By the end of February, there was not a single British commercial carrier left in operation. As a result, throughout the year, the focus was on ways to subsidize the British air carriers.

On March 14, 1921, Sykes addressed the members of the Institute of Air Transport about the reasons for the failure of British civil aeronautics:

> Above all, there is a general financial stringency and the difficulty of obtaining capital. Yet without capital, it is impossible to initiate or run a new commercial concern, and without the experience only obtainable from the practical operation of air services, British commercial aviation will disappear.[34]

Sykes returned to the themes stated in 1918 by the Commercial Aerial Transport Committee as a solution to the problem faced by British aeronautics:

> If commercial aviation dies, we not only lose a great potential reserve for our Service aviation in time of emergency and thus risk our national security, but we neglect the use of the fastest means of intercommunications yet devised and surrender commercial air supremacy to those nations which are already full aware of its importance.[35]
>
> The solution of this problem, according to my firm belief, lies in the development of civil aviation. We look for an analogy in the Navy and the Mercantile Marine. . . . A large commercial air fleet will provide a reserve of men and machines, though it must be remembered that Service and Civil types of machines will diverge.[36]

In the summer of 1921, the RAF helped boost commercial aviation in an unanticipated way. An armed rebellion in Iraq and deep budget cuts forced the military services to devise new ways to deal with the conflict. Trenchard submitted a plan that promised that four to six squadrons of aircraft could quell the rebellion in comparison to the estimated 27,000 ground troops. First, the RAF had to map an air route from Cairo to Baghdad, without which pilots could become quickly lost in the featureless terrain while searching for the rebels. Teams created a series of markers and tracks across the desert to assist navigation throughout the area. The trail also included emergency landing sites constructed every fifteen to twenty miles.

The air route proved to be a military necessity. Flying long hours searching for roving bands of Iraqi rebels, RAF pilots found the track provided them with a vital navigational reference point. The army and the air force established a system of mutual support. RAF aircraft spotted and attacked the rebels. They also directed newly formed armored car units to the rebel locations for additional fire support. The trail also served as a path of rapid movement for the armored car units in the desert.

Along this route, the RAF began to provide regular air service to government officials traveling through the Middle East as well as carry the official mails. In constant use from their inception in 1921, the air routes received continual maintenance and improvements. When Imperial Airways took over transport responsibility from the RAF in 1924, the airline continued to maintain and extended this important desert air route for commercial and military purposes.

By the middle of 1922, the Air Ministry had begun to take actions to support commercial air carriers. That summer the Air Ministry gave the three reconstituted air carriers route monopolies and began to transfer the duties from the RAF to the private carriers. Handley-Page Transport won the most valuable route between London and Paris; the revitalized Instone Air Line received the London-Brussels-Cologne route; and Daimler Airways flew the London-Amsterdam-Bremen-Berlin route.[37] This scheme eliminated competition between the three officially recognized carriers. The Air Ministry hoped that by giving exclusive routes to these airlines they could guarantee a small operating profit. Through these designated route monopolies, the government was able to subsidize the carriers inexpensively. In July 1922, the "First Report of the Civil Aviation Advisory Board" took further steps to enhance the British air transport system through direct and indirect subsidies with the underlying goal of improving imperial air defense. The advisory board first wanted to establish financially sound companies:

> If civil undertakings are making an efficient attempt to keep open the civil airways of the Empire by means of aid and direct air communications, they can fairly claim a considerable measure of financial assistance from the Government until they have been able to establish themselves on a sound financial basis.[38]

The government removed that additional financial burden for the companies by constructing airway markers and airfields in direct cooperation with the RAF:

> We contemplate that the actual route to be followed by the civil company would be selected after discussion and agreement with the Royal Air Force so as to provide the most suitable route for Service purposes, and that the aerodromes, if not already in possession of the State, would be acquired by the State and after preparation of the ground, the erection of the necessary plant and construction of shed accommodation, would be rented to the operating company.[39]

The report later further elaborated on this point:

> We recognise that there are many advantages in the civil air route being the same as the R.A.F. route, and have accordingly inquired from the Chief of the Air Staff as to the assistance that the Service would be prepared to give to a commercial company adopting the longer or Arabian coast route to meet the strategic requirements of the R.A.F.[40]

By early 1924, the subsidies and route monopolies did not solve the problems for the private carriers. Following the recommendations of the Hambling Committee, the British government paid the private carriers £1 million over ten years and merged them into Imperial Airways in March 1924. The creation of Imperial eliminated all vestiges of commercial operations by the RAF except airway development.

By 1926, linking the empire by air routes became imperative to its political leaders. Noted long-distance flying pioneer Capt. Alan Cobham, at a speech in Melbourne before representatives of the British

Imperial Oil Company, stated, "Commercial success is not the issue. What is absolutely the issue is that aerial routes between the Dominions and the Motherland are essential for the defence of the Empire, and for all that the Empire stands for."[41] In October at the meetings of the 1926 Imperial Conference, Air Minister Sir Samuel Hoare, in a presentation before all of the attendees, stated that it was the goal of the London government to completely link the empire with aerial routes and make it possible to reach its most distant corners within two weeks.[42] No matter what the rhetoric called for, unfortunately, aircraft at this time were technically unable to perform the tasks of carrying heavy loads of passengers and cargo for long distances. The perceived promise that an airship could fill these duties was also problematic. They remained cost prohibitive and the British airship program remained mired in developmental and funding troubles; and the crash of the R 101 brought the British airship program to a halt.

On December 20, 1934, Sir Philip Sassoon, undersecretary of state for air, announced on the floor of the Commons that the government would increase the airmail capabilities of the empire within a two-year period. This public announcement had its origins in a plan presented to the cabinet on May 30 titled "Scheme for the Carriage of First-Class Mails by Air," which became known as the Empire Air Mail Scheme (EAMS).[43] The plan would remove the carriage of first-class mails from the contracted shipping companies and transfer this responsibility to Imperial Airways. Like all of the commercial plans outlined before it, the scheme had the underlying purpose of its importance for imperial defense.[44] The government also had a willing partner with the formation of the joint private/government-supported airline, Imperial Airways. Sir Eric Geddes, known for wielding the budget axe in the early 1920s, now served as the chairman of Imperial. He believed that transporting the mails and passengers could not be separated from each other and recommended that flying boats would be the best aircraft to make the lengthy trip from London to Sydney via Singapore. The goal for the government was to connect the two cities within seven and a half days. From Geddes's perspective Imperial Airways could "operate any kind of service and [it] is for the Governments concerned and our customers to say and demonstrate which class of service and which scale of charges they wish to have."[45] For such a service to take place, however, it would be the responsibility of the British taxpayer to find the money for this service. In a word, subsidies, which were somewhat of an anathema to Geddes.[46] He was a realist and understood that the service could not operate on postage and paying customers alone.

The plan ran into an immediate roadblock. When presented with the plan, the Australians objected to its basic premises. They opposed their proposed share of the annual subsidy of £90,000, but more important for them was maintaining control of the last stages of the flight from Singapore to Sydney. Australia's QANTAS airline was already flying this route and had negotiated overflight rights with the Dutch over their territories of the Netherlands East Indies. According to the British plan these routes would now be the concern of Imperial Airways. The Australians were not willing to give up these responsibilities. Inflexibility of both the British and Australians delayed the implementation of the scheme for the next four years and regular service would not take place until 1938. The EAMS never would become successful, within a year the outbreak of the war interrupted service, and it would not see any progress until the postwar period.

For strategic reasons, throughout the 1920s and 1930s, the British Empire's airways planning remained the responsibility of the RAF. The primary intent of these routes was to move military aircraft from one strategic point of the empire to another and was not their commercial viability. Although licensed for public or private, all airfields in Britain and throughout the empire gave "all military aircraft" the absolute right to their access. During the interwar period, the concept of commercial entities providing a ready reserve for the RAF lingered. In fact, the opposite was true. As commercial aviation became more viable, the lucrative career opportunities lured pilots and technicians away from military service. In addition, by the middle of the 1930s the needs of commercial operators and the RAF came into direct conflict. As both entities faced growing demand for larger and more modern types of aircraft, production of commercial models took away vital and limited production capacity from military types. It would not be until 1938 that Imperial Airways finally established regular commercial air service between Britain and Australia.

CHAPTER 5

AIRSHIPS AND THE EMPIRE: DEFENSE, SCHEMES, AND DISASTER, 1919–1930

> *The Airship of to-day, as far as its adaptability is concerned, should be compared to the sailing vessels of Elizabethan time, ready at her country's need to become a ship of war and capable of rapid conversion.*[1]
> —Air-Commodore E. M. Maitland

In this age of supersonic aircraft and jumbo jet airliners, the military and commercial utility of an airship seems almost quaint. In the aftermath of the first aerial bombing raids of London by German zeppelins, the military application of a dirigible was especially real in the 1920s. Like Germany, Britain manufactured numerous rigid and nonrigid airships during the war, and by war's end, operated a significant fleet of seventy-three nonrigid and three rigid airships whose primary function was long patrols against the U-boat threat.[2] Following the war, the airship continued in this capacity, but military planners devised strategic plans for the airship to act as a transport and communication link for the British Empire and as an adjunct to a commercial transportation system. The British airship program was a microcosm of the problems of Britain's postwar aviation network: private versus public funding, airplanes versus airships, the Royal Air Force (RAF) versus the Royal Navy, and commercial enterprises versus military endeavors.

Four days before his appointment as the first controller-general of the Department of Civil Aviation, Sir Frederick Sykes read a speech titled "Commercial Aviation in Light of War Experience" before the London Chamber of Commerce on January 7, 1919. To an audience of prominent business leaders, Sykes outlined the advantages that the airship had over the airplane and how it would enhance the transportation system of the British Empire.[3] During this session, Sykes referred to one particular airship mission during the war. In November 1917, the German Zeppelin L59 left from Jamboli, Bulgaria, carrying twelve tons of ammunition to resupply the German troops fighting in German East Africa. The L59's commander, Kapitanleutnant Ludwig Bockholt, abandoned the mission when he received a radio message indicating that the troops that he was to assist had already surrendered. Although the mission failed to deliver the supplies, the flight was a significant accomplishment. The zeppelin remained aloft over four days and flew 4,198 miles nonstop. The airship demonstrated its heavy lift capabilities over vast distances as well as its potential for strategic military transport.[4] For these reasons, Sykes felt that the mission of the L59 confirmed the airship's utility for both military and commercial purposes.[5]

Sir Hugh Trenchard was not as impressed with the airship's capability as was Sykes. Trenchard recognized the airship's capability for variable speed and ability to hover, its value as an observation and communication platform, endurance, ease of handling in fog and darkness, and finally its considerable lifting abilities for commercial work.[6] For Trenchard, these positive aspects of airships were counterbalanced by their lack of airworthiness, ground handling and housing difficulties, vulnerability even with the employment of nonflammable gas, and the extravagant requirement in personnel required for their operation. Because the Air Ministry and especially the Royal Air Force faced diminishing budgets in the postwar period, Trenchard argued correctly that it was better to direct the limited funds available toward the development of the airplane. Trenchard also questioned both the commercial and military capability of the airship in the strongest terms: "The work performed by the existing rigid ships is at present negligible and does not justify the absorption of personnel and expenditure on constructional and housing facilities involved."[7]

In January 1919, airships were the last aspect of aviation still under the Admiralty's control. The airship's primary function during the war was for naval reconnaissance against German U-boats. Rather than disrupt their operations, airships remained the navy's responsibility until after the war when the navy transferred the airship organization to the Air Ministry. Although he was not a great supporter of the airship, Trenchard was more than willing to take over the Admiralty's responsibilities to consolidate all of Britain's air functions under the Air Ministry's umbrella.[8]

With the end of the war and no need for a sizable airship fleet, negotiations began between the Air Ministry and the Admiralty to transfer these assets to the Air Ministry. This was not an insignificant matter for either service. During the war, the Admiralty spent more than £40,000,000 on airships and their support facilities. By May 1919, the two parties agreed to complete the transfer of the airships, infrastructure, and personnel to the Air Ministry by October 22, 1919.[9]

In the summer of 1919, the successful transatlantic flight of the R.34 bolstered Britain's airship program. On July 2, R.34 took off from East Fortune, Scotland, and after a four-day flight, arrived at Roosevelt Field, New York. The following week, the airship returned safely to Pulham, England, on July 12, after a three-day flight. The R.34 became the first aircraft to complete a return crossing of the Atlantic.[10]

Figure 5.1. British airship R.34 moored at Roosevelt Field, Long Island, New York, on July 6, 1919, after completing the successful crossing of the Atlantic Ocean. Following the R.34's return to Britain on July 13, the mission demonstrated the hope that in the near future airships could link the vast British Empire by air. (Photograph courtesy of the Smithsonian, National Air and Space Museum)

The success of the R.34 did not silence the critics of the British Airship service, a number of whom backed Trenchard's opinions. In a parliamentary debate on July 24, 1919, airship opponents raised their objections to their further development. Labour Party backbencher Lieutenant Colonel Joseph Montague Kenworthy echoed Trenchard's position that government money was better spent on airplanes.[11] Aerial pioneer and Conservative MP Lieutenant Commander John Theodore Cuthbert Moore-Brabazon echoed Kenworthy's position that airships were dangerous to operate as long as hydrogen remained the principal lifting gas. To replace the hydrogen with inert helium, Brabazon correctly argued, was a costly proposition.[12]

Even with the successful flight of the R.34, the future for British airships still did not appear bright. Negotiations continued between the

Air Ministry and the Admiralty concerning the details of their transfer. Nevertheless, not until August 22, 1919, did the Admiralty finally report in a letter to the secretary of state for air the final disposition of Britain's airship establishment. The Admiralty agreed that the R.34 and R.38 would remain in commission with the RAF but were obligated to support any future naval requirements.[13]

While the Air Ministry and the Admiralty continued negotiations, the full British cabinet decided to reduce the airship program to a minimum.[14] The cabinet felt that the future of airships was best left to private enterprise but with the caveat that civilian personnel could be recalled to national service in the advent of an emergency.[15]

On September 8, 1919, a meeting took place at Australia House, London, between representatives from the Air Ministry and prominent members of Britain's aviation industry. The central theme of the meeting concerned the future government policy regarding airships and the involvement of private industry. The ultimate goal was to transfer Britain's lighter-than-air assets over to a commercial syndicate.[16] Under-Secretary of State for Air Maj. Gen. John Seely opened the session:

> Our service needs will compel us to build some [airships]; but if we were to confine ourselves only to service needs, we should run a great risk of falling behind in the race for supremacy in lighter-than-air.[17]

During this meeting, Sir Lionel Fletcher recognized the value of decreasing transit times within the empire and wondered if the government considered possible route structures to South Africa, India, Australia, and New Zealand. In addition, Fletcher wondered about the disparity between the commercial and the military utility of airships. He believed that converting a commercial airship for war might present an insurmountable problem.[18] General Seely replied that in the future, there would be a divergence between military and commercial airships, but the current fleet could easily be converted for both purposes.[19]

In the months following the Australia House meeting, the Air Ministry submitted offers and negotiated with the principal aviation firms such as de Havilland and Vickers on a proposal to turn over all of the airships and support equipment in the government's possession. The value of the equipment was significant. In October 1919, the Air Ministry notified the cabinet that completion of the R.36, R.37, R.38, R.39, R.40, and the R.80 would cost approximately £670,000.[20] Once again, the lighter-than-air advocates within the Air Ministry justified this expense by stressing the important commercial and military value of these airships.

The budget shortages were becoming so acute by the beginning of 1920 that the only possibility of a British airship service surviving was to commercialize the system. Throughout the early months of 1920, the Air Ministry proposed that any commercial entity that obtained this material would be obligated to operate the airship to the benefit of the government and would absorb the military personnel and maintain their proficiency in case of national emergency.[21] For the British aviation corporations, the financial risk was too great even with the offer of "free" equipment. The unproven use of airships in a commercial role, the "onerous" financial risks to the companies, and the demand for the return of equipment in times of national emergency compelled these firms to reject the Air Ministry's offer.[22]

In June 1920, the Air Council addressed the need to dispose of Britain's airships. The Air Council's membership, comprised of the Air Ministry's branch heads that included the chief of the Air Staff, controller-general of civil aviation, director general of aircraft production and research, finance member, and administrator of works and buildings, was chaired by the air minister.[23] The council was particularly concerned about the loss of capital, putting Britain behind other nations with airships, and the potential military loss for the empire if the government scrapped the airship program.[24] In addition, the Air Council was frustrated by the lack of interest in their privatization plan.[25] In response, the Air Ministry submitted another proposal that would have been more appealing financially to private industry. Unfortunately, the Treasury felt that the plan gave away too much and killed the new proposal. On June 22, 1920, George L. Barstow, permanent secretary to the chancellor of the exchequer, wrote to the secretary of state for air, Winston Churchill, that the Treasury believed that the airships should "be scrapped."[26]

The harsh position taken by the Treasury once again raised the whole question of Britain's future airship policy, especially from the military aspect. In response, the Air Ministry approached the Admiralty to determine its commitment to the airship. On November 20, 1920, the Air Council's representative, Sir Walter F. Nicholson, wrote to the Admiralty's Lord Commissioners requesting their requirements regarding airships, but he also questioned the airship's future for financial reasons.[27]

In a rare moment, when examining the value of the airship, the Royal Navy agreed with the Air Ministry. The Admiralty's Lord Commissioners' representative, W. J. Evans, responded that money directed toward airships would be better spent on "heavier-than-aircraft."[28] Without a commercial entity willing to take over Britain's airship program, the commissioners reluctantly concluded that the industry must be allowed to lapse.[29]

By the early months of 1921, British commercial and military airship policy had come to a complete standstill. In those uncertain economic times, business was reluctant to invest in airships without significant government financial guarantees or subsidies. With support lacking from both services, it appeared that there was little hope for any future British airship service. In February, the RAF closed the Howden

Station and transferred the base's equipment to the Air Ministry's Civil Aviation Branch, confirming the service's lack of interest. For the next several months, the editor of *Flight*, Stanley Spooner, lamented the dilapidated state of Britain's airship industry and its bleak future.[30]

Spooner identified new support for airships that probably saved or at least prevented the termination of the airship program in Britain in 1921—the Dominions. With the airship branch slated for elimination on August 1, it appeared that their use in imperial air transportation was no longer viable. At this point, the Dominions' leaders stepped in to save the British airship fleet from the scrap heap and prevent the closure of the remaining airship station at Carrington.

The first strong indication of Dominion interest in and support for an airship service came in April 1920 when Alfred H. Ashbolt, the agent general for Tasmania, sent a memorandum to the Australian House of Lords that stressed the importance of an airship service for the Dominion. Although he recognized the huge expense of such a service, Ashbolt felt that it would also be incumbent upon the Dominions to provide a small percentage of the funding to develop them for the empire and repeated the common arguments for the need of an airship service.[31] The Dominion prime ministers attending the 1921 Imperial Conference gave the airships a new lease on life. At the conference, one of the significant discussion points was imperial communications. Airship supporters in the Air Ministry prepared a memorandum for the Dominions' officials entitled "Development of Civil Air Communications within the Empire." The Air Ministry provided all the conventional arguments in support of the airship but they also expressed them in terms of their interests on behalf of the Dominions: "The development of the rigid airship during the last ten years has now reached a stage at which the future utilisation of this class of aircraft has become a matter of considerable importance to the Empire as a whole."[32]

At the meetings the Air Ministry also introduced information regarding a new technology that they felt could significantly reduce the operating cost of an airship system. The single most expensive item to operate an airship was the large number of ground personnel. Moreover, airships needed huge hangars to house them and extensive hydrogen-gas production facilities. When plotting a route across the empire the Air Ministry determined that it would require eight major air stations to Australia, each of which needed approximately 300 to 400 people to operate and maintain them.[33] To eliminate these extensive costs, in the spring of 1921 the airship service successfully tested the airship mooring tower Vickers Ltd. had patented in 1919.[34]

The mooring tower, placed in the center of a circular airfield, enabled an airship to make landing approaches into the prevailing wind. To dock the airship to the mast, a special fitting on the nose of the craft slipped into a coupling basket at the top of the mooring tower. Once secured to the mast, the airship could swing into the prevailing wind while remaining secure without the need for large numbers of ground handling personnel. The Air Ministry predicted that mooring masts would reduce operating costs by significantly reducing ground staff and ensuring service that was more regular.[35]

Before the Institute of Transport, Sir Frederick Sykes expressed his hope for the future that the mooring mast offered:

> [The airship's] main disadvantage is the large outlay required for the construction and upkeep of sheds and the numerous personnel necessary for its handling. The difficulties we believed could be overcome by mooring ships to a mast. . . . We are, therefore, considerably nearer to overcoming one of the main obstacles to economic use of airship[s].[36]

A £15,000 mast eliminated the need for a £150,000 storage shed at each site, according to one Air Ministry estimate.[37]

With these new cost-saving figures presented at the Imperial Conference, some members of the Dominion delegations enthusiastically encouraged further development of the airship. H. Ross Smith, an Australian representative, urged the acceleration of demonstration flights to Australia and said that the Australians wanted the route opened at the earliest possible date.[38]

At the final session of the Imperial Conference on July 29, 1921, three days before the August 1 shutdown date for Britain's airship services, the focus was specifically on the future of the empire's airship operations. With a sense of urgency in his opening commentary, Secretary of State for Air Frederick Guest warned the conference of the imminent demise of the British airship program. He announced that Britain's airship fleet was insufficient for a fully developed service.[39]

Following Guest's speech, support from Australian prime minister Billy Hughes and New Zealand's prime minister William Massey averted the termination of Britain's airship service. If the airship delivered the benefits that its advocates promised, the two most distant Dominions had the most to lose by its cancellation. Hughes asked for a delay to see if the Australian Parliament would provide financial assistance or subsidies to the program.[40] Massey concurred with Hughes and felt that he should have the opportunity to consult with New Zealand's Parliament about future support for airship service. It was also clear from Massey's statement that he was not totally convinced about the airship's potential. Massey concluded, "I doubt if it is possible for the Government to hand the business over to private individuals for quite a long time to come. . . . it will certainly be five years before any service of the sort can reach Australia and New Zealand."[41]

While the Imperial Conference took place in London, the first new airship completed since the war launched in Cardington on June 23.

The British did not intend to use the R.38; they sold it to the U.S. Navy. During the first three test flights, there were indications of problems regarding the ship's performance and structural integrity. On the R.38's fourth trial flight on August 23, the ship's aluminum structure collapsed during a low-altitude maneuver and the ruptured hydrogen gasbags exploded. Only five crew members of the ship's complement of forty-five survived the disaster.[42] The course of the British airship policy and its setbacks clearly frustrated Prime Minister Hughes:

> If you ask me whether I am satisfied with the proposal to cast aside the instrument of Empire communication which, I may remind you, cost something like £40,000,000 and which offers the most hopeful means of bringing this world-wide Empire of ours within a narrower compass, then most emphatically I am not satisfied.[43]

In spite of the disaster, support continued. Prime ministers attending the Imperial Conference gave the program a new lease on life when they agreed to use the next six months to rally financial support in their respective Dominions to sustain some form of imperial airship service. In December, Hughes brought the issue of Australian assistance before the Australian Parliament. Despite the continuous misfortunes of the British airship service, he continued to regard airships highly and encouraged Australia to support these efforts financially.[44]

By February 1922, the six-month reprieve for the cessation of the British airship program agreed upon at the Imperial Conference was about to end. Once again, hope for continuing an imperial service was waning. Examining the financial benefits versus the cost of airship operation, both South Africa and New Zealand declined participation in any government-operated system. On the sixteenth, the British secretary of state for air, Frederick Guest, announced in Parliament that:

> In accordance with the agreement made with the Dominion Prime Ministers during the conference last summer, the Government agreed to suspend disposal of airships and airship material until the Prime Ministers had had an opportunity of consulting their Parliaments in regard to the establishment of an Imperial airship route. Replies from the Dominions and India are not yet complete, but the Governments of South Africa and New Zealand have stated that owing to financial reasons, they are unable at present to participate in such a scheme.[45]

While politicians and policy makers argued about keeping or eliminating the British airship establishment through 1919 and 1922, research continued in an attempt to develop the airship's capability and versatility. Many of these new ideas centered on the airship's military application. In spite of the unrelenting threat of cancellation, these experiments provided airship advocates with evidence that demonstrated the airship's importance.

In December 1919, Group Captain Charles R. Samson had reported to the Air Ministry that it was feasible for an airship to launch and retrieve fixed-wing aircraft and operate as an aerial aircraft carrier.[46] For Samson, the aircraft carrier airship provided four advantages that increased the practicability of the airship for military use. Not only did the fixed-wing aircraft operating from an airship increase its reconnaissance ability, but also the airship's attached aircraft could provide an aerial defense from hostile aircraft. They also could attack enemy airships that might be scouting the British fleet, and finally, conduct long-range attack raids. Air Vice Marshal Arthur V. Vyvyan concurred with Samson's proposal. He noted the difficulties of fixed-wing aircraft operations in high seas from the aircraft carrier HMS *Argus* during a postwar fleet exercise. Vyvyan argued that the government pursue an airship aircraft carrier program as vigorously as surface aircraft carriers. Vyvyan also believed that the 5,000,000-cubic-foot R.38 or L.71 could each accommodate a full squadron of the Parnall Panther or Sopwith Snipe aircraft and estimated that an airship aircraft carrier could operate at forty knots for five to six days. To extend the airship's endurance, Vyvyan also advocated close ties between the airship and the surface fleet.[47]

Although Samson and Vyvyan's concept of an aircraft carrier airship seemed rather fanciful, this concept remained a constant consideration in later British airship designs. In addition, designers submitted proposals for airships armed with howitzers and acting as an aerial gun platform. In spite of these far-fetched proposals, the primary military function of any airship remained aerial reconnaissance and heavy lift strategic troop transport.

In March 1922, a new plan floated to establish an imperial airship system with the collaboration of government and private industry was the first new proposal that was acceptable to both parties. Known as the Burney Airship Scheme, it was named after its author, Commander C. Dennis Burney.[48] On March 27, 1922, Burney submitted a letter to the Air Ministry and to the governments of India and Australia calling for the creation of an airship monopoly run by Vickers Ltd. and Shell Oil Group with £1,800,000 of common shares and £2,200,000 debentures guaranteed by the government.[49]

Burney felt that substantial direct and indirect subsidies from the government were required for this fledgling entity to survive. Like the government's 1920 plan, Burney suggested that the government would provide in-kind support by giving the new company the existing fleet of airships and the production and maintenance infrastructure. In addition, the government would provide free of charge its wireless and meteorological services. In the form of an indirect subsidy, Burney advocated that dividend and interest payments should be free of income tax, thus strengthening private awareness and investment in the company's capital stock. In return for this generous backing, the new airship company would provide biweekly scheduled service to India with weekly extensions to Australia. In addition, the company immediately would construct five new airships valued at approximately £750,000 each and spend an additional £1.2 million on capital expenditures such as bases, manufacturing facilities, and mooring masts. Burney anticipated the company's annual operating expenses at £390,000 but in return estimated £1.5 million in revenue from mail and passengers.[50]

Burney took the matter of British airship development public. On the day he sent his proposal to the Air Ministry, he also issued a press release in an attempt to generate public support and awareness. Even though the focus of Burney's proposal was commercial, the military component was also a primary concern. Burney worried about the elimination of the airship program and its effect on national security. For him, airships remained the ideal platforms for U-boat patrols and, when equipped with aircraft, could strike at an enemy a thousand miles away.[51]

For the remainder of 1922, the Burney Airship Scheme became the focus of a vigorous debate between the pertinent government agencies. Chancellor of the Exchequer Sir Robert Stevenson Horne found it difficult to accept that the Burney Scheme was financially viable and felt that government participation in the proposed stock venture would be "almost uniformly unsuccessful."[52]

Winston Churchill, not far removed from his dual post as secretary of state for air and war, now served as secretary of state for the colonies. He had a great interest in and direct knowledge of the difficulties surrounding Britain's airship system. Like Stevenson, Churchill questioned the economics of the Burney Scheme. He felt that the £2,200,000 of government capital was inadequate and that Vickers Ltd. and Shell Petroleum would not incur any financial risk.[53] In his criticism of the Burney Scheme, Churchill cited the crash of the R.38 in August 1921 as evidence against the airship's safety and its utility versus the airplane.[54]

Sir Frederick Guest was more inclined than his predecessor to pursue an airship construction plan based on Burney's proposal. Although the Burney Scheme centered on commercial operation, Guest felt that Air Ministry support for the airship program was essential for national and imperial defense:

> [The Burney Scheme] is capable of producing practical flying results, though owing to the many uncertain factors involved there can be no guarantee of its commercial success. . . . I am of [the] opinion that the sum [£80,000] named is the maximum financial assistance which should be provided from the funds available for defence.[55]

In matters of aerial defense, Trenchard was hardly reluctant to question his superiors at the Air Ministry. He remained skeptical of the airship's value to aerial defense, especially because it would redirect money from the Royal Air Force's fixed-wing assets.[56]

By July 1921, the Committee of Imperial Defence recommended that the government should not proceed with an airship program for financial reasons. Countering the committee's suggestion, Prime Minister Lloyd George decided to pursue a commercial airship venture based on the Burney Scheme and appointed a commission to ascertain the commercial and military value of the airship.[57] Lloyd George's support confirmed the continuation of the British airship system and the subsequent Conservative governments of Andrew Bonar Law and Stanley Baldwin continued the program. The focus of the airship development remained on the Burney Scheme or a slight modification thereof. Facing ministerial support for an airship program, Trenchard reluctantly accepted these proposals but in a series of letters to the air minister, he wanted to prevent the diversion of the RAF's limited funds to airships.[58]

Trenchard remained skeptical of Burney's economic claims and feared that the navy might reacquire responsibility of the British airship program. He reluctantly backed its continuation but only under the control of the Air Ministry.[59] In early 1923, momentum grew within the British government in support of the airship. Throughout the spring and summer of 1923, a special subcommittee of the Committee of Imperial Defence chaired by the First Lord of the Admiralty, Leo Amery, met to determine if the technical details of the Burney scheme were realistic. The Admiralty reversed its earlier position and now attached great importance to the airship in a naval reconnaissance role.[60] Secretary of State for Air Sir Samuel Hoare emphasized the importance of airships to the British Empire and contended that the airship was essential because of its long range and endurance.[61]

Amery's committee issued a final report in favor of the airship to the Committee of Imperial Defence. Hoare confirmed in Parliament on August 2, 1923, that the Conservative government would continue the airship program despite the many concerns surrounding their development. Hoare argued that though the airship was a strategic instrument for the Far East and Australia, the government would encourage its development through the private sector rather than by state operation.[62]

In the fall of 1923, the British airship program seemed to be going forward on a dual military and commercial track with Dominion participation. In a statement before the 1923 Imperial Economic Conference, Hoare indicated that the British government would establish airship routes to the Dominions regardless of their participation financially.[63]

Three months later the British airship program and the Burney Scheme was once again in disarray. In January 1924, a significant shift in the British political landscape took place. In the November 1923 general election, Stanley Baldwin's Conservatives in Parliament shrank from 345 seats to 258. Without a majority in Parliament, Baldwin declined to form a coalition government with the Liberal party. This left it to the Labour Party, then under the leadership of Ramsay MacDonald, to form a coalition government with Liberal Party support. Almost a year to the day after the announcement of the Burney Scheme, the Labour government rejected the plan because it felt that it created a "virtual monopoly."[64]

The socialist Labour government opposed the privatization Burney Airship Scheme but not a government-administered airship program. In fact, Labour felt more comfortable nationalizing airships under government control rather than subsidizing them with commercial entities. Within a month of taking office, Labour's secretary of state for air, Christopher B. Thomson, issued a long memorandum outlining the government's position concerning airships. Like so many who preceded him, Thomson highlighted the important link between a commercial airship system and military applications.[65]

The Labour government placed a high value on the utility of the airship vital to the empire. The government authorized to the Air Ministry in the 1924–1925 Air Estimate £1,400,000 over four years to proceed with a program of governmental airship development on the broad lines of the commercial and military applications. On May 6, 1924, the Airship Development Committee established the parameters of Labour's airship policy with a decision to start the construction of two massive airships. For the remainder of the 1920s, British airship construction focused on these two ships. The government financed and built the first ship at Cardington, a 5,000,000-cubic-foot-capacity airship whose primary application would be for the military—in particular for naval reconnaissance. In addition, the design of the ship would include provisions for a squadron of twelve aircraft, their equipment, and personnel for the Royal Air Force or 200 fully armed soldiers for the army. The government ship became the R.101 and was known as the "Socialist" ship.

The Vickers Company designed the second airship, designated the R.100 and referred to as the "Capitalist" ship, primarily for commercial applications. Vickers received the construction contract so as not to deprive the company of its earlier investments. The Air Ministry would allow Vickers to buy the airship for a modest sum of £150,000 contingent upon the company making the airship available to the government in the case of a national emergency.[66] On May 14, 1924, Prime Minister MacDonald confirmed the government's two-ship program.[67] A week following the prime minister's statement in the Commons, Thomson justified the government's position of the two-path airship development process before the House of Lords:

> These proposals should enable two ships to be placed in commission in a shorter period than under the original scheme. The Government ship and the commercial ship will be laid down simultaneously. This will also result in the maintenance of two separate airship manufacturing plants and other ground facilities on a scale which will admit of rapid expansion.[68]

MacDonald's government fell after only ten months in office. With Stanley Baldwin's return, many wondered if he would reintroduce the Burney Airship Scheme. Sir Samuel Hoare, reappointed as air minister, decided to proceed with Labour's airship plan for the sake of continuity, although he was not fully satisfied with the Labour scheme.[69]

With the Labour airship program confirmed, the old conflict between the Royal Air Force and Royal Navy over control of airships resurfaced. Because the primary military function stated was naval reconnaissance, the navy wanted again to become the organization that ultimately had control of the equipment and funds. In October 1925, Trenchard intercepted a copy of an unofficial memorandum sent by Alex Flint, a permanent undersecretary at the Admiralty, to Lord

Haldane at the Committee of Imperial Defence that argued in favor of the navy's control of the airship program.[70] From the Admiralty's perspective, only trained naval personnel understood how airships cooperated with the fleet.[71] In a sharp rebuttal, Trenchard defended the Royal Air Force and the Air Ministry's responsibility for all air assets to Air Minister Samuel Hoare:

> At the meeting under Lord Haldane's Committee today I stated that it was clear that the Admiralty were raising the question of ownership and control of Airships now and in the future, and that under the terms of reference to our Committee such a claim was out of order. . . . Lord Haldane over-ruled me affirming that was a Cabinet decision. . . . I am clearly of the opinion that Lord Haldane's view is incorrect.[72]

Trenchard's foremost concern was the possibility that the air force would become subordinate to the navy if the Air Ministry relinquished its control of airships.[73] However, even more critical to Trenchard was the Admiralty's challenge to the future control of airpower.[74] In the end, the cabinet confirmed Trenchard's position and the airship program remained under Air Ministry control.

With production of the R.100 and R.101 progressing, albeit slowly, the Air Ministry now decided to include the Dominions in the planning of the future use of airships within the empire. In May 1927, Group Captain Peregrine F. M. Fellowes received orders from the Directory of Airship Development to conduct an inspection trip to "advise the Dominion Governments as to possible sites for airship bases with a view to future Empire airship development."[75] For the next six months, Fellowes and his party toured the Dominions discussing policy with leaders and making site surveys. Interestingly, in reference to Australia and New Zealand, the Directory of Airship Development instructed

Fellowes to lower their expectations for regular airship service. The directory felt that demonstration flights to the Pacific Dominions could not take place before 1929.[76] More realistically, the Air Ministry did not foresee a regular service operating to the Pacific Dominions until 1933 at the absolute earliest.[77] Presenting this timeline to the Australians and New Zealanders, Fellowes reassured them that "the Dominions need not commit themselves to anything but a very minor expenditure prior to the partial completion of the home trials."[78]

Even with the extended time presented to Australian prime minister Bruce, Fellowes provided detailed blueprints and cost analysis for three airship stations in the Commonwealth located at Perth, Melbourne, and Sydney. In response to the plan, Bruce responded that following the trial flights, "[the Australian] Government will take all steps necessary to carry out the recommendations of the report."[79]

Fellowes's mission also explored areas of New Zealand for potential airship bases and discussed the future prospects of airship service to the most distant Dominion from London. Planning for such service was much more difficult for Fellowes. Suitable landing sites, more erratic weather, and problematic terrain in New Zealand were a few of the difficulties he encountered. On the North Island, he selected potential sites near Auckland and the capital, Wellington; however, they were very distant from these cities' centers. On the South Island, Fellowes scouted sites near Dunedin and Christchurch but varied weather patterns made them both problematic for operations.[80] New Zealand's prime minister, Joseph Gordon Coates, like Bruce, responded positively to Fellowes's report. Coates's government committed only £1,400 for meteorological services and deferred commitment of major funding until he ascertained Australian intentions.[81]

Throughout 1926, 1927, and 1928 construction of the R.100 and R.101 continued at a glacial pace. Air Minister Hoare continued to state how vital airships were for imperial defense and communications even

Figure 5.2. The R.101 moored at Cardington, England, on March 10, 1930. The R.100 privately funded and designed "Capitalist" and the R.101 government-funded and designed "Socialist" airships were part of the British Air Ministry's final attempt to link the empire by rigid airships. The crash of the R.101 on its maiden flight on October 5, 1930, killed forty-eight of the fifty-four passengers and crew including the former and current air ministers, Lord Christopher Thomson and Sir Sefton Brancker. The crash ended all British interest in airships. (Photograph courtesy of the Smithsonian, National Air and Space Museum)

though the program was behind schedule.[82] The fiscal realities of 1920s Britain could not accommodate the luxury of a government-sponsored airship service no matter how vital it was to imperial defense. The Air Estimates for 1926–1927 directed toward the continued construction of the R.100 and R.101 reflected these fiscal constraints and reduced their construction budget from £400,000 to £335,000.[83]

Throughout 1929 and 1930, the British airship program continued to lag behind air programs of other nations. Particularly discomforting for the British airship establishment was the success of the German airship *Graf Zeppelin*. In 1929, the *Graf Zeppelin* completed an around-the-world flight in just over twenty-one days. Following the German success, the British stepped up the pace of construction of the R.100 and R.101.[84] In the summer of 1930, the R.101's designers modified the airship with an extra gas cell to compensate for the ship's excessive weight. By September, the changes were complete. To accommodate the new gas cell, the engineers at Cardington lengthened the airship more than thirty-five feet. On the afternoon of October 1, the ship made its first successful test flight. With this test flight completed, there was tacit pressure to fly the R.101 to India and return before the start of the Imperial Conference. Air Minister Lord Thomson wrote on October 2, "You mustn't allow my natural impatience or anxiety to start to influence you in any way. You must use your considered judgment."[85]

On the afternoon of October 4, the R.101 left for India with a full crew and numerous Air Ministry representatives, including Lord Thomson. As the airship crossed the coast of France, the flight encountered stronger than expected winds from a storm. The ship went through a series of climbs and dives. An emergency landing was attempted but the nose of the R.101 struck the ground and the resulting collision collapsed the structure, rupturing the gasbags and producing a violent explosion. There were only eight survivors. With the crash of the R.101, Britain's pursuit of the airship for commercial and military purposes came to an abrupt end.[86]

In the 1920s, the airship provided some hope of shortening the vast distances of imperial travel with increased speed but ultimately failed to deliver upon its promise. With hindsight, airships were an unsuitable aerial technology to pursue. While the airship's advocates acknowledged their limitations such as high operational costs and vulnerability to weather and enemy action, they believed that their military potential, long range, and high passenger and payload capacity outweighed their constraints. By the mid-1920s, the rigid airship was a stagnant technology that had already reached the extent of its development, whereas aircraft technology continued to progress and ultimately surpass the airship during this period. Though this technical stagnation was not initially recognized, the repeated failures of the British airships and the fiscal realities of the period compelled the British governments of the day to follow the correct path and abandon the pursuit of airship development. This temporarily left the Dominions without the prospect of an air connection within the empire until aircraft technology became available in the middle of the 1930s in favor of heavier-than-air craft.

CHAPTER 6

AIR DEFENSE AND THE LABOUR PARTY: SINGAPORE NAVAL BASE AND THE 1926 IMPERIAL CONFERENCE, 1924–1926

> *The policy of the Labour Government in throwing over the Singapore scheme, and at the same time voting more money for the aerial defence of this country, was not understood in the Dominions, where it had an unfortunate effect. Unless we could satisfy the Dominions that we were working on some consistent policy, we're not likely to obtain their financial co-operation.*[1]
>
> —Commander C. Dennis Burney

By 1924, it appeared that many of the animosities between the powers of France, Germany, and Great Britain were on the decline. Even the chiefs of the Imperial General Staff could not contemplate conditions in the current atmosphere that could instigate another major war except for "the small wars incidental to our Imperial position."[2] Even so, planning for national defense in the event of war continued. Britain's first Labour government, led by Prime Minister Ramsay MacDonald, was determined to achieve his foreign policy objectives through international cooperation. MacDonald brokered an agreement between France and Germany to end the French occupation of the Ruhr, gained French acceptance of the Dawes Plan to restructure German reparation payments, opened negotiations with Soviet Russia, and supported international security through the League of Nations.[3]

When MacDonald came to power, he confronted two courses of action for imperial air defense: achieve parity with France or disarmament. British air strategy at this time was based on Stanley Baldwin's supposition that "British air power must include a home-defence Air Force of sufficient strength adequately to protect us against air attacks by the strongest air forces within striking distance of this country."[4] Because France possessed the largest air force in Europe and was within striking distance of Britain, the French air force became the standard to judge Britain's air strength. For MacDonald and the Labour government, disarmament was a reasonable and primary means to reduce international tension and competition. Parity no longer was a necessity. Before Labour came to power in January 1924, the previous June, MacDonald had called for limiting air armaments along lines "similar to the Treaty of Washington."[5] Before any formal statement by MacDonald's government regarding the future direction of Britain's defenses, the Air Staff assumed that drastic air defense cuts would take place. In anticipation, the Air Staff prepared a long memorandum for MacDonald on the hazards of limiting air armaments. The views expressed in this memo echoed many of the arguments and difficulties confronted at the Washington Conference, such as limiting air force budgets, the number of squadrons, an aircraft's lift capacity, and engine displacement.[6] In addition, the Air Staff claimed that unlike naval construction, it was nearly impossible to monitor a nation's air force structure. In fact, the air attachés in British embassies throughout the world sent back remarkably detailed reports about their host nation's aviation activities. Another dubious assertion put forward by the Air Staff claimed that air power skewed traditional military power structures by allowing smaller nations or those of limited economic means to achieve greater strength by substituting air forces for more expensive navies and armies. Finally, the Air Staff argued that for the above reasons it would not be possible to obtain international agreements about limiting air forces.[7] Once again, the British Air Staff disregarded the infrastructure expenses, such as factories, the large skilled workforce, and the airbases required to build and operate a modern air force. Such expenses would be just as daunting for a "small" nation as those required to build a substantial naval force would. In addition, existing aviation technology simply did not enable air forces to deliver the "knockout" blow that the air power advocates envisioned.

In comments regarding the Air Staff's memorandum, the vast majority of the Royal Air Force officers who commented on the draft supported the Air Staff's opinion.[8] There was, however, some dissent regarding the paper. Air Vice-Marshal Henry Brooke-Popham, commandant of the RAF Staff College, warned the Air Staff that it was not in the best interest of the service to take such a stance with MacDonald's government, "that the non-possumus attitude adopted by the memorandum is unwise in view of the present attitude of mind of the Government."[9] The Air Staff did not have to wait long before they learned the position of the MacDonald government on the subject of the air defense of Britain and the empire, but the result was unexpected.

A heated debate in Parliament on February 19, 1924, forced the Labour government to make known its position regarding Britain's air defense. The debate was opened by the former Conservative air minister, Samuel Hoare, who asked the undersecretary of state for air, William Leach, if the Labour government would keep in place his December 1923 program to expand the Royal Air Force (RAF) to 52 squadrons.[10] Leach's reply noted the Labour Party's aversion to the use and buildup of military armaments, which created instability rather than security:

> Preparedness is not the best weapon in diplomacy. The best weapon in diplomacy is to have a sound and righteous cause. I always think that preparedness indicates a fear of one's neighbours, a disbelief in the righteousness of the intentions of those neighbours.[11]

Leach's philosophy on international relations was idealistic and the continuing mistrust of nations toward one another made his position untenable. Even MacDonald did not recommend a policy of unilateral disarmament. Dissatisfied with his response, Hoare and the opposition continued to press Leach on the matter. In an interesting twist, with the question concerning air defense and the 1924–1925 Air Estimates there was a real possibility of the government losing a parliamentary vote.

Leach acquiesced to the pressure of the opposition and maintained the previous government's policy.[12] He cautioned the members that if there were a chance to reach an international agreement in the direction of aerial disarmament the Labour government would take full advantage of the opportunity.[13] About an arms race, Leach warned: "If we continue to put fear at the helm and folly at the prow we shall steer straight for the next war."[14] Some members of the Tory opposition were somewhat sympathetic to Leach's views. Maj. Gen. John E. Seely, in particular, seemed to admire Labour's stance concerning disarmament and international cooperation, stating, "It seems to me that unless some of that idealism can be translated into action we shall never make any progress."[15] Seely was not prepared to trust other powers in matters of imperial security. For Seely, the unified strength of the empire was Britain's greatest asset in any negotiation. During this debate regarding the Royal Air Force, Seely appealed to the secretary of state for the Colonies, James Henry Thomas, to persuade the Dominions' leadership to cooperate in the establishment of an "adequate" imperial air defense.[16] Lt. Commander C. Dennis Burney was less than congenial about Dominion cooperation with imperial aerial defense, demanding, "We should make the Dominions do their share of the economic upkeep of our defence forces. They do not do it to-day in any respect in comparison with the taxation upon this country."[17]

The Labour government's 1924–1925 Air Estimates aimed to expand the air force while attempting to remain fiscally responsible. Under-Secretary of State for Air Leach agreed with the expansion of fifteen new squadrons completed by the end of the budget cycle in April 1925 and in achieving an ultimate goal of expanding the Royal Air Force by thirty-four squadrons. To attain this, Labour increased the Air Estimates by £2,500,000 from the previous year.[18] To realize savings while expanding the air force, thirteen of these new squadrons would consist of a new reserve formation or the Auxiliary Air Force. The structure envisioned for the auxiliary force was similar to the organization of Territorial units within the British Army.[19]

During a subsequent debate on the Air Estimates, Leach now found himself arguing with the pacifist wing within the Labour Party. The government's policy corresponded in most respects to the Conservative policy of Sir Samuel Hoare. The general trend of the criticism that followed was that the government was ostensibly planning to carry on the agenda of the previous government and that what it proposed to do would send the country down the dangerous path of an aerial arms race, particularly with France. Leach now found himself having to defend the government's policy to his own party's backbenchers, arguing that he could not ask that Britain unilaterally "disarm" itself.[20] The 1924–1925 Air Estimates submitted by Labour passed by a wide margin with strong support from the opposition.

Even though there was growing interest in the use of air power to defend the empire in the early 1920s, the Royal Navy remained the primary symbol and force of British imperial strength. On

March 25, 1924, MacDonald made a clear departure from the previous government in relation to the empire's Far Eastern defenses. In Parliament, he announced the cancellation of further construction of the Singapore naval base. Ten days before this formal announcement, Secretary of State for the Colonies James Henry Thomas informed the Dominions' leadership of the reasoning behind the government's decision to cancel the Singapore base:

> It seemed clear, apart from any other considerations, that to continue the development of the Naval Base at Singapore would hamper the establishment of this confidence [to allay international suspicions] and lay our good faith open to suspicion. As a result we should almost inevitably drift into a condition of mistrust and competition of armaments in the Far East.[21]

The new British stance dismayed the governments of Australia and New Zealand. The Australian governor-general, Sir Henry William Forster, conveyed the Australian response: "[If Singapore is abandoned] incalculable harm will be done to the Empire's prestige, the confidence of smaller nations will be shattered, the ambitions of lesser powers will be increased, and deep distrust will be caused throughout the whole Empire."[22] Admiral Jellicoe, author of the Singapore base plan and now serving as New Zealand's governor-general, delivered the most vehement protest:

> On behalf of New Zealand, I protest earnestly against the proposal to make Singapore a strong and safe naval station being abandoned, because I believe that as long as Britain holds supremacy of the seas the Empire will stand, but if Britain loses naval supremacy, the Empire may fall to the detriment of not only its own people but of humanity as a whole.[23]

With the Labour government's decision to suspend the construction of the Singapore naval base, the Australians recognized the need to become more self-sufficient in their own defenses. At the beginning of 1924, Australia had no active defense policy except the assumption of British assistance. Britain's suspension of the Singapore base coincided with a series of events in the Pacific that confirmed Australian fears of Japan. In April 1924, the Sempill British Aviation Mission to Japan reported Japan's advances in aviation, noting the operations of the *Hosho*, the first aircraft carrier in the world built from the keel up and the expansion of Japan's carrier force. The conversion of the battle cruiser hulls of the *Amagi*, *Akagi*, and *Kaga* to aircraft carriers (as agreed upon at the Washington Conference) was nearing completion.[24] The *Akagi* and *Kaga* became the nucleus of Japan's carrier forces during World War II. The Japanese abandoned the conversion of the battle cruiser *Amagi* whose hull structure was heavily damaged in the 1923 earthquake. That same spring, both the Canadians and Americans closed their borders to new Japanese immigration. At the League of Nations, moreover, Japan now openly challenged the "White Australia Policy." All of these actions combined confirmed Australian fears that Japan might then turn on the Pacific's largest and least populated land region.[25]

The Air Staff in Britain in 1925 wrote several assessments of the threat posed against British interests in the Pacific by new Japanese aircraft carriers. In their view, Japan would be unlikely to jeopardize their aircraft carriers in a direct attack against Australian ports and the scale of bombing that carrier-borne aircraft could deliver would be limited.[26] In the opinion of the Air Staff, a more likely scenario would be for the Japanese carriers to blockade and attack British, Australian, and New Zealand merchant shipping.[27] The probability of air attack against New Zealand was even more remote. Regarding a major war in the Pacific, the Air Staff felt that an attack by surface ships against New Zealand was more likely and the country would remain isolated for a number of

Figures 6.1 and 6.2. To meet the limits set by the 1922 Washington Naval Treaty, the Imperial Japanese Navy converted the battle cruiser hull *Akagi* and battleship hull *Kaga* into aircraft carriers. RAF planners dismissed the threat these carriers posed to Australia and New Zealand, believing that the Japanese would not risk the ships in waters so distant from their home bases and their lack of striking power from the biplane aircraft. The Japanese proved RAF planners wrong when both carriers participated on a raid on Darwin, Australia, on February 19, 1942, inflicting heavy damage and sinking eight ships in the port. (Photographs courtesy of the Yamato Museum [Kure Maritime Museum])

weeks or months before a significant British relief force could arrive. In this scenario, the Air Staff felt that New Zealand should concentrate their aviation efforts in reconnaissance and torpedo bombers.[28]

Defending Australia with its own naval force, while attractive to the Dominion's defense planners, was cost prohibitive. The belief that aircraft offered the Dominion an inexpensive defense remained a principal consideration for the Dominion's military leaders. Australia's new prime minister, Stanley M. Bruce, believed that Australia could disregard sea defense altogether and rely instead upon air power.[29]

Since the gift of the war surplus aircraft in 1919, the Australian government had failed to maintain and upgrade its air force. By 1924, the Royal Australian Air Force (RAAF) deteriorated beyond obsolete. The RAAF at this time consisted of 65 officers and 300 men and it had only two machines fit for war.[30] With the focus of defense spending on capital improvements such as the purchase of land for airfields, the Air Force had not kept pace with aircraft developments since the war. In addition, while the country demonstrated an ability to manufacture aircraft during the war and in the immediate postwar period, the lack of government and private orders forced all of these firms into liquidation.[31]

In March 1924, the Australian Council of Defence met to reexamine the Dominion's defenses and attempted to reverse the decline of the previous five years. With the new concerns, the Australian Defence Ministry prepared to recondition the air force's current equipment and to provide funds to purchase aircraft that were more modern. The Australians' de Havilland D.H.9 army cooperation and light bombers as well as their Fairey IIID naval cooperation aircraft were particularly in need of replacement.[32] Even though the members of the Australian Defence Council recognized the inadequacy of the Royal Australian Air Force, Defence Minister Eric K. Bowden pointed out that "it was not likely that we should get more money for the Air Force."[33]

In June 1924, the Air Board and the RAAF delivered a paper to the government reporting on the force's current condition. The board offered a grim assessment of the force's condition, indicating, "Australia cannot yet be said to possess even a reasonably satisfactory foundation on which to build up an adequate Force for its Air Defence."[34] Australia's budget was still too limited to correct the situation. Even if the air force could recondition existing equipment, there would still be only a sufficient number of aircraft to keep three flights of six airplanes operational for approximately eight months under war conditions.[35] Without making any specific numerical commitments, the government agreed at least to expand the pool of available pilots and mechanics.[36] By the end of 1924, the Royal Australian Air Force's existing squadrons were reequipped and "brought up to their normal establishments."[37]

As the Australians recognized the inadequacy of their air force, they attempted to make corrections. In New Zealand, there was no such concern. Even the British Labour government, like its Conservative predecessor, expressed concern for the lack of any semblance of an air force in New Zealand. On January 16, 1924, the Air Ministry sent New Zealand's Air Board a request to participate in the air training scheme outlined at the 1923 Imperial Conference. New Zealand officials "expressed the view that it was premature at the present time to consider extensive schemes of co-operation as regards personnel."[38]

In November 1924, Britain's first experience with a Labour government ended. The Conservatives under Stanley Baldwin returned to power with a wide majority in Parliament. By the middle of December, the new Baldwin ministry repeated the RAF's offer to train New Zealand's pilots and officers. They recognized that the "present financial position does not permit [the New Zealand government] to take immediate advantage of the offer, they hope that they may be enabled to do so . . . in the ensuing year."[39]

With the return of a Conservative government led by Stanley Baldwin in 1924, Baldwin revived Conservative defense policies. Because the Labour government had adopted their plans in respect to the Royal Air Force, there was some continuity. Baldwin's government supported resuming construction of the Singapore naval base, but it focused on the review of its design and scope with no real progress in physical construction. In connection with this naval base, the Royal Air Force began planning for the construction of a large air station.[40] This request to some extent was significant because the Singapore proposals to this point had been exclusively a naval matter and for the first time the RAF's imperial defense responsibilities would stretch into the Pacific. Even with the continuance of the Singapore strategy, the Committee of Imperial Defence did not consider a war between the British and Japanese Empires as a serious contingency for the next ten years.[41] Foreign Minister Austin Chamberlain confirmed this position and agreed that resumption of the Singapore base was a prudent measure for imperial communication and defense but also viewed the prospect of war in the Far East as "very remote."[42]

In February 1925, Air Minister Sir Samuel Hoare introduced the government's Air Estimates for 1925–1926. Once again, the Royal Air Force received a modest budget increase of £652,000 with £2,500,000 specifically directed for the purchase of new aircraft and £1,500,000 for naval aircraft.[43] At this time, the majority of Britain's air force and naval aircraft were now woefully obsolete. When Hoare presented the Air Estimates to Parliament, he introduced the Royal Air Force's new concept of a ready mobile defense for the empire:

> I would ask the honorable members to keep constantly in their minds the great potentialities of air power for Empire defence. If we could succeed in putting our Empire defence upon a more mobile basis, might we not save both large numbers of men and great sums of money?[44]

With several years of operational experience in Iraq and Afghanistan, Air Minister Hoare also referred to successful cooperation between the army and the air force. In May 1924, the RAF transported a fully armed contingent of sixty-six officers and men of the Inniskilling Fusiliers from Baghdad to Kirkuk who quickly quelled clashes between the local Christian and Muslim groups.[45] In another instance, the combined use of air and ground forces, where aircraft bombed the insurgents and directed the ground forces to trouble spots through reconnaissance, helped to subdue a local insurgency.[46] In Hoare's opinion, the government should encourage the development of large aircraft to increase further the mobility of even larger forces and help "solve the problem of defending a vast Empire at a period when we are short both of men and of money."[47]

In the subsequent debates over the Air Estimates, Maj. Gen. John Davidson, Conservative MP for Hemel Hempstead, supported Hoare's concept of mobile defense, noting, "We are defending our strategic points in an expensive and inefficient manner by maintaining fixed armament defences instead of utilising aircraft."[48] Davidson accepted the air power advocates' assumptions and did not take into account the technical limitations of aircraft of the period, the expenses of infrastructure, and the workforce requirements of a modern air force.

Inexpensive and mobile imperial defense became the emerging theme for the Air Staff. In a meeting of the Chiefs of Staff Sub-Committee, Hugh Trenchard argued that aircraft could become the primary weapon in the defense of the Singapore naval base. He alleged that aircraft could replace the fifteen-inch naval guns estimated to cost £1,250,000.[49] In addition, a Japanese invasion fleet's capital ships would be particularly dependent upon lightly armored auxiliary ships that would "offer an easy target to attack by aeroplanes" at least 150 miles away from their intended target.[50] First Sea Lord Admiral David Beatty opposed Trenchard's views and requested that the Air Staff needed to put forward concrete proposals rather than present abstract concepts. Chief of the Imperial General Staff Lord Cavan thought that the base would require only the necessary reconnaissance aircraft to spot for the guns.[51] In his opinion, "bombers and torpedo-carrying aeroplanes would be unnecessary [and] the provision of those types of aircraft would be in the nature of a luxury and not a necessity."[52] All of the chiefs were guilty of blindly defending the responsibilities of their particular service. Successful military operations would require the close cooperation and coordination of the three services, and interservice bickering hindered the successful defense of the empire.

In a major address before Cambridge University on April 29, 1925, Trenchard delineated the role of the Royal Air Force in the future in the defense of the empire:

> If there were aerodromes suitably arranged and built, even though they cost a few millions, it would save in expenditure. You need not tie air squadrons in every spot of the British Empire to defend it, and so long as you have these facilities and arrangements the actual unit becomes very mobile and will be a thousand times still more mobile when great aircraft carriers of the future come into being.[53]

The Air Ministry and the Royal Air Force from that point forward would continue to make the case that the service provided a mobile and economic defense for the empire. Trenchard's proposals for a mobile defense and the reexamination of the Singapore concepts opened new dissension among Britain's chiefs of staff.

Before the creation of the Royal Air Force, navy and army had clearly defined responsibilities regarding imperial port defense. The navy's responsibility was to defend imperial ports by intercepting hostile naval forces at sea. The immediate security of any port was the charge of the local army garrison whose duties included operating coastal defense batteries as well as repelling any invasion force. Trenchard's ideas about Singapore and Pacific defense alienated both services and disrupted their traditional balance. Trenchard claimed that aircraft could cover local port defenses by replacing the expensive gun batteries with aircraft as well as using them to augment or even supplant the navy's interdiction responsibilities.[54]

Throughout the spring and summer of 1925, the British chiefs of staff continued to bicker about their respective roles regarding Singapore and the empire's Pacific defenses. On one point, the chiefs were in agreement. They now viewed Japan as the one power that could and would threaten the status quo in the Pacific. Admiral Beatty believed the Japanese to be:

> A race who considered themselves to possess a mission in this world and were a military race from beginning to end. . . . He [Beatty] considered that the menace from Japan was most serious and that to believe that there was no possibility of war during the next ten years was in reality living in a fool's paradise.[55]

The Chiefs of Staff Committee also noted a new airbase that the Japanese began to build on Formosa, and they believed this was a clear violation of Article 19 of the Washington Treaty that forbade the expansion and construction of military facilities south of Japan. At a distance of 450 miles from Hong Kong, the base was still just beyond the operational range of the larger military planes in 1925, but the chiefs recognized that continuing improvements in aircraft would eventually place this important port in jeopardy. Field Marshal Frederick Rudolph Lambert Lord Cavan, chief of the Imperial General Staff, reported that the current state of the Formosan aerodrome was in "somewhat bad order" and that the Japanese used planes based there only for internal policing.[56] Likewise, Air Marshal Trenchard was not quite as concerned, indicating that the Japanese were at least ten years away from developing aircraft that could threaten Hong Kong. Trenchard was prepared to abandon Hong Kong in the face of any Japanese military strike. Once the Japanese base became operational, the geographic limitations of Hong Kong would prevent the RAF from basing a significant force at the port that could prevent or limit Japanese air attacks.[57] The British chiefs of staff concluded that they were limited in responding to Japan's actions:

> Although the Japanese Air station at Formosa as at present equipped does not constitute a menace, nevertheless, it contains essential elements which could rapidly be expanded into a formidable military air base and its existence can consequently be held to be a violation of Article 19 of the Washington Treaty. It is desirable that the Foreign Office should enter a protest on the first convenient opportunity, but it is recognised that the appropriate moment for such action must be subordinated to wider considerations of which the Foreign Office are the judge.[58]

As for the Singapore base, considered by all the chiefs of staff as pivotal to the empire's eastern defenses, Trenchard was not prepared to station a significant RAF contingent there. The RAF only assigned a small airfield maintenance staff of thirty officers and men to Singapore. Touting the advantages of air mobility, the RAF's Pacific defense aircraft would be stationed somewhere in India and moved to Singapore in the event of a security crisis or threat from the Japanese.[59] Trenchard believed doing so would provide cost benefits for the government and would not antagonize the Japanese even though the British airbase at Singapore would remain.[60]

Air Marshal Trenchard also envisioned a growing need for the participation of the Royal Australian Air Force in that country's and the empire's Pacific defense. Despite the potential threat of the new Japanese aircraft carriers, Trenchard still believed that "Australia is in no danger of being attacked by Air."[61] Even so, Trenchard thought that if the Australians expanded the country's aviation infrastructure and provided more money to expand the force, Australia would be in a position more adequately to defend itself from invasion than was possible under existing methods.[62] Trenchard concluded:

> The Air could amplify and partially replace some of the functions of the Navy and Army; it should be possible to obtain a more efficient defence of Australia itself, and a system of greater value to the Empire as a whole with no increase in cost. In order to render effective such an inter-connected scheme, it would be necessary that for a term of years, the air should be allotted a reasonable proportion, say one-third, of the funds available for defence; I feel convinced that the deterrent to Japanese aggression would exceed that now provided, at a cost not exceeding the existing defence votes.[63]

The rhetoric coming from Whitehall about potential reductions in overseas commitments made it obvious to the Pacific Dominions that they would have to become more dependent upon themselves for defense. The false arguments that aviation provided an economical method of defense still appealed to the Australian leadership. The concept of mobile air defense or a rapid reaction force outlined by Trenchard was always a contingency for the Australians. They believed that a small well-trained air force could move to prepositioned airfields at any threatened location. These air units then could augment the local land

and naval forces. It was clear that Australia's small budget could not afford an expansion of the nation's permanent air force.

On July 1, 1925, the Royal Australian Air Force created three new squadrons in an attempt to bolster its diminishing air defenses. No. 1 and No. 3 Composite Squadrons consisted of a flight of day bombers, a flight of army cooperation aircraft, and a flight of single-seat fighters. No. 101 Squadron, located at Point Cook, contained fleet cooperation aircraft. These new squadrons became the origin of the Australian Citizen Air Force (CAF).[64] The personnel framework of the CAF squadrons consisted of one-third permanent air force members and the remaining two-thirds were reservists.[65] Those who joined the CAF were obligated to serve eight years: four years actively in the CAF and the remaining four in reserve. The CAF was essentially an air militia subject to call-up during a national emergency and, like Britain's Auxiliary Air Force, it would depend upon volunteers to fill the ranks. The Australians hoped that the CAF would become a low-cost solution to expand their air force, but the CAF was of questionable military value. These units' subsequent and highly publicized accidents and lack of military discipline earned the force the reputation and nickname of the "Flying Club."[66]

By the fall of 1926, the Royal Australian Air Force had made some progress toward expansion. In August the RAAF's annual budget more than doubled from £347,000 to £728,000. The dramatic increase was a result of £250,000 directed for the purchase of a flight of nine Supermarine Seagull patrol aircraft and a naval seaplane carrier, HMAS *Albatross*, to service these aircraft.[67] In addition, the RAAF planned for a steady increase in personnel. By 1929, the Australians intended to expand the permanent air force from 89 officers and 780 airmen to 110 officers and 872 airmen, and expand the Citizen Air Force from 54 officers and 259 airmen to 98 officers and 456 airmen.[68]

While the Australians demonstrated a small but serious effort to expand their air force, New Zealand's lack of any substantial force remained a concern for the British Air Staff. With four officers, eleven airmen, and about 100 pilots in reserve, one military airfield located at Christchurch, and only eighteen operational aircraft of all war types, the RAF simply did not consider the RNZAF in imperial military strength calculations.[69]

In late 1925 and into early 1926, European tensions eased as the League of Nations seemed to function smoothly and the Locarno Pact reduced Franco-German animosity. The British chiefs of staff therefore began a top to bottom reassessment of British and imperial defense priorities. Even the Committee of Imperial Defence concurred with a report by the Foreign Office that "there is no present reason to anticipate a war among the Great Powers of Europe."[70] With this as a consideration, Trenchard argued that Japan should be the empire's primary defense priority.

With the introduction of the 1926–1927 Air Estimates, the fifty-two squadron expansion plan was curtailed. While the Royal Air Force's budget saw an overall increase of £486,000 from the 1925 estimates, the need for government economies and the reduction of international tensions made it more difficult to justify such growth. The most dramatic cut introduced by the Air Ministry was the reduction of money for the Fleet Air Arm from £1,320,000 in the 1925 budget to £299,800 in 1926.[71] Even if the government wished to continue with its expansion plans, it would not have been possible. Secretary for Air Hoare had to admit during his introduction of the Air Estimates that the RAF was unable to meet its expansion goals. The inability to recruit personnel to fill the needed slots, the lack of airfields to base the expanded force, and the need for more training facilities and equipment all combined to restrain any growth.[72] For Secretary Hoare the RAF's expansion plans remained in place but were now subject to a "temporary deferment."[73]

With expansion on hold, the Air Ministry and the RAF's leadership focused greater attention on the role of air mobility in imperial defense. In a series of speeches before the Royal Academy and the British Empire League, Secretary Hoare argued that with a well-marked imperial route structure RAF squadrons could move swiftly from one imperial territory to another.[74] According to Hoare, for this vital communication system to be economically viable and practical required the active support and participation by the Dominions.[75] At the end of the summer of 1926, the celebrated British aviator Sir Alan Cobham made a dramatic flight from England to Australia and back. Cobham's success seemed to support the Air Ministry's position concerning imperial air communication and defense.

At the end of 1926, the Dominions' prime ministers traveled once again to London to meet for another imperial conference. Of the many agenda items discussed at these meetings, one of the central defense issues was aviation. In preparation for the meeting, Cabinet Secretary Maurice Hankey specified a focus on "Air Policy generally and in particular the progress made with Air Defence and also the proposed development and co-ordination of Strategic Air Routes for purposes of Empire Defence and Communications."[76] The progress regarding air defense by the Pacific Dominions there was reason for both optimism and pessimism for the British Air Ministry.

In his address to Dominion premiers at the Imperial Conference, Trenchard again emphasized the theme of mobile air defense. He recognized that a system of linked airfields was ambitious and expensive but if they methodically built them in peacetime, in the event of a future crisis the network would be in place.[77] At the end of the conference, the ministers came to a general agreement about the empire's air defense, reconfirming proposals from the 1923 conference to maintain an imperial standard for equipment, training, and doctrine.[78] In addition, there was a consensus to establish Trenchard's airfield network and to place regional air defense needs in the hands of the respective Dominions.[79]

During the period from Ramsay MacDonald's first premiership to the 1926 Imperial Conference there was a growing recognition of the value of aircraft for imperial defense. Successful aerial operations, particularly in the Middle East, seemed to bolster the Air Ministry claims of an inexpensive imperial defense. Once again, the upstart Royal Air Force infringed upon the traditional defense spheres of the British Army over port defense and the Royal Navy's protection of the British Isles from invasion and safeguarding of imperial trade routes. While the goal of fifty-two combat squadrons remained a consistent, though modest, goal through the successive Labour and Conservative ministries, the ability of Britain to achieve this benchmark was not possible. The Royal Air Force could not attract the personnel to fill its permanent ranks; the continuing postwar apathy toward the military, and the long seven-year enlistment were the principal reasons cited for public disinterest in joining the air force. The creation of the part-time Auxiliary Air Force in Britain and the Citizen Air Force in Australia were attempts to solve this problem. While the British Auxiliary Air Force units demonstrated some success in attracting personnel, the poor operational record of the CAF indicated its questionable value as a supplementary fighting force for the RAAF. Even with the minor expansion of both the RAF and the RAAF with auxiliary units, the easing of international animosities of the period made it difficult to justify an air force of the size proposed by the Air Staff.

CHAPTER 7

IMPERIAL AIR MOBILITY, THE SALMOND REPORT, AND AIR MARSHAL TRENCHARD'S LAST SALVO, 1927–1929

Even when the present programme of expansion has been completed, and, even reckoning upon the co-operation [of] the air forces of Australia, Canada, and South Africa, our Empire air power will remain all too small for its responsibilities. . . . In the meantime it is of prime importance to compensate for smallness of numbers by extra mobility.[1]
—Maj. F. A. de V. Robertson

Consideration of international conflict was hardly a priority for Stanley Baldwin's government from 1927 to 1929. With the Locarno Treaty in place, the signing of the Kellogg-Briand Pact renouncing war, and new disarmament discussions planned and taking place, large and expensive armament programs seemed a waste of the taxpayers' money. With the need for budget savings, the British reduced military spending and directed the money elsewhere. The British essentially adopted a tacit policy of unilateral disarmament. With new spending cuts looming and the potential for conflict among the services for limited monetary resources, the leadership at the Air Ministry and within the Royal Air Force (RAF) attempted to design a plan of imperial defense. The Royal Air Force touted "air mobility" as their new fundamental operational concept.

The 1927–1928 Air Estimates demonstrated these growing budgetary pressures upon the service. At the end of the 1926–1927 budget cycle, the service was subject to a "super cut" and returned £500,000 of unspent funds to the Treasury. The RAF originally intended this money for equipment and personnel for the four new squadrons approved in the 1923 expansion scheme.[2] These squadrons were never created because of the RAF's inability to attract enough recruits to fill the ranks, and there was little chance that the recruiting conditions would change. Postwar apathy toward the military, the long seven-year enlistment cycles, and poor pay rates were the most likely causes for the RAF's failure to draw personnel. This resulted in the decision to reduce its 1927–1928 estimates by £450,000.[3] One segment of the Air Estimates that did expand was £92,000 designated for imperial air communications links or airfields.[4] This was the first significant amount of money directed to the imperial air route system.

When the secretary of state for air, Samuel Hoare, presented the Air Estimates to Parliament, he now placed "the greatest possible importance to the development of these strategic air routes, which are essential to the effective and economical employment of the Air Arm in the field of Imperial defence."[5] In addition to the £92,000 for airfield development and construction, the RAF designated another £30,000 to conduct a series of long-distance flights to South Africa, India, and the Far East.[6] Though an air route system was the subject of previous discussion, it did not receive the money required to make it practical because of the quality of available aircraft. Developing this imperial air route system now became a top priority for Hoare, who gained a clear understanding and firsthand experience of the system's commercial and military potential when he participated in the inaugural flight opening the route from Britain to India. The flight left England on December 27, 1926, and arrived in Delhi on January 8, 1927, making thirteen scheduled stops along the way. In his report to the cabinet about his imperial air tour, Hoare stressed both the commercial and military potential of this accomplishment. During his six-week absence, Hoare inspected the Royal Air Force units in four different overseas commands and discussed with these aviators ways to further the development of British air power.[7] For Hoare, the flight was a "conspicuous example of the mobility upon which our Empire depends for its defence and its communications."[8] For the next several years, air mobility became the axiom touted by the Air Ministry and the RAF's contribution to imperial defense.

In March 1927, the Committee of Imperial Defence (CID) issued a comprehensive review of the principles of the British Empire's defenses. This assessment was the first such review attempted by the CID since 1910, and it was long overdue because of the changing political and technological landscape since the previous analysis. Even though there had been significant changes in the political makeup of the empire and new technological advances, for the CID the protection of sea communications and the maintenance of naval supremacy remained as the pillars of imperial defense.[9] The committee acknowledged the growing independence of the Dominions within the imperial framework and felt that it was of the highest priority that "general organization of our defence should be in complete harmony."[10] The growing independence of the Dominions concerned the committee because it could lead to the fragmentation of the empire and weakening of its overall military capability. In addition, the committee also saw the need to review the defense capability of the empire because of the dramatic changes in military technology.

Many obvious advances in military technology had taken place in artillery, submarines, automatic small arms, and wireless and telephone communication. The airplane made the most significant advances over the previous seventeen years. The committee concluded:

> The increased efficiency and reliability of aircraft, which, in their infancy in 1910 have proved their value as a weapon and as a means of communication, and, in fact, have introduced a new dimension into the art of war, besides revealing the possibility of further developments which must be considered in preparing for future eventualities.[11]

The advent of aircraft increased the vulnerability of British sea communications by subjecting shipping lanes to another means of attack. The CID also acknowledged the corollary of this danger by recognizing that aircraft could provide a defense against air attack, be of great value for reconnaissance, and supplement the local defenses against sea or land attack.

Understanding this, the committee adopted the Air Ministry's concept that mobile air forces could strengthen the empire's position at vulnerable strategic points by the ability to move aircraft to those locations along well-organized air routes and to have air force detachments permanently located at points where assistance might be required. The CID stated, "Air security depends not so much upon the strength of any air units maintained locally, but upon the efficiency of our arrangements rapidly to bring large air forces to a threatened point when the need arises."[12] Once again, the CID emphasized that it would be each Dominion's responsibility to organize its resources to delay aggression until assistance could arrive from other parts of the empire as well as providing relief to threats elsewhere in the empire.[13]

The committee also specified the basic oversight of aircraft use in times of peace and war. In times of peace, the air force would prevent or suppress frontier raids or outbreaks of internal disorder in "semi-civilized" countries where suitable conditions and terrain existed. Successful air operations to suppress insurgencies in the open regions of Sudan and Iraq in particular seemed to confirm the view of the CID. To this end, the CID decided that the underlying principle of rapid deployment depended upon a chain of interconnected airfields with adequate ground protection provided by both army and RAF ground security forces.[14] With this principle of mobile deployment in place, the air force would be required to operate in compliance with the empire's established strategic goals and supplement or cooperate with naval or ground forces when required.

With mobile deployment now as the established policy, even the Air Staff recognized that it was not a panacea and that the strategy had numerous and serious limitations. The most serious of these shortcomings for the Air Staff related to aircraft and their supply. The staff argued that once the air routes were finally established, large stocks of aircraft would still need to be kept or held at certain main airbases within the likely theaters of war.[15] In addition, the question of where to establish large ammunition and bomb depots needed to be addressed. Finally, how were these large stocks of munitions in quantities needed to make the aircraft a viable fighting force to be transported to any crisis point?[16] Another aspect that was not addressed by the Air Staff concerning these ammunition depots was the vast sums of money that would be required to buy enough munitions to supply a fighting force at a remote location. The existing ammunition stocks were so small that air operations would cease well before they could be replenished.

Even with these potential complications, defensive air mobility remained the operational concept for imperial defense upon which the leadership of the Royal Air Force concentrated its efforts during the next several years. Secretary of State for the Colonies Leo Amery, in a letter to the Air Staff, praised air mobility for the future defense of the empire:

> As the administrative mobility of Air Forces develops, and air routes spread across the world, the advantages attendant upon centralization in peace and immediate speed of action in emergency, which have already been so amply illustrated in local air control, will be extended, in conjunction with naval and military action, to the whole system of Imperial Defence.[17]

As the Committee of Imperial Defence reconsidered the changing needs of the empire's defense in 1927, so too were defense planners in Australia and New Zealand reexamining their own conditions and how their forces fit within the imperial defense system. At the 1926 Imperial Conference the parties concurred that the primary responsibility of local defense was the responsibility of each Dominion, which made them more self-reliant for their own defense.

Of particular concern to military planners in Australia was the completion of Japan's naval air expansion program between 1928 and 1930. Moreover, the 1921 Washington Naval Agreement would expire in 1931. The Air Staff in Australia took a particularly candid review of the condition of the Royal Australian Air Force (RAAF). From the 1926–1927 estimates to the 1928–1929 estimates, the staff expected a modest increase of the air force's budget from £458,144 to £500,144, a level of funding still woefully inadequate for the service's needs.[18] The RAAF was still flying their surplus World War I fighters and trainers.[19] One of the main pillars of Australian air defense for the previous five years had been that even though these aircraft were obsolete, they would be sufficient to train a cadre of pilots and mechanics for future expansion. The Australian Air Staff now recognized that these aircraft were so obsolete that they did not have "the necessary machines for the training of pilots to provide for a reasonable reserve."[20]

Of even more concern for the Australians, the RAAF was now about to be outclassed and outnumbered by the Japanese Naval Air

Service, which would soon be increased by two large fleet carriers. The construction of the *Akagi* was completed at the Kure Naval Yard on March 25, 1927, and the *Kaga* was finished a year later on March 31, 1928, at the Kawasaki Naval Yard in Kobe. These two carriers were converted battlecruisers of 36,500 tons and 38,200 tons respectively and were similar in size and displacement to the USS *Lexington* and *Saratoga*.[21] These new Japanese aircraft carriers outweighed the largest British carrier, HMS *Courageous*, by 14,000 to 17,000 tons respectively. The British would not have similar sized aircraft carriers until they launched the four 29,000-ton HMS *Illustrious*-class carriers just after the start of World War II.[22] An intelligence study correctly determined that Japan would be capable in 1928 of operating 130–150 aircraft from these ships and that all of Australia's important cities, mobilization areas, oil reserves, and munitions factories were within range of aircraft operating from them.[23] With potential Japanese air superiority over Australia, previous strategic assumptions now had to be revised. To overcome their current weakness, the Australian Air Staff estimated that they required an average annual expenditure of approximately £2,500,000 per year from 1927 to 1931 for aircraft, equipment, workshops, hangars, and machinery.[24] A sum of £10,000,000 over five years was far beyond the Australian government's ability to take in. The only optimistic aspect of the Air Staff memorandum was that the country's air routes were fairly well organized, with established connections between Darwin, Sydney, Melbourne, Adelaide, Perth, and Derby. Only the coastal region north of Brisbane required attention.[25]

New Zealand's government was still unwilling to direct funds toward their own air arm. In February 1927, the British Air Staff submitted proposals to New Zealand's government suggesting that the Dominion give aircraft a greater share of the coast defense responsibilities by replacing gun emplacements with aircraft. The leadership of the Dominion decided to defer a decision on expanding the Air Service because of the rapid pace of aeronautical technology and capability and the heavy expenditure required for their purchase.[26] Even though the New Zealanders were unwilling to buy new aircraft, they did not totally abandon their imperial defense responsibilities. In August 1927, Prime Minister Gordon Coates announced that New Zealand would contribute £1,000,000 toward the construction of the Singapore Naval Base. Coates intended that the money would be paid in annual installments over the next eight years.[27] Some New Zealanders, influenced by the air power advocates, objected to the Dominion contributing to the construction of the Singapore base:

> Capital ships (i.e. battleships and battlecruisers) are fast becoming obsolescent owing to the steady increase in the effective power of airships and aeroplanes; and that the huge expenditure proposed to provide a Singapore for the wants of these ships will be almost entirely wasted.[28]

The 1927 Air Estimates directed £30,000 for the Royal Air Force to conduct a series of long-distance flights to South Africa, India, and the Far East. On October 14, 1927, a flight of four Supermarine "Southampton" twin-engine flying boats commanded by Group Captain Henry M. Cave-Browne-Cave departed Felixstowe, England, for the Far East, their mission designated as the "Great Cruise." In the wake of many famous flights that took place earlier in the year, most particularly Charles Lindbergh's solo flight from New York to Paris in late May, Hoare wanted to reassure the British cabinet that the intent of the "Great Cruise" was to prove the practicality of the Royal Air Force's air mobility mission:

> The cruise is to be undertaken with the object of gaining experience in the problems involved when flying-boats carried out an extended independent cruise. It is also hope to gain experience

of the problems involved in the reinforcing of points on the Imperial routes with aircraft drawn from England or other parts of the Empire. In no sense is the cruise to be regarded as a "stunt," and no attempt will be made to cover the route between London and Australia in "record" time.[29]

For the next several months the all-metal-hulled "Southamptons" would fly more than 23,000 miles on a route from England to Singapore, then on to Australia. In Australia, the flight finished a complete circuit along the coastline of the continent and the aircraft returned to their ultimate destination, Singapore. Except for alighting at a few isolated locations, the "Great Cruise" called at existing air stations, successfully tested the aircraft's duraluminum hulls in a wide range of climatic conditions, tested for fuel evaporation, and explored remote corners of the empire.[30]

By the end of 1927, the Royal Air Force was winning the public relations battle against the army and the Royal Navy in matters relating to imperial defense. The argument that mobile defense offered a rapid and inexpensive method to defend the empire appealed to frugal politicians. The success and goodwill generated by the "Great Cruise" seemed to provide evidence for the air force's position. That November, after a careful analysis of the RAF's strategy, the Imperial General Staff formulated a series of arguments that countered the air force's plans.

One of the army's primary imperial security responsibilities focused on coastal and port defense. In 1925, Trenchard, without any evidence that aircraft could replace fixed gun defenses, proposed their elimination at Singapore. He stated, "I would urge that no precipitate step be taken now which may involve the locking up of money in fixed defences whose function can be so admirably fulfilled at less cost by utilizing the mobility of aircraft."[31] The use of aircraft to replace the fixed guns had many drawbacks from the army's perspective. First, mobile defense by its nature implied that aircraft would not be located in the immediate vicinity of a port and would take time to stage to the threatened area. Meanwhile, the port would be subject to constant attacks until the air force could assemble a defensive strike force. The ability of this concentration was subject to factors beyond the control of the air force such as weather or enemy attacks elsewhere.[32] According to the Army General Staff, aircraft were more vulnerable than the air force would care to admit. These fragile craft were subject to constant mechanical breakdown and would face defensive fire from antiaircraft guns and enemy defensive aircraft to and from the target. The success and accuracy of any bombing mission was dependent upon the ability of the air force to concentrate a large number of aircraft and the "intensity of their fire is very low."[33] Finally, there were factors relating to costs that the air force ignored:

> As regards [to] the financial aspect its not possible to make any general comparison; . . . The life of guns is long, and the initial expenditure not great, since in most cases existing armament can be economically converted; the life of aircraft, on the other hand, is small, even in peace, and continual changes must be made to keep up to date; owing to liability to temporary mechanical defects, a considerable reserve must always be held in hand; large auxiliary establishments have to be maintained; and the defence if provided by aircraft, cannot simply be placed in "care and maintenance," and yet be ready for immediate action.[34]

For these reasons, the General Staff maintained that the clear role for aircraft in coast defense was in cooperation and as a supplement to the fixed gun emplacements rather than an expensive replacement for them.

In January 1928, the British chiefs of staff began a series of meetings to review the status of imperial defense in the Far East. The British Air Staff had made projections earlier that the entire southern half of the British Isles was now subject to aerial attack. In the Far East, the trade routes throughout the entire Dutch East Indies and Hong Kong were vulnerable without the RAF having the forces in place to defend them.[35] In a small war or a war in the Far East, the Mobilization Committee of the Air Staff had already projected a monthly wastage rate for single-seat fighters and day bomber/reconnaissance aircraft of 50 percent, and 30 percent for their pilots; for army cooperation aircraft the rate of loss was projected to be 40 percent and 20 percent respectively.[36]

The naval base at Singapore remained the focal point of these discussions. Trenchard was committed to completing the air base at Singapore but was not concerned about stationing aircraft there. He argued that a major war with Japan was still unlikely within the next ten years and was unwilling to assign a squadron to the base before 1933.[37] He did confirm with his colleagues that the "Southamptons" at present flying to the Far East as part of the "Great Cruise" would ultimately be permanently stationed at Singapore.[38] To Trenchard, the present status of Britain's relations with Japan did not warrant a large commitment of air force materiel at Singapore, and "If we started to have little bickerings with Japan . . . that the Air Ministry would insist on putting in our Squadrons, even a Home Defence Squadron, out at Singapore."[39] Among the chiefs of staff, however, there was a growing doubt as to whether reinforcements from India for the garrison of Singapore were likely to be available on or just before the outbreak of war.[40] They intended that these forces should be held safely in India and moved to Singapore after the initial attacks.[41] Significantly, the chiefs ultimately concluded:

> A hostile landing on the mainland of Johore, with the object of an attack on Singapore Island from that direction would, owing to the difficulties of the terrain to be traversed and various other factors, be an operation of so difficult a nature, that the probability of an enemy attempting it on a large scale may be excluded.[42]

The chiefs thus dismissed the exact strategy and tactics that the Japanese employed to capture the island base in 1942.

By 1928 some progress on the airfield's construction could be seen. The "L" shaped landing ground suitable for use by light aircraft was available, barrack accommodations for the construction and maintenance crews were nearly completed, and the seaplane slipway, jetty, and maintenance buildings were also under construction.[43] The Air Staff anticipated that the airbase could be operational for most types of aircraft by 1932 or 1933 but would be finally completed only by 1937. No specific provisions were made for the number and types of air units designated for Singapore's defense.[44]

The Singapore airbase was the last link in the chain of planned strategic bases that the Royal Air Force intended to build for the air route to the Pacific Dominions. In 1928 well-organized air routes were in place from Cairo to Basra and across the Indian subcontinent from Karachi to Calcutta. The locations for the airfield chain from Calcutta to Singapore were being surveyed, and the financial arrangements to pay for these air routes were being worked out between the British government and the governments of India and the Malay States.[45] But the important link from Iraq to Karachi over Persian airspace had yet to be settled. The Air Ministry preferred a route along the northern Persian Gulf but the Persian government would only allow the east-west passage of aircraft once per week.[46] The Air Ministry attempted to get agreements with Persia opening up the air space but also began to plan out a less desirable contingent route along the southern coast of the Persian Gulf. At the July meetings of the chiefs of staff, Trenchard argued that the development of the imperial air routes "should be in the first order of priority."[47] But in November 1928, the CID disregarded Trenchard's view by delaying completion of the airbase at Singapore until 1937 and reducing the capital expenditure estimate from £705,000 to £601,000.[48] In addition, the committee's expenditure schedule did not include any money for the "provision for aircraft or the maintenance of air squadrons."⁴⁹

The Australian Defence Committee acknowledged the importance of the Singapore base for their defense needs and that of the entire Pacific region. They concluded that until the base was completed, the British battle fleet, "despite the numerical superiority conferred by the Washington Treaty, cannot meet the Japanese on equal terms."⁵⁰ The growing unease about Japanese intentions remained the focus of Australia's defense planners. The Defence Committee warned, "The traditional policy of Japan is to commence hostilities without warning and to attack the foundations of her opponent's sea power from the start."⁵¹ In addition, the council also concluded that a Japanese invasion of Australia should not be dismissed. They believed that the Japanese army and navy were capable of transporting and maintaining in the field a maximum of three infantry divisions.⁵² As part of the review of the Pacific defenses and how the Australian services fit into the imperial scheme, Prime Minister Stanley Bruce invited the RAF to comment on the current condition and needs of the Royal Australian Air Force. The British Air Ministry accepted the Australian invitation and sent Air Marshal Sir John M. Salmond to conduct a formal assessment of the Dominion's air defenses.⁵³ Salmond had broad experience in imperial air defense. He was the supreme military commander in Iraq during the uprisings of 1919–1923 and had reorganized and commanded the home air defenses from 1923 to 1928. From January through July 1928, Salmond visited Australia and New Zealand and in September issued a detailed comprehensive report concerning the air defenses of the Pacific Dominions.

Salmond was particularly concerned about the rapidly increasing obsolescence of the Royal Australian Air Force's equipment. His report began by stating, "I consider that the RAAF would be totally unfit to undertake war operation in co-operation with the Navy or Army."⁵⁴

Australian airplanes and equipment were long overdue for replacement and their poor quality had a detrimental effect upon the quality of airmen being trained. He found that in the two years proceeding his report, 10 officers and 136 airmen voluntarily left the service to take advantage of lucrative offers of civilian employment.[55] The undersized RAAF could ill afford the loss of this number of personnel and remain a viable force. Salmond's report also harshly criticized the part-time Citizen Air Force. For Salmond, modern air warfare required the highest degree of competence and efficiency that could only be obtained through "constant training in a 'full time' permanent unit."[56] The RAAF would be better off without these CAF units, or at the least should restrict these units to a single type of plane rather than comprising multiple types of aircraft:

> I do not find the stability in these squadrons to justify this policy, well intended as it is, and I consider better value would be obtained in future by confining these or any future Citizen Air Force squadrons to one service type machine and one operation role only.[57]

Touting the current vogue of air mobility, Salmond felt that sheer size of the Australian continent and the sparse distribution of the country's population made air power the most economic and efficient means for self-defense.

To correct the deficiencies of the RAAF, Salmond proposed a relatively modest nine-year plan to reverse the deterioration. For Salmond, the first priority was to reequip the existing five squadrons with new aircraft. In addition, Salmond recommended the following new units should be established: one army cooperation squadron based at Canberra; one fighter squadron and one flying boat reconnaissance flight at Point Cook; one flying boat reconnaissance flight at Sydney

IMPERIAL AIR MOBILITY

Figure 7.1. Sir John Maitland Salmond. In the summer of 1928, Salmond toured Australia and New Zealand to assess the current state of the Dominions' air defenses. Salmond's report determined that the Australian Citizen Air Force and the New Zealand Permanent Air Force (NZPAF) were not capable of sustained cooperation with the army or navy, acting independently in defense against air attack, or as a deterrent to seaborne attack. He recommended very specific increases and modernizations for both Dominions' air forces. Both Dominions' governments dismissed these recommendations for lack of funding. (Photograph courtesy of the National Portrait Gallery, London)

in New South Wales; one bomber-reconnaissance squadron and one fighter flight at Richmond, New South Wales; and finally, one bomber-reconnaissance squadron at Leverton, Victoria. With such an aerial force, Salmond believed that the RAAF would become a useful deterrent as well as increasing the effectiveness of Australia's army and navy.[58]

Salmond's modest Air Force expansion proposal was consistent with his assessment of the likely threat to Australia. Salmond gave little credence to a large-scale invasion and thought that attacks on Australia by "enemy" battleships and large aircraft carriers was highly improbable.[59] More plausible forms of attack would be small raids by cruisers, armed merchantmen, and submarines; small landing raids or modest air attacks by small aircraft carriers or seaplane tenders; and most likely extensive attacks upon Australian trade routes.[60] Citing the American aerial bombing trials against the German battleship *Ostfriesland* in July 1921 and the encouraging experiments with aerial torpedoes in a 1926 British

Mediterranean Fleet exercise, Salmond felt that "in aircraft we have a weapon . . . of such vast capacity for development that it must be a primary consideration in framing all future schemes of defence."[61]

While Air Marshal Salmond conducted his review of Australia's air defense, Prime Minister Stanley Bruce faced an ever-burgeoning budget deficit that had a long-term ripple effect upon the air defense of the Dominion. Bruce informed the Australian Defence Council that:

> In view of the present state of our finances, the absence of any likelihood of an immediate international crisis, and the fact that the experts do not by any means agree as to the best means of defending ports, [I am] of the opinion that it would be most unwise at this state to incur heavy expenditure in forms of defence which, bearing in mind the possible developments in aircraft, might be out of date and ineffective before many years have passed.[62]

Both Minister for Defence Sir William Glasgow and Chief of the Air Staff Air Commodore Richard ("Dickey") Williams accepted the prime minister's views.[63] Prime Minister Bruce informed the Defence Council that "there [is] not the slightest hope of increasing the amount of money available for Defence in 1928–1929."[64] In Australia, action on the Salmond Report was over before it was delivered.

Following the formal presentation of the Salmond Report to the Australian government in October 1928, the Australian Military Board, composed of the Dominion's service chiefs, challenged almost every premise of Salmond's conclusions.[65] The board considered Salmond's strategic ideas "an unsound starting point on which to frame a comprehensive defence policy for Australia."[66] Salmond's disregard for a significant attack upon the Dominion also distressed the Australians. The limited expansion of the air force in the Military Board's view was "of such comparatively small dimensions that an air force so constituted cannot be regarded as meeting any of our strategical problems."[67] The board continued, "We are mainly concerned with the preservation of our national security and integrity, and it would be unwise to ignore the major possibility and to delude ourselves that their defence can be entrusted to a few squadrons of aeroplanes, however mobile."[68] The Military Board went one step further and now questioned how committed the British were to the defense of the Pacific Dominions. In so doing, the board made an eerily accurate supposition of future events:

> It is a reasonable assumption that, if war were to break out with a Pacific power, it would be at some time when Great Britain was involved in war in Europe. Under such circumstances it is doubtful if the British Government, under pressure of British public opinion, would sanction the dispatch of the fleet to the Far East until the local problem, in Europe, had been dealt with; and since a modern battle fleet cannot operate effectively unless it has available a suitable base it is clear that a delay such as which is apprehended would afford an enemy an opportunity to attack the base in the Pacific, and, if the attack was successful, to prevent the main fleet from coming to the Pacific.[69]

Following his investigation of air defense conditions in Australia, Salmond went to New Zealand to conduct a parallel examination of the conditions there. Salmond's evaluation was the first such reassessment of conditions in New Zealand since Group Captain A. V. Bettington's report issued in 1919. In 1927–1928, the NZPAF was an anemic force. During an inspection by the Duke of York, the photographers following the duke outnumbered the personnel drawn out for his inspection at the Wigram Aerodrome outside of Christchurch.[70] When Salmond arrived at Wigram, the New Zealand force consisted of only five officers and seventeen enlisted personnel, six training aircraft and twelve service aircraft, nine of which were completely obsolete.[71] Unambiguously, Salmond concluded:

> Consequently, from a defence standpoint the Dominion is lacking in Air Forces capable either of sustained co-operation with the Army or Navy, or of acting independently in defence against air attack or as a deterrent to sea-borne raid attack.[72]

Following visits to points of strategic value on the North and South Islands and consulting with the Dominion's army and navy leaders, once again, Salmond advised that only modest measures were needed to correct New Zealand's air defense conditions. On the North Island at Auckland, Salmond recommended the formation of one reconnaissance flight, one torpedo bomber flight, and one full fighter squadron, and on the South Island at Blenheim, he called for one torpedo bomber flight. At Christchurch he recommended basing one army cooperation squadron and a fighter squadron and establishing a service-run flight school.[73] Salmond was highly critical of New Zealand's training scheme, which consisted of government-subsidized local aero clubs to train the Dominion's pilots and encourage interest in aviation. Salmond observed that "the military value of the flying training activities of the Aero Clubs is very small."[74]

Salmond also encouraged the Dominion to expand its air force officer pool. Of New Zealand's fourteen air force officers, only five—two majors, two captains, and a single lieutenant—were considered to be on permanent duty. Salmond recommended that this pool be expanded to include a single lieutenant colonel, three majors, six captains, and sixteen lieutenants to command the expanded force. In addition, these officers would require formal training and should be sent to London for instruction at the RAF War College at Cranwell as the New Zealanders had agreed to do at the 1926 Imperial Conference.[75]

Figure 7.2. At the time of Air Marshal Salmond's inspection, the New Zealand Permanent Air Force still flew World War I vintage Bristol F2B fighters. Here an F2B prepares for a demonstration flight at the Trentham Racecourse. (Photograph courtesy of the National Library of New Zealand)

Finally, Salmond suggested the elimination of the New Zealand Air Board within New Zealand's Defence Department and the creation of a separate Air Ministry or Department. New Zealand's current command structure, Salmond thought, made the Dominion's air force more vulnerable to budget reductions by authorities within the country's defense establishment. For Salmond, "any subsequent [budget] reductions rendered inevitable by financial stringency [could] be ordered by the cabinet only."[76]

Financially, Salmond's proposals were reasonable, considering that New Zealand's prime minister, Gordon Coates, was prepared to spend £1 million over the next eight years for Singapore. To build and man this air force expansion would require an initial commitment of £348,300 in capital outlay for equipment, hangars and barracks, emergency landing sites, and the loan of an RAF officer to assist with the expansion. Salmond then estimated that such a force would require an annual budget of £168,000 for maintenance of equipment, personnel, and training.[77]

Salmond hypothesized that the reinvigorated New Zealand Air Force would contribute to the defense of New Zealand. Where Salmond viewed an air attack against Australia as "improbable," he believed that "the scale of possible air attack as visualized by the CID against which provision is required at New Zealand ports is nil."[78] Realistically, Salmond deemed a seaborne attack in the form of raids by cruisers, armed raiders, and submarines as the most likely scenario.[79] Some form of air force was required to serve as an effective deterrent to an invasion and to support New Zealand's ground and naval forces. Like the RAAF, the NZPAF's primary missions would include long-distance reconnaissance, long-range torpedo and bomb attacks on enemy warships and transports, antisubmarine patrol, convoy escort, and observation for long-range fire.[80]

The Salmond Report received the same reaction in New Zealand as had the Bettington Report in 1919. The Dominion's leaders recognized the need for air defense but were unwilling to commit the meager funds available to them in funding an air arm of significant size or strength.

By the beginning of 1929, the local economic conditions throughout the empire were strained. The British economy, stagnant at best since 1921, was in crisis. Even though there were plans for air expansion, demands for lowering expenditure made these plans prohibitively expensive. With looming budget cuts, Hoare still had to cope with the air force's increased operational costs brought on by extended imperial responsibilities in Iraq, Aden, the North West (Indian) Frontier, and Sudan. In addition, the RAF needed to replace its existing stocks of obsolete and dilapidated aircraft.[81] Once again, the Royal Air Force's expansion scheme was the first victim of the budget cut when Lord Birkenhead's committee recommended that the air force postpone any growth until 1935.[82]

The growing economic crisis once again brought a shift to Britain's political makeup. In the May general election, the Labour Party won 288 seats in Parliament to 260 for the Conservatives; fifty-nine Liberals held the balance of power. Once again there would be another reevaluation of the strength of the Royal Air Force.

In Australia, the financial situation was even worse. The Dominion's economy was almost totally dependent upon its agricultural exports. Worldwide and imperial demand for its primary commodities, wool and wheat, disappeared. With declining revenues, the government would nearly default on payments on the debts accumulated during the 1920s for infrastructure improvements. Finally, the unemployment rate, like that of the other industrial nations, neared 35 percent, even before the onset of the Great Depression brought on by the collapse of the American stock market that October.

At the July 8, 1929, meeting of the Australian Council of Defence, Prime Minister Stanley Bruce informed his military advisers about the dilemma the Australian budget faced. According to Bruce, if the present rate of expenditure and revenue continued, the budget would incur a deficit of £5 million by the end of the present year.[83] In response, the minister of defence, Maj. Gen. Sir William Glasgow, agreed to reduce the military's budget by eliminating a planned five-year program for the improvement of the Dominion's military equipment, expansion, and training. The prime minister informed the air force's representative, Group Captain Stanley J. Goble, that "Air Force expansion under Sir John Salmond's scheme was out of the question at present."[84] Group Captain Goble informed Bruce that the RAAF had made reductions significantly below the minimum force requirements recommended by Salmond. For example, Salmond recommended that the RAAF required a minimum aircraft reserve of 125 percent of those actively flying, but the RAAF reduced their reserve aircraft figure to 50 percent of the current force strength.[85] Glasgow warned Bruce that these reductions would "probably result in the Air Force being left in the future with an equipment of obsolete machines." Bruce simply replied, "There was no hope of more money."[86]

The growing financial difficulties in Australia brought political difficulties. In response to labor unrest, Prime Minister Bruce attempted to eliminate the Labor Conciliation and Arbitration Court, which would return arbitration power from the federal government back to the state level. On September 10, 1929, eleven months into Bruce's third term, former prime minister William Hughes and five other Nationalist Party members crossed party lines and voted with the Labor Party against Bruce's proposal. The actions of these men forced Bruce into another general election, which resulted in the first Australian Labor government, led by James Scullin, taking office on October 21, 1929. Unfortunately for Scullin, his government had to face the worldwide depression triggered by the Wall Street crash that took place a week after he took office.

Within two weeks of becoming prime minister, Scullin faced a struggle among his service chiefs. The military budget reductions that Bruce had instituted pitted the three services against one another. In an attempt at least to maintain their current funding, Chief of Staff of the Royal Australian Navy Rear Admiral William M. Kerr, Sir John Monash, the commander of Australia's forces during World War I, and Sir Brudenell White, the former and future chief of the General Staff, would argue for the elimination of the Royal Australian Air Force at the Council of Defence meeting on November 12, 1929.[87] With such an influential group of current and former military leaders aligning against the RAAF, its elimination as a separate service was a real possibility. News of these events soon reached London. A day prior to the Australian Council of Defence meeting where discussion about the elimination of the RAAF took place, Secretary of State for Dominion Affairs Sidney Webb in London cabled Scullin about the imperial defense implications of such action. Webb warned Scullin that different command structures would have a detrimental effect on the ability of the Royal Air Force to cooperate with Australian units and that the "Aim hitherto has been the establishment of the closest possible correspondence in methods of training and organisation between the air forces of the Empire."[88]

The debate between the service leaders and the prime minister took place at the November 12 Council of Defence meeting. Speaking on behalf of the Royal Australian Air Force, Air Commodore Richard Williams provided the air force's now familiar position that it was a cost-efficient deterrent and a rapid, mobile defense force; moreover, land-based aircraft could cope with the threat presented by the new Japanese aircraft carriers.[89] Scullin supported reducing national expenditures but was unwilling to take such a dramatic step as elimination of the RAAF so early into his tenure as prime minister. In the end, Webb's arguments swayed Scullin's decision.

In June 1929, Air Marshal Sir Hugh Trenchard, the chief of the Air Staff, announced that he would retire at the end of the year. For the first twelve years of the RAF's existence, Trenchard had served as its chief. He oversaw its creation during the war and protected the service from being dismantled in the postwar years. With economic dislocation now becoming chronic, Trenchard issued a paper, "The Fuller Employment of Air Power in Imperial Defence," which summarized all of the activities of the Royal Air Force during his tenure as chief of the Air Staff. The themes of the paper centered upon the successful operations of the RAF in the Middle East and the advantages of air mobility. Most importantly, Trenchard once again repeated how the service provided an economical defense. Along this line, Trenchard called for substituting air power to replace the army and navy's coast defense responsibilities.

Trenchard's paper would once again bring to the forefront the interservice rivalries that had been repressed since 1923. In considering 25,000 miles of the empire's coast defense, Trenchard felt that "the whole of our system of coast defence requires re-examination in the light of modern conditions."[90] In addition, Trenchard believed that the

Dominions had the most to gain by utilizing aircraft but were hesitant to act because of indecision on this matter in London:

> the Governments of Australia, South Africa and New Zealand while recognizing that their present coast defences are out of date, are taking no action until agreement has been reached on the air question between the three Fighting Services at Home, and a definite policy for coast defence can be adopted by the Imperial Government.[91]

For Trenchard, the Dominions needed direction from London, and he felt their air units would become a key component of imperial defense.

Figure 7.3. Air Marshal Sir Hugh Trenchard. Trenchard is best known for the strategic bombing theories that he developed after World War I. In the immediate aftermath of World War I, he fought numerous political battles to maintain the independence of the Royal Air Force from the British Army and Royal Navy. He argued that a mobile air force could defend the vast British Empire more efficiently and economically than the other services. (Photograph courtesy of the National Portrait Gallery, London)

> The Dominions are awaiting a lead from the Imperial Government in this matter and are especially interested in the possibilities of air power in coast defence; and any units which may be provided in the Dominions for this duty will also be available in the event of war with a non-maritime Power to form part of any Dominion contribution to an Imperial striking Force.[92]

The heads of the army and navy were quick to condemn the newest assault on the respective services' defense responsibilities. Throughout December, a series of memoranda were issued by the respective departmental secretaries in defense of their current responsibilities as well as attacking Trenchard's proposals. Secretary of State for War Thomas Shaw informed the cabinet that his military advisers completely disagreed with the entire premise of Trenchard's paper.[93] Shaw made his own proposal for economy by once again calling for the elimination of the Royal Air Force as a separate service.

> I desire equally an examination, in conjunction with the Treasury, of the question of the present constitution of the Royal Air Force as a separate service, with what seems to me to be duplication of staff and administrative services. I am of the opinion that a close scrutiny of this problem will reveal the fact that substantial economies, without any loss of efficiency, can be thus effected.[94]

Secretary of State for Air Christopher Birdwood Thomson quickly responded to Shaw's memorandum, protesting that Trenchard's proposals should not "degenerate into an interdepartmental wrangle."[95] Thomson defended Trenchard, whose suggestions, he felt, "deserve serious consideration."[96] Albert Victor Alexander, First Lord of the Admiralty, though not as vitriolic as Shaw about Trenchard's proposals, agreed "with the Secretary of State for War that in a matter of such prime importance to Imperial defence we cannot afford to be precipitate."[97]

The 1920s ended as they began, with Britain's military services fighting among themselves for meager defense funds. In response, the leadership of the Royal Air Force forwarded the strategic concept of mobile air defense as a means to achieve defense economies while providing protection to the vast empire. As the Great Depression took hold of the world's economies, the military services budgets would become even more strained. With still no looming threat, the second Labour government continued to look to collective security through the League of Nations, the Locarno Pact, and its imperial partners as the principal means to maintain international peace. Abhorring armaments, MacDonald embraced disarmament as the primary means to solve the mounting economic crisis.

CHAPTER 8

DEPRESSION AND DISARMAMENT, 1929–1933

> *We venture to suggest that no opportunity should be lost to open the door, however little, to practical co-operation in Empire Defence and to relief of the disproportionate burden at present borne by the United Kingdom.*[1]
> —*George F. Milne, Frederick L. Field, and John M. Salmond*

In June 1929, the Labour ministry under Ramsay MacDonald took office for a second time. The primary themes of election, unemployment, and the quest for international peace through collective security dominated. Though all of the political parties promised relief in these spheres, the electorate viewed Labour as the best party to deliver results. MacDonald took office in a precarious position with a thin plurality of 287 Labour seats to 261 Conservative seats and 57 Liberal seats. Like the government in London, the governments of the Dominions were preoccupied with combating the Depression. The key weapon utilized by all of them was the reduction of government expenditures in an attempt to bring budgets into balance. The curtailment of defense expenditure once again was the principal means of achieving this budgetary goal.

In December 1929, the secretary of state for air, Christopher Thomson, decided to postpone the RAF's fifty-two squadron expansion plan for eight years. The fifty-two squadron scheme had been the foundation of RAF defense planning since 1923. Thomson took into consideration the current international situation and fiscal emergency and determined that the completed program would not be needed until 1938.[2] He immediately cut money intended for the planned expansion for three regular squadrons slated in the 1930 Air Estimates. He based this decision "on the grounds of the wholly exceptional exigencies of the financial situation."[3]

At this time the Royal Air Force was also in transition with Trenchard's retirement and replacement by Air Marshal Sir John M. Salmond as the chief of the Air Staff. During his tenure as the chief of the Air Staff, the British government's main goal in foreign policy once again became naval and air disarmament. Salmond viewed disarmament as a foolish principle because other powers would not keep their pledges.[4] Foolish or not, for the next three years Salmond had to guide the Royal Air Force through the disarmament minefield. In addition, Salmond expressed concern as to how the Dominion air forces would fit into an international air disarmament accord, which in any case ran counter to his 1928 recommendations.[5]

The Dominions' prime ministers met once again in London for the 1930 Imperial Conference. The world economic crisis obviously dominated discussions at the meeting but defense matters were not forgotten. In preparation for the conference, the Committee of Imperial Defence established the Sub-Committee on the Reduction of Armaments. This committee began to outline the British position on disarmament that would later be followed in Geneva in February 1932 when general disarmament talks began under the auspices of the League of Nations.

The subcommittee also prepared recommendations for the Dominions' military strength and how their militaries fit into the British imperial defense scheme. The subcommittee's chair, Lord Robert Cecil, a veteran of the 1927 Geneva Naval Conference, recognized the growing independence of the Dominions within the imperial system. On December 4, 1931, this independence was formally acknowledged when the British Parliament passed the Statute of Westminster that gave formal recognition for the sovereignty of the Dominions within the British Empire. The statute declared that the British Commonwealth of Nations was now a free union of self-governing Dominions, bound by a common allegiance to the throne, and that the British Parliament might not legislate for the Dominions except at their request and subject to their assent. Although the statute was a year away from passage, Cecil was still anxious to get the views of the various Dominions on questions regarding disarmament; but he also emphasized that each Dominion would speak for itself in international forums.[6] Cecil also argued that since the Dominions were responsible for the composition and scale of their military forces, each would have to be a separate signatory to any disarmament convention.[7] The position prescribed by the committee became Britain's negotiating stance at Geneva over the next three years.

Like Lord Cecil, Air Minister Thomson was concerned about the Dominions' ideas about imperial air defense and disarmament. In preparation for the Geneva talks, Thomson wanted to coordinate a joint air disarmament policy between the different parts of the empire.[8] Thomson also requested the Dominions' estimations on how disarmament would affect their home defenses and the operation of imperial air routes to the Dominions, and how limited budgets would curtail aviation activities and technical development in each Dominion.[9] In response, both Australia and New Zealand would use the coming Imperial Conference to review the status of their respective defense establishments.

Australia's first Labor government, led by James Scullin, looked to MacDonald's disarmament plan as its model for defense. The minister of defense, Albert E. Green, wrote to Scullin with his assessment of Australia's military preparations and was most concerned about the lack of unanimity among Australia's military leaders. The service chiefs echoed the same arguments of the British political leaders in Whitehall. The navy maintained that sea power was economical, essential to protect Australian trade routes, and afforded the best security against invasion.[10] The army's leadership disputed the navy's claims because the naval force was too small and the army's defense responsibility remained port defense, and it needed a sizable land force to repel invasion.

The Royal Australian Air Force (RAAF) leaders continued to rely on the third option argument that air power could potentially supplant both naval forces and army shore batteries. Naturally, both naval and army leaders dismissed the air force's position.[11] In February 1930, Green suggested to Scullin that he appoint a committee whose members were "not holding office" to review Australia's existing defense policies to reconcile the disputes between the services as well as enable the government to determine its future defense policy.[12] The services were too intransigent, defending their limited budgets against each other.

In March 1930, Scullin informed the Australian Defence Committee of the pending budget cuts. The inability of Australia's service chiefs to agree on the basic principles of defense forced the government to distribute the reductions on a "pro rata basis."[13] In April, the cuts drove the air force to eliminate its aeronautical research station outside Sydney.[14] Later, when Scullin took over the Treasury portfolio in July, he cut RAAF permanent personnel by three officers and thirty-seven other ranks.[15] Even with these cuts, Green, who supported a strong Australian air force, managed to implement a limited expansion training scheme for Australian pilots and bought a few new aircraft for the service.

Air power in New Zealand continued to remain an afterthought in the Dominion's defense scheme. In 1930, the New Zealand Permanent Air Force (NZPAF) consisted of only nine officers and forty-one enlisted men. There were only nine combat aircraft in the inventory, consisting of six obsolete Bristol fighters and three Gloster Grebes. Half of the Dominion's eight training aircraft were World War I vintage Avro 504s and four de Havilland Moths.[16] In addition, ninety officers in the Territorial Air Force supplemented the NZPAF.

In January 1930, an incident in Western Samoa illustrated the pathetic state of the NZPAF. A small uprising of the indigenous Mau population broke out against New Zealand's mandate. When the riots resulted in a dozen deaths, New Zealand dispatched the cruiser HMS *Dunedin* and a company of naval militia to suppress the disorder. To avoid being locked out of the operation, the NZPAF contributed a de Havilland Moth D.H.60 light training biplane, piloted by Flight Lieutenant Sidney Wallingford, and two mechanics. The use of the aircraft became a series of almost comical errors. To aid communication with ground troops and the *Dunedin*, a radio set was installed in the aircraft, which because of its size had to be mounted in the front cockpit, thus displacing the observer who was supposed to operate it. The radio ultimately proved to be worthless. Wallingford could not reach it and tune it while flying, and it broke down in the tropical weather conditions. The set was soon removed from the aircraft and Wallingford and his observer resumed delivering messages to the ground with streamer bags. When attempts were made to use the airplane for mapping and aerial photography, the vibration and an inadequate camera resulted in blurred and useless images. The tropical weather also made maintenance difficult, and the frequent pop-up storms caused numerous forced landings. The final indignity came on January 23, when a rock-throwing Mau attacked the airplane. Unarmed, Wallingford's only means of retaliation was to fire his emergency signal flare at the assailants. In response, the mechanics hastily mounted a

Lewis machine gun in the observer's seat and lashed a second Lewis gun to the aircraft wing struts.[17] This second gun was useless because it was impossible to aim as well as reload in flight. The poor performance of the NZPAF in Samoa convinced the conservative United Party government of Joseph Ward that changes needed to be made.

The first step to improve NZPAF was an immediate increase to the force's budget. In March 1930, New Zealand appropriated £53,097 for military flying, almost doubling the preceding year's budget.[18] Though a paltry sum, it still demonstrated a new commitment to the Dominion's military aviation. In May, Joseph Ward resigned the premiership for health reasons and was replaced by George Forbes. In preparation for the Imperial Conference later in the year, Forbes's government informed London about New Zealand's plans for participating in imperial air defense. First the government planned to implement Salmond's 1928 air defense recommendations, "insofar as the finances of the country permit."[19] With the new infusion of money, the priority was to continue infrastructure improvements to the Dominion's principal airbase, Wigram, outside Christchurch, as well as to establish a new flight of coastal reconnaissance flying boats at Hobsonville.[20] Second, the government intended to send, within two months, fully trained pilots and mechanics to fill two Royal Air Force squadrons and to staff another two squadrons within another two months. The Forbes government informed the British that they were willing to send these men to any destination required by the imperial government at New Zealand's expense.[21] Training for these four squadrons was programmed into the 1930 budget and initiated under a "Territorial Scheme."[22] The chiefs of the Imperial General Staff welcomed this support from New Zealand, stating, "Even if it were not found practicable to send aircraft to this country, . . . a reserve of fresh pilots, arriving at a time when the personnel at home . . . might be expected to be feeling the strain acutely, would have the most far reaching effect."[23]

Figure 8.1. HMS *Dunedin* moored in Apia Harbour was sent to suppress the local Mau uprising in 1930. A contingent aircraft of the New Zealand Permanent Air Force accompanied the operation. (Photograph courtesy of the National Library of New Zealand)

Figure 8.2. The deHavilland Moth of the New Zealand Permanent Air Force being unloaded and prepared for operations in Western Samoa. The single Moth was the NZPAF's only contribution to the Samoan operation. (Photograph courtesy of the National Library of New Zealand)

The NZPAF sent Squadron Leader Thomas M. Wilkes to London to establish a "permanent" liaison office in Whitehall to coordinate the activities of the NZPAF with the Royal Air Force. The British reciprocated by appointing Wing Commander S. Grant Dalton as director of New Zealand's aviation services. The appointment combined the duties of officer commanding the NZPAF and comptroller of civil aviation. To encourage both military and commercial aviation, New Zealand's government directed £8,300 in subsidies to various flying clubs with the goal of training ninety new pilots each year.[24]

In September, the government purchased four new Hawker "Tomtit" trainers to replace the aged Avro 504s. The £7,200 spent for the aircraft and £3,000 spent on spare engines and parts "swallowed up the balance of the funds available this year for aircraft and spares."[25] Although the government made attempts to improve the Dominion's aeronautical situation, its efforts were still feeble. By the middle of 1931, because of the continuing effects of the Depression, Forbes reversed all of the previous year's "improvements." The NZPAF budget returned to £30,000 and was "barely sufficient for the maintenance of existing personnel and equipment."[26] In addition, Squadron Leader Wilkes was recalled and the Air Liaison office in London was closed. The government's policy hinted at how New Zealand would later benefit imperial air defense. Clearly, they could not provide much in the way of material assistance, but New Zealand was willing to provide trained personnel to Britain for use and deployment at their discretion and would help fill the wartime ranks of the Royal Air Force.

Imperial defense matters at the 1930 Imperial Conference almost were left off the agenda because economic issues were the primary concern. Even though defense was a peripheral topic at the conference, the subject remained important since the economic discussions had a direct effect on military decisions and policy. The conference confirmed the agreements of the 1926 conference on imperial defense but there were some interesting and important new developments. The British chiefs of staff, Field Marshal George Milne, Admiral Frederick Field, and Air Marshal Salmond, felt that the Dominions needed to expand their imperial responsibilities even further:

> If arrangements for Imperial defence are to be a practical proposition, the Dominions will have to regard themselves as responsible for more than "local defence" and we suggest that before long, perhaps at the next Imperial conference, serious consideration should be given to the question of allotting larger "areas of responsibility" in defense.[27]

Even though the chiefs wanted a larger commitment from the Dominions for regional defense, they were concerned about the growing independence of the Dominions within the imperial system: "The extent of co-operation by the Dominion forces, if even where it is assumed that the latter would be cooperating, cannot be gauged, and the Dominion forces have to be regarded largely as an extra asset not to be taken into account."[28]

Naturally, the southwestern Pacific would become Australia's and New Zealand's "area of responsibility." The military forces of the Dominions were still weak and would continue to depend upon the British for their defense. The Australians and New Zealanders insisted that construction of the Singapore naval base continue. Unfortunately for the Dominions, with the Labour Party again in power, interest in developing the base again waned. On April 22, 1930, Britain, the United States, France, Italy, and Japan signed the London Naval Treaty, agreeing not to start construction of any new capital ships until 1937 and further reducing their respective fleets. MacDonald felt "[f]ully justified in taking advantage of the favorable international situation to slow down the work on the naval base at Singapore and obtain some relief from the large expenditure involved, at a time when the United Kingdom's Exchequer is heavily burdened."[29]

Even the British air staff was prepared to postpone any new work on Singapore's aviation facilities until 1936, unless "the political situation vis-à-vis Japan changed suddenly for the worse."[30] It was also the opinion of the British in the current political environment that "Japan was unlikely to disturb the peace."[31] This assessment was soon proved wrong when the Japanese invaded Manchuria within a year. The leaders of Australia and New Zealand understood the financial situation but once again opposed MacDonald's decision.[32] In their opinion, no changes should have been made to the progress of the base. The Australian Air Staff continued to view the Singapore base as vital to the defense of the Pacific and Australian interests. The Australian Air Staff also felt the base's air defenses must be developed to counter any Japanese air attack, and to enable aerial reinforcement to reach the Dominions. In addition, these facilities, when completed, would become an important economic link between Australia and India.[33]

While lobbying for the continued construction of the Singapore base and the expansion of the air route to India, the Australians stepped up their presence in the Solomon Islands to enlarge the buffer between the Australian continent and the Japanese. The Australian Defence Committee, believing that Japan would not risk an attack on the islands in greater force than a raiding party, organized a chain of coast-watching stations throughout the islands to counter this possibility.[34] These stations proved to be invaluable during World War II. In addition, they felt that if the Japanese sent a strong expeditionary force more than 3,000 miles to the Solomon Islands, they would expose their communications to attack by British forces.[35] The committee assumed that a Solomon Islands operation would be difficult for Japan because the resources of the islands were not sufficient to support an army of occupation for any length of time.[36] Even though Australia's military leaders concurred with the British and felt that Japanese occupation of the Solomons was unlikely, they were not prepared to surrender them to Japan. The view declared by Prime Minister Billy Hughes at Versailles in 1919, that "no 5,000,000 people can possible hold this continent when, 80 miles off, there is a potential enemy. There are literally hundreds of other islands stretching out, every one of them a point of vantage from which Australia could be attacked," remained more persuasive to Australian planners.[37] Expanded occupation of the Solomons would reduce the threat of air attack on Australia by denying Japan the islands as bases for Japanese bombers.

As the 1930 Imperial Conference came to an end in November, a British delegation departed for Geneva to participate in general League of Nations discussions on disarmament. Between 1925 and 1933, Germany had been training pilots and ground crews on fifty Fokker D XIII fighter aircraft in Lipetsk, Russia.[38] This was expressly forbidden by the Versailles Treaty. At Geneva, the British negotiators faced a near-impossible mission, trying to reconcile the German desire for equality with the other powers and the French desire for security. As new aircraft with improved speed, payload, and size became available, the predictions of mass destruction by aircraft now seemed closer to reality. For these reasons air power now became a primary disarmament topic at Geneva.

The Committee of Imperial Defence Sub-Committee on Air Disarmament examined the many aspects of aerial disarmament and outlined the British position for the negotiations. The subcommittee first rejected any attempt to limit aircraft horsepower. Sir Harry Batterbee, the assistant secretary at the Dominion Office, was concerned that such a limitation would be detrimental to the continued development of imperial civil air communication. Other members of the committee disregarded Batterbee's concerns because they believed that civil aircraft now were not suitable for military purposes. The committee ultimately concluded that horsepower restrictions would be ineffective because this principle could be easily evaded.[39] Like horsepower limitation, limiting the size of aircraft was also deemed impractical because this could potentially encourage designers to develop smaller aircraft armed with smaller but more powerful bombs.[40] The subcommittee would also concur with the British Air Staff in rejecting the idea of arms limitation through limiting air force budgets. Limited budgets would still allow a power to build any particular type of aircraft and easily evade treaty obligations through "the undisclosed diversion of monies ostensibly provided for other purposes."[41]

As in naval agreements, the subcommittee eventually decided that the most practical means of aerial disarmament would be to limit the number of a power's operational and reserve aircraft and personnel to a predetermined ratio. This provided the most flexible means to manage the Royal Air Force. This fixed number of aircraft could then be distributed in proportion to the specific strategic needs of the empire. The committee concluded that there was "nothing to prevent us concentrating the whole of our air forces at home, or, if we wish, overseas."[42] This action was highly improbable. The concept of a numerical air strength ratio as a negotiation position was the weakest stance for British diplomats at Geneva. Because the Royal Air Force was the fifth largest behind France, the United States, the Soviet Union, and Italy, there was no incentive for the other powers to set limits or reduce the size of their air forces. Moreover, Britain would be obliged to accept a status of continued inferiority.

During the summer of 1931, the economic conditions in Britain continued to deteriorate, and the Labour Ministry faced massive budget deficits. The government's inability to respond to the situation led to MacDonald submitting his resignation on August 24, 1931. King George V convinced MacDonald to stay in office and address the crisis by forming a National government with representatives in the cabinet from the Conservative and Liberal parties. This first National government was short-lived, falling under Conservative pressure to hold elections. On October 8, 1931, Parliament was dissolved and new elections took place on October 27. Within a week, the king asked that MacDonald form the second National government. Weakened by the election, Labour chose Arthur Henderson as its leader, and MacDonald became a prime minister without a political party. The election tilted parliamentary power in favor of the Conservatives.[43]

This Conservative shift was most influential in the change of direction of Britain's foreign policy. As disarmament talks continued in Geneva, negotiators at the conference discussed the possibility of outlawing the aerial bombing of civilians. The British delegation rejected the proposal outright. The new air minister, Lord Londonderry, argued that such a proposal would limit the RAF's peacetime imperial policing duties.[44]

Meanwhile, Scullin's government in Australia supported the endeavors of the League of Nations and the attempts at Geneva to reduce arms and promote collective security. At the same time, Scullin recognized that the country was still dependent upon Britain for all aspects of its defense. The Australians looked to the future and determined the country might need to strengthen its three military branches to "further safeguard against invasion based on that aspect of deterrence."[45] For this reason, the Australians, while supportive of general disarmament, thought that the subject should be approached with caution.

Echoing many of the concerns of the British Air Staff, the Australian Air Staff opposed any sort of limitation on aircraft size and horsepower because "our geographical position and great distances . . . [would] constitute a far more serious restriction to us than countries more favorably situated and with shorter distances to contend with."[46] As Lord Cecil had argued earlier, the Dominion aircraft needed to be regarded separately from British aircraft totals. The major powers needed to recognize that Australia, like other small nations, was also "faced with the problem of raising forces compatible with national security."[47] Unfortunately for the Australians, powers such as France and Italy still did not view the Dominions as sovereign countries. If a numerical ratio was to be established, as it had been at the Washington Naval Conference in 1922, they wanted the Dominions' aircraft included in the British air force strength.

The worsening economic conditions in Australia in late 1931 threatened Scullin's Labor government. In the fall of 1931, Joseph Lyons with several other Labor ministers abandoned the party in a dispute over Labor's economic policies. As a result, Lyons and his political allies joined with members of the conservative Nationalist Party and formed the new United Australia Party (UAP) under Lyons's leadership. In the elections held that December, Lyons became the first national candidate to utilize the airplane for campaigning across the country. Following the victory of the UAP, Lyons, a fiscal conservative, served as both prime minister and secretary of the Treasury. His principal concern was to reduce government debt and to maintain balanced budgets. At the same time, Lyons determined that "the provision made for Defence has been inadequate for some years" and increased military spending from £3,105,188 in 1932 to £3,522,820 in 1934 with £438,000 directed to the RAAF.[48]

Unlike the Australians, who demonstrated the desire for some autonomy outside the imperial system, the New Zealanders would not even consider taking an independent path. The declining economic conditions increased the Dominion's dependence on Britain. Air Marshal Salmond was most disappointed about the continued weakness of the NZPAF and that New Zealand's leaders had not implemented any of his earlier recommendations.[49] The fragile political divisions in New Zealand prevented the government from even considering an expansion of the air force at this time. The United Party's minority government (a remake of New Zealand's Liberal Party) of Prime Minister Forbes could not alienate the Labor Party's pacifists wing, nor could it afford to lose the support of the fiscally conservative rural farmer constituency that was highly sensitive to public money being "wasted." Neither group would support the expansion of the Dominion's military forces, especially at a time when there was no obvious threat to the empire or the Dominion.[50] This view would soon change.

On September 18, 1931, Japanese troops occupied Mukden on the pretext of a Chinese attack on the South Manchurian Railroad. By the end of the year, the Japanese, faced with only feeble Chinese resistance, completed their occupation of Manchuria. The Japanese offensive placed British diplomats in a difficult position. Some, such as Sir Francis Lindley, Britain's ambassador in Tokyo, were sympathetic to Japanese claims in Manchuria, did not wish to antagonize the Japanese against British Far Eastern interests, and also warned that a false step might also develop into a general war between the powers.[51] Other voices in the Foreign Office, however, opposed this blatant Japanese aggression and wanted strong action taken by the League of Nations.[52] In the opinion of Cabinet Secretary Maurice Hankey, the league was unlikely to persuade the Japanese to cease their offensive, and he was "very glad that the utter futility of the present covenant has been demonstrated in the Far East. . . . no one is ever likely to believe in sanctions, and they will become more and more a dead letter. Personally I would like to see them got rid of."[53] Hankey was opposed to Britain's participation in the league because it constrained Britain's ability to enter independent negotiations. Economic sanctions might have had some effect upon the Japanese because of the fragile state of their economy. Even though the members agreed that this was clearly an instance of Japanese aggression, the league was never able to come to a consensus and take the steps necessary to implement these sanctions. Although New Zealand ultimately followed the British position at Geneva, the Dominion's representatives joined with the Soviet Union and pressed for sanctions against Japan.[54]

The Manchurian crisis brought an end to discussions at Geneva relating to aerial disarmament and inspired the British military to reevaluate its defense network in the Pacific. Japanese aggression had a disquieting effect in Whitehall. From the perspective of the service chiefs, the crisis developed out of the "clear sky" and "the suddenness [with] which Japan took action and the success with which her intentions were concealed notwithstanding the glare of worldwide publicity to which she was exposed at the League of Nations."[55] The chiefs of staff also made another prediction that proved to be accurate: "If Japan were ever to prepare for operations of a wider scope, it must be assumed that these preparations would be concealed with equal ardor and a blow struck with equal suddenness in order to gain the initial advantage."[56]

Even before the Manchurian crisis, the British Air Staff reported that "our most serious deficiency is the shortage of aircraft for the duty of assisting in the maintenance of sea communications."[57] In addition, the staff felt that there was also a severe shortage of heavy bomber/transport aircraft capable of "effective and versatile air action."[58] In a discussion at the Joint Planning Sub-Committee of the CID, the RAF's representative, Group Captain Charles Portal, and navy representative Captain Andrew Cunningham (both future chiefs of their respective services) highlighted the difficulties that faced British imperial defense. The talks also revealed how dangerously thin their respective forces were spread. The debate concerning the Pacific's defenses remained centered on Singapore.

Portal believed that it would take at least eighteen months to station three squadrons of aircraft there, and this move was still dependent upon the construction of new facilities to service these aircraft.[59] Portal's disclosure ran counter to the RAF's argument that they could defend the empire through rapid redeployment. Cunningham also questioned whether or not these aircraft would even be available and if the aircraft and trained crews even existed. The subcommittee's discussions focused on Singapore's shore-based guns and permanently assigned eight air force squadrons and a naval division of ships to the base. Cunningham argued that the group's fixation on Singapore's defenses would have an adverse effect upon the military services' mobility and increase the "possible dangers elsewhere in the empire."[60] Portal was not as pessimistic as Cunningham about the availability of squadrons and personnel, pointing out that the RAF were making the necessary armaments available along the imperial air routes and at strategic points throughout the empire. Finally, Portal claimed unrealistically that the sixty-five aircraft designated for the air defense of the Far East would "put [the Japanese] carriers out of action, or alternatively, if the landing were attempted, would create havoc, amongst the transports and tows."[61] Even at this time this number of aircraft would be inadequate compared to the 220 aircraft carried by Japan's three fleet carriers, *Ryujo*, *Kaga*, and *Akagi*. Portal and Cunningham both believed that the Japanese would not risk all of their carriers on a combined attack on Singapore.[62]

In the opinion of the British chiefs of staff, the crisis in the Far East now made the Pacific Dominions even more unreliable partners in imperial defense. "It must be remembered that in a war with Japan, public opinion, in both Australia and New Zealand, would likely at the outset press for an exaggerated amount of local protection."[63] The chiefs were also concerned that the military forces in Australia and New Zealand were considerably reduced and it was doubtful whether they could even be made available.[64] The 1932 "Annual Review of Imperial Defence Policies" summarized the overall situation in the Pacific and put the blame for this weakness on the Ten Year Rule,

> The report points in particular to our own unreadiness to deal with the situation in the Far East owing to the weakness in the defenses at Hong Kong, Singapore, and Trincomali. This section attributes our weakness in the Far East a good deal to the Ten Years assumption underlying the Service Estimates.[65]

As a result, the chiefs of staff recommended and the government accepted the cancellation of the Ten Year Rule.

As in Britain, the crisis in Manchuria created two camps in Australia. John G. Latham, Australia's attorney general and minister for external affairs, summarized Australia's position before the Committee of Imperial Defense:

> The only nation which could be regarded as a potential invader was Japan. As regards the latter, [my] government felt that owing to Japan being so involved on the mainland against Manchuria, not to mention places like Shanghai, the risk to Australia by an invasion force for many years was small.

Even though military planners viewed the burden placed on Japan by their military adventures in Manchuria as diminishing the threat to Australia, the Dominion remained dependent upon the promise of the British fleet being sent to the Pacific if the Japanese decided to move south.[66]

From the Australian perspective, the greatest danger from Japan were raids rather than a full invasion. The sources of these raids would be limited to naval aircraft launched from limited numbers of aircraft carriers. With their maritime defense dependent upon the Royal Navy, the Australians decided to emphasize air power. Latham felt that a strong air force would act as a deterrent against the Japanese, and for this reason he believed that it would be better to put "a large amount of their money into bombing aeroplanes."[67] There was one important caveat to Latham's position. He indicated that Australia would abide by any aerial convention agreed upon at Geneva and would defer to the position adopted by the British delegation. Unbeknownst to the Australians, the disarmament discussions were essentially over by this time.

Many in Australia were opposed to disarmament. The warnings of Australia's former prime minister, Billy Hughes, summarized the situation for the British Empire and Australia in the Far East in September 1933:

> I regard the position here as serious as the days preceding 1914. Japanese are a fine race but their ways are not our ways. In the nation with great armed forces behind it should rather choose the risk of war than certainty of national oblivion. If we want to hold Australia, we must be prepared to defend Australia, and we know that Australia was never so open to attack as she is now. Disquieting use of British fleet's backwardness shows that, despite all goodwill, the British navy is no longer in a position to come immediately to our aid. Recent events in the Pacific show that Australia must be prepared to hold her own until the British navy arrives. We must have air force, submarines, surface craft adequate to patrol our coast and efficient land forces.[68]

The Great Depression devastated national economies across the world. With people starving in the streets, many believed that it was a waste to spend money on the military. The solution favored by the Labour government was to entice the other powers to reduce military spending in preference for domestic programs instead; so, arms reduction was as pragmatic as it was altruistic. Although indeed naïve in retrospect, this is also an understandable viewpoint given the breadth and severity of the Depression. So at the same time diplomats met in Geneva in attempts to reach agreement on reductions in the military, Germany, Italy, and Japan preferred to solve their economic problems through military preparation and expansion. The British government realized the path these powers were following, but there was still hesitancy to rearm for fear of further weakening the British economy. The collapse of the economy was seen as just as dangerous to Britain's survival as an attack on the country by these powers. The British leaders did not dismiss the threat posed by Germany, Italy, and Japan and soon began the expansion of their military forces and industrial infrastructure, albeit in a more restrained manner. To accuse Britain and the Dominions of ill-preparedness overlooks their dire economic circumstances and concerns over military expenditures.

CHAPTER 9

THE INTERNATIONAL CRISES AND IMPERIAL REARMAMENT, 1934–1936

> *But the time has come when we can no longer afford to ignore the fact that, while other nations talk of disarmament, almost all nations but ourselves are increasing their air armaments extensively. If other nations will not come down to our level, then, inevitably, our national and Imperial security demands that we must begin to build up towards theirs.*[1]
> —*Sir Philip Sassoon*

In response to Hitler and the Nazi Party's acquisition of power in 1933 and walking out of the League of Nations in October, the British military leadership recognized the need to reassess the empire's defenses. On November 14, 1933, they responded to this need by forming the Defence Requirements Sub-Committee within the Committee of Imperial Defence. With depleted armed forces, the British faced the ominous scenario of a rearmed Germany and an aggressive Japan. To counter this state of affairs, the British wanted to improve relations with Japan, strained since the termination of the Anglo-Japanese Alliance in 1922. The British also began to rearm, especially air power. The worsening international situation was just as obvious to the leaders of the Pacific Dominions, who, like the British, undertook to reevaluate the conditions of their wholly inadequate armed forces.

In the spring of 1934, the British chiefs of staff rated the Royal Air Force (RAF) fifth among the world powers behind France, the Soviet Union, the United States, and Italy, blaming the current deficiencies on the Ten Year Rule.[2] The Defence Requirements Committee (DRC) had been appointed on November 3, 1933, to examine the current state of national and imperial defenses and determine what actions were required to improve the situation.[*] There was one important new strategic assumption: these changes were to be based on a rearmed and aggressive Germany. During the meetings from January to March 1934, members of the DRC concluded that Nazi Germany was not an immediate threat, but that it was the greatest threat to peace and stability in the long run.[3] Secretary of State for Air Lord Londonderry, the British Air Staff, and the cabinet agreed with the DRC's assessment, predicting that Germany could not deploy an effective air force for about five years, estimating that Germany would require this amount of time to instruct pilots, aircrews, and ground crews, and manufacture aircraft to equip a modern air force from scratch.[4] The Royal Air Force at this time would have to cope with some of the same expansion difficulties as Germany including the expansion of manufacturing capabilities and addressing the need for skilled workers. Londonderry pressed MacDonald to make a rapid decision to help "lay the foundation" for the expansion of the RAF.[5] MacDonald assured Londonderry that this was his intention.[6]

---

[*]The full-time members of the committee were: chair, Stanley Baldwin, Neville Chamberlain, chancellor of the exchequer, Sir John Simon, Sir Robert Vansittart, permanent undersecretary at the Foreign Office, Sir Warren Fisher, permanent secretary to the Treasury, Sir Maurice Hankey, cabinet secretary, the imperial chiefs of staff, First Sea Lord Admiral Ernle Chatfield, Gen. Sir George Milne, Air Marshal Edward Ellington.

The chiefs of staff agreed that the present strength of the Royal Air Force was "wholly inadequate for the requirements of Imperial security."⁷ The committee also determined that:

> We are still short of what was as long ago as 1923 regarded as the *minimum* number of squadrons required for home defense and this despite the rapid process of air expansion which has been taking place continuously since that date abroad. War reserves are non-existent.⁸

Once again, the committee returned to the fifty-two squadron proposal.⁹ Londonderry saw this goal as the "bare minimum" and felt that the Royal Air Force would require twenty-five additional new squadrons for a total of seventy-seven.¹⁰ He warned the cabinet that before implementing such a policy, public opinion would have to be persuaded to fund these dramatic increases. There was also the practical concern with planning the rapid expansion of airbase infrastructure, training, and recruitment.¹¹ Londonderry gave no indication of how the air force would solve these problems. Most important was the development of new methods of aircraft construction.

Similar to the launch of HMS *Dreadnought* in 1906 that made all other capital warships of the period obsolete, the development of all-metal aircraft in the mid-1930s rendered all existing fabric-covered aircraft obsolete as well. Increased horsepower from turbochargers, retractable landing gear, and the ability to carry a greater number of guns contributed to the rapid increase in aircraft performance and capability. Weakened by the economic dislocation of the Depression, Britain's feeble aircraft industry had to adapt to the production of these new designs as well as expand rapidly to build the aircraft necessary to equip seventy-seven squadrons. The pressure created by aerial rearmament on the British aircraft industry would not be seriously addressed until 1935.

In 1930, the Air Ministry issued Specification F.7/30 to encourage Britain's manufacturers to come up with new and innovative designs in fighter aircraft. These changes called for increases in armament to include four machine guns or heavy cannons, a service ceiling of more than 30,000 feet, a speed of more than 250 mph, and improved rates of climb and maneuverability.[12] By 1934, aircraft such as the Hawker Fury series, the Gloster Gladiator, and the Westland P.V.4 were among the improved biplane designs introduced, but the innovative monoplane designs such as the all-aluminum Bristol Type 133 and Supermarine Type 224 showed more promise for the future. In 1934, the most significant designs were started by Sidney Camm at Hawker Aircraft with the Hurricane and by Reginald Mitchell at Supermarine with sketches for the Spitfire. The government and the Air Ministry now faced a difficult decision. Should money be spent to reequip the existing and newly formed squadrons with obsolete equipment or should expansion be put off until the advanced monoplane designs became available?[13] To make this technological transition, the RAF, like the Luftwaffe, would essentially have to start from scratch. The responsibility for this conversion fell to Stanley Baldwin's new government.

In May 1934, a select group from the cabinet—Lord Londonderry, Foreign Secretary John Simon, Chancellor of the Exchequer Neville Chamberlain, and Permanent Secretary Maurice Hankey—met to formulate a five-year plan for the expansion of the RAF. Simon argued for increasing the air force by forty new squadrons, consisting of ten squadrons for home and Far Eastern defense respectively and twenty squadrons for the essentially nonexistent Fleet Air Arm. At this meeting, Londonderry changed his earlier position regarding the expansion of the RAF beyond the fifty-two squadron proposal. He now feared that it would be uneconomical and detrimental to the efficiency and quality of the force.[14] Chamberlain seemed surprised by the Air Ministry's reluctance about a rapid expansion, but he was willing to overlook these concerns and forwarded to the cabinet a five-year plan calling for "some 1287 aircraft."[15] The committee's proposal designated eighty-eight aircraft specifically for the Far East, a provision that concerned Chamberlain, who wondered if "they were to be considered as definitely locked up there?"[16] To alleviate Chamberlain's concerns, Hankey explained that the production of these aircraft came toward the end of the five-year program and were essentially a reserve. Hankey indicated that if the "situation vis-à-vis Japan improved and deteriorated in Europe, it might be possible to take some of these aircraft for home defense."[17]

At the group's May 15 meeting, the issue of Far Eastern air defenses continued to concern Chamberlain, who wondered if the ten new squadrons designated for home defense were enough and whether it was necessary to send another ten squadrons to the Far East. His primary concern was the growing German menace. From 1933 to 1934, German military spending grew from RM7.4 million to almost RM4.2 billion.[18] Correspondingly, the German air budget increased from RM78,348,450 in 1933 to RM210,187,650 in 1934.[19] For Chamberlain:

> There should be no difficulty in convincing public opinion of the necessity for increasing our air force's at home, but [I do] not think that arrangements to increase air forces at such places as Penang would carry very much conviction.[20]

With support from the former Air Minister and now First Lord of the Admiralty Sir Samuel Hoare, Londonderry repeated his support for the fifty-two squadron home defense plan. He noted that expansion of the Royal Air Force had been prevented in the past by financial stringency, and although he welcomed the relaxation of that limitation, "he saw no need for panic."[21] The addition of ten new squadrons to the existing forty-two home defense squadrons was sufficient, but other squadrons were required overseas. Hoare added that the overseas air defenses were actually weak because the existing twenty-six squadrons overseas had been drawn from home. Simon and Chamberlain continued to press Londonderry and Hoare on the adequacy of the fifty-two squadron plan. Chamberlain considered sixty-five home defense squadrons a more appropriate force with an additional twenty squadrons formed by 1940. In Hoare's opinion, the fifty-two squadrons were sufficient for home defense even though the DRC concluded earlier that this was the "bare minimum."[22] Chamberlain replied, "[I]f the Air Force agreed that this was all that were required, it was another matter. Personally, [I am] inclined to think that they had been asking for too little."[23] Chamberlain's distaste for a large British land commitment on the Continent ultimately overrode both the DRC and Londonderry. Through his control of the budget Chamberlain significantly changed Britain's defense priorities by expanding the Air Ministry's budget 94 percent above the DCR's request.[24]

With an influx of new money from the Exchequer, Chief of the Air Staff Edward Ellington issued Air Defence "Scheme A." This new plan deemphasized Britain's global commitments and focused on the German menace. The scheme required numerous changes and redesignations as the situation changed in Europe, but it was the first redress to the weakened state of the Royal Air Force. The plan called for the expansion of the RAF to seventy-five home defense squadrons with a progressive increase to the budget from £2.4 million to £10.85 million between 1934 and 1939.[25] Ellington was not comfortable with the plan's focus on Europe and thought that "it may be difficult to justify exclusive concentration on home defense requirements for the next five years to the entire neglect of the Fleet Air Arm and Far Eastern requirements."[26] Chamberlain insisted on refocusing Britain's defenses on Europe and Germany. Realizing that Britain did not have the military resources to fight both Germany and Japan at the same time, he believed that Britain should reestablish friendly relations with Japan and free all of the nation's resources to meet Germany: "We cannot overstate the importance we attach to getting back, not to an alliance (since that would not be practical politics), but at least to our old terms of cordiality and mutual respect with Japan."[27] Foreign Secretary Simon thought it was dubious to take any concrete actions to improve Britain's relations with Japan. He still believed that Japan and Germany were the two main sources of anxiety for which military provisions should be made. Londonderry concurred with Simon's assessment and felt that "we must be ready to fight on two fronts against both Japan and Germany."[28]

In May, the proposals of the Defence Requirements Committee were brought before the cabinet for review. The cabinet's general consensus agreed with Chamberlain's view that Germany was the primary threat to peace. This did not alleviate their worries about Japanese intentions in the Far East:

> The most striking feature of the Report of the Defence Requirements Committee in dealing with the situation in the Far East is the extent to which our Empire security depends on the avoidance of hostilities with Japan. . . . We agree of the importance of improving relations with Japan. Possibility of our being menaced in the Far East at a time when we might be faced with a dangerous situation in Europe is one that we ought to do our utmost to avoid. It would involve war on two widely separated fronts and would strain our resources to the uttermost.[29]

Japanese aggression in China and subsequent withdrawal from the League of Nations, as well as the pressure created by competition over regional trade were just a few of the obstacles to improving Anglo-Japanese relations that needed to be addressed.[30] If British policy and security in the Far East depended upon "a permanent friendship with Japan," specific proposals were needed to bridge the divide between the two countries. The cabinet, unlike Chamberlain, was not prepared to abandon the security of the region by a strategy exclusively focused on Germany. First Lord of the Admiralty Eyres Monsell, Lord Privy Seal Anthony Eden, and Secretary of State for Dominion Affairs James H. Thomas felt that steps needed to be taken to remedy the serious weaknesses in the Far East.[31]

The most troubling aspect of Chamberlain's proposal was his belief in coming to some accommodation with Japan. Thomas warned Chamberlain of the obvious unease that this position would have for the Pacific Dominions, "For them Japan was the danger. If we were to adopt a policy such as was now suggested, it would create a very serious situation, because it would be quite impossible to convince the Dominions that there was no danger from Japan."[32] Secretary of State for War Douglas Hogg accused Chamberlain of abandoning the empire in the east to the mercy of Japan.[33] Baldwin considered both Germany and Japan as "political mad dogs," but he was actually less nervous about the threat from Germany and believed that Japan posed a wider threat to peace.[34] Baldwin's concern about Japanese intentions was supported by a Defence Requirements Committee note that informed the cabinet that Japan's defense expenditure had risen from ¥407,000,000 in 1931–1932 to ¥936,000,000 in 1934–1935, and this did not include expenditures in Manchuria.[35] Although Japanese actions concerned Baldwin, he would ultimately support Chamberlain's position because "finance was necessarily the guiding consideration and it has been felt that the needs of the Far East must be sacrificed to a considerable extent for the more pressing demands of Home Defence."[36] Baldwin also tried to reassure his cabinet colleagues that the intent of the plan was to remain as flexible as possible: "If it should be found at any time there's an intensification of the danger from one quarter or another whether in the East or in the West, then the programme may have to be expedited or adjusted in accordance with the circumstances of the moment."[37] On June 11, the German delegation walked out of the Geneva disarmament talks, an event that strengthened Chamberlain's position to concentrate British efforts in Europe. He delivered a long and sharp rebuke to his cabinet colleagues and the Defence Requirements Committee over Britain's policy in the Far East:

> The proposals of the Defence Requirements Committee were designed to enable us to defend our possessions and interests in the Far East, to defend India, and to fulfill our European commitments. A layman cannot contend that for this purpose the Programme is excessive. Nevertheless, the result of our deliberations is to put it bluntly, that we are presented with proposals impossible to carry out.
>
> But today it can hardly be disputed that the anxieties of the British people are concentrated on Europe rather than on the Far East, and that if we have to make a choice we must prepare our defence against possible hostilities from Germany rather from Japan. My first proposition then is that during the ensuing five years our efforts must be chiefly concentrated upon measures designed for the defence of these islands.[38]

For Chamberlain, a global strategy was impossible to carry out because the government could not pay for it. As chancellor, he believed that a strong economy was as important to Britain's defense as a sound military, and he did not want to forsake one for the other. In addition, Chamberlain concluded that the immediate defense of Britain was more vital than its global commitments.

If reconciliation with Germany, Italy, and Japan was of benefit to the economy and limited the need for spending on the military, so much the better.[39] To this end, Chamberlain concluded his argument by questioning the validity of Admiral Jellicoe's Fleet to Singapore Plan, the pillar of Britain's interwar Far East defense planning. He wrote, "We must postpone the idea of sending out today a Fleet of capital ships capable of containing the Japanese Fleet or meeting it in battle."[40] Chamberlain's position created uproar in the cabinet, although Simon's opinion also corresponded closely with Chamberlain's. He argued, "If the British Empire in the East were to break up, that would be a terrible calamity, but it would not be quite so desperate as if we were attacked and defeated at the heart of the Empire."[41] Sir Philip Cunliffe-Lister, secretary of state for the colonies, recognized that "[i]f we were to become involved in a war with Germany and in the Far East at the same time, it would be just about the end of all things for us."[42] British and imperial defense policy was now split between East and West with British concerns centered in Europe, and Australia and New Zealand focused on the Pacific. Former South African prime minister Jan Smuts suggested a departure from the traditional model of the empire's defense:

> The Dominions have even stronger affiliations towards the [United States] than Great Britain . . . therefore, our Far Eastern policy should be based on friendship with all and exclusive alliances or understanding with none, the ultimate objective of that policy should continue to conform to that general American orientation.[43]

Smuts recognized the prevailing isolationist view in the United States at this time but thought that the Americans would not tolerate further Japanese expansion, especially if it threatened their interests in the Philippines.[44] The Australians and New Zealanders at this time did not accept Smuts's proposal and for the moment continued to maintain their exclusive affiliation with Great Britain, though London's Pacific policies were hardly reassuring. As the situation deteriorated later in the 1930s, the Dominions heeded Smuts's proposal and turned their defense orientation to the United States.

Knowing the likely negative reaction of the Dominions' leaders to new priorities regarding the Pacific, the British cabinet was not disposed to inform them of the details. By early 1934, both Australia's and New Zealand's leaders recognized the deteriorating situation in Europe and Asia. There was a growing realization in Australia that Britain might not or would not fulfill its commitments to imperial defense in the Pacific. Following the advice from London to create a better relationship with Japan, Australia's minister for external affairs, Sir John G. Latham, created and led the Australian Eastern Mission. From March 22 through May 22, 1934, the Australian delegation traveled throughout the Pacific to advance imperial as well as Australian diplomatic and trade affairs, but its primary objective was to improve relations with Japan.[45] The Eastern Mission, however, had no success at reaching diplomatic accommodation with Japan; its failure, on the contrary, motivated the Australians to improve their military preparations. The third option of air power figured prominently in the Dominion's new security measures.

E. V. Crutchley, Australia's representative in the Dominions Office, indicated that the Australians were "rather shocked" that British air strength was ranked fifth in the world by their own admission.[46] This, according to Crutchley, stimulated the Australians' "desire to strengthen their defences."[47] It is doubtful that the British ranking was the actual motivation for increased aerial preparation; that Britain was not willing to increase Far Eastern defenses was probably more of a concern. The Lyons government looked at the international situation and noted the failure of the disarmament conventions at Geneva, the inability of the League of Nations to impose sanctions on aggression, and the obvious weakness of the Commonwealth's armed forces. Lyons initiated the Three Year Programme as "a stepping stone" toward improving national security and increased by £8,000,000 Australia's military budget.[48] The primary goals of the government's new policy were to supplement British sea power in the region, strengthen and reorganize Australia's army as a deterrent against invasion, and expand the air force's ability to cooperate with the army and navy.[49]

Australia used the 1928 Salmond Plan as a point of reference for its air defenses. Owing to the Depression, the Salmond Plan had not been implemented, but in September 1933, Prime Minister Lyons reaffirmed the recommendations in the proposal. When Lyons presented the 1934 budget to the Australian Parliament, he specifically noted that it contained £430,000 for "provision of seaplanes and land aircraft for the strengthening of the aerial defences of the Commonwealth."[50] This money was to be spent in replacing obsolete types of aircraft and to start raising new squadrons. In March 1934 the Australians placed an order for eighteen Hawker Demon fighters and later increased this order to sixty-four aircraft. Hawker Aircraft took a full year in filling Australia's order and did not deliver the aircraft until March 1935.[51]

In Australia's Parliament, former prime minister James Scullin doubted that enough money was being spent on the air force and questioned whether money budgeted to purchase a new cruiser would be better spent on aircraft. For Scullin, aircraft would be a better defense against raids than a single cruiser.[52] Defending the government's position, Assistant Minister for Defence Josiah Francis spoke of the recent purchase of Hawker aircraft and the planned purchase of an additional twenty-four Supermarine Mk.V Seagull amphibian patrol aircraft. In Francis's opinion, "At no time has Australia been better equipped."[53] This may have been the case, but five squadrons of aircraft were still pathetically little to defend the Australian continent.

The Hawker Demon purchase was just one aspect of the aviation component of the Three Year Programme. The plan included money for four new "general purpose" squadrons with one each based at Leverton,

Victoria, and at Perth, Western Australia, with two squadrons designated for Richmond, New South Wales. A coastal reconnaissance squadron was also planned for Leverton, a new aircraft repair and supply depot was to be built at Richmond, and the naval cooperation flight at Richmond would be expanded to a full squadron.[54] This growth was not insignificant for Australia's budget. The allocations for the Royal Australian Air Force (RAAF) would more than double from £334,143 budgeted in June 1933 to £860,885 in June 1934.[55] The Australians projected that the £860,885 figure would again double to £1.6 million by 1939.

The British Air Staff welcomed the Australians' expansion plans and hoped that the RAAF would be of value both to local and overall imperial defense. This contingency, however, was not specifically discussed with the Australians at the time.[56] The British Air Staff wanted Australian squadrons to replace the RAF units in Singapore because of the growing demand for squadrons for home defense:

> In view of our own concentration during the next few years on the provision of air forces for the defense of the United Kingdom, it is probable that we shall be short of aircraft at the outbreak of the war in the Far East and any contribution which Australia could make would be of great value.[57]

In cabinet discussions regarding Far Eastern defenses, Maurice Hankey pressed for expanding Australia's role and wanted to "see what they might be willing to do."[58] Chief of the Air Staff Ellington replied that "reinforcements of [Australian] squadrons would be very useful, but even if this was not possible; a supply of trained pilots would be almost equally valuable."[59]

Like Australia, New Zealand also recognized the deteriorating international situation and initiated its own military expansion, the Six Year Programme. Their plan called for an additional £840,000 directed toward the three services with £267,000 specified for the purchase of new aircraft.[60] In January 1934, the New Zealand Permanent Air Force (NZPAF) ordered a full squadron of Vickers Vildebeest torpedo bombers as the first phase of this expansion. On February 3, Sir James Parr, high commissioner for New Zealand in London, attended a demonstration flight and accepted delivery of these aircraft on behalf of the Dominion.[61] Later that month, on February 27, the New Zealand Permanent Air Force by royal decree officially changed its title to the Royal New Zealand Air Force (RNZAF).[62] With only 20 officers and 100 airmen, the title was more grandiose than the force. Unlike the Australians, New Zealand's air planners worked closely with the British Air Staff in the expansion of the RNZAF. Initially, the British recommended a force of fifty-one combat aircraft that would include eighteen army cooperation, fourteen torpedo bombers, fourteen fighters, and five flying boats.[63] The British Air Staff also noted the growing improvement in the strength and capabilities of Japanese carrier-based aircraft, in view of which, New Zealand should develop "at some future date for a quota of aircraft for naval purposes."[64] In all, the Air Staff recommended that New Zealand required a force of 100 aircraft to "cover all contingencies."[65]

With Pacific Dominions strengthening their defense measures, concern surfaced in Britain that each might follow a different strategic plan. Under the pretense of serving as Britain's official representative to the centennial celebration of the founding of Melbourne, Cabinet Secretary Hankey toured the Pacific Dominions to discuss and attempt to coordinate Imperial policy.[66] Hankey had the delicate task of "communicating . . . the particulars of the defensive policy they [the British] have recently adopted, together with the reasons for that policy, including a review of the general international situation."[67] Hankey informed the Dominions' leaders that Britain meant to "continue efforts to secure a permanent basis of friendship with Japan," but admitted the obvious difficulties of carrying out this policy.[68] Hankey expected the

THE INTERNATIONAL CRISES AND IMPERIAL REARMAMENT 197

Figure 9.1. With the growing global crisis, New Zealand finally began to take steps toward rearmament with the purchase of new Vickers Vildebeest aircraft and the creation of the Royal New Zealand Air Force. (Photograph courtesy of the National Library of New Zealand).

Pacific Dominions to play a greater part in imperial defense. Hankey's discussions ranged over numerous topics including the complete reorganization of Australia's civilian control of its military organizations. On the topic of air defense, Hankey informed the Dominions of the accumulating evidence of Germany's rearmament program, especially in aviation, and of the new measures that the Air Ministry was taking to correct the condition of the RAF.[69] Hankey encouraged the continued buildup of the RAAF to the level envisioned by Air Marshal Salmond. He also felt that the RAAF needed to be more cooperative with the navy on coastal defense and in developing ground support capability to assist the army. Focusing the mission of the RAAF as an auxiliary to the navy and army would require the air force to reconsider its current force composition.[70]

For Hankey, "the defence of Australia's interest might easily require the co-operation of Air Forces, whether with or without military forces, in the first line of Australian defence."[71] In addition, Hankey now wanted Australia's leaders to think beyond defending their own borders. He considered it desirable for them to organize their military forces to enable them to be sent abroad in an emergency and felt that doing so was "necessary to the safety of Australian interests."[72] Hankey thought the RAAF could be particularly useful for general imperial security. He warned the Australians that it was probable that the British could not provide the necessary air defense in the Far East:

> In view of the heavy commitments in the air, His Majesty's Government in the United Kingdom cannot yet provide in time of peace all of the Air Forces needed for the naval bases and coaling stations in the Far East. The provision of landing grounds at certain ports is being considered with a view to a possible scheme of air reinforcements in an emergency. The provision of these reinforcements from India and the Middle East might prove difficult, and any assistance that Australia could provide might prove invaluable and important strengthening of one or other of the strong points on the eastern route—Australia's first line of defence.[73]

When Minister of Defence Archdale Parkhill presented Hankey's proposals to Lyons, the prime minister simply marked them as "approved."[74] The government soon began to take the steps to extend Australian assistance in the Far East. The largest commitment for independence was reestablishing a local aircraft industry by direct support for the creation of the Commonwealth Aircraft Corporation. In addition, the government also provided a £30,000 annual subsidy to Qantas Empire Airways to build, maintain, and staff the strategic flying boat air route from Sydney to Singapore.[75] Lyons was committed finally to completing the expansion of the RAAF to the levels recommended by Salmond in 1928.

Hankey next traveled to New Zealand accompanied by Australia's minister for external affairs and former minister of defense, Sir George Pearce. The two men had a series of discussions with New Zealand's prime minister, George W. Forbes, and Minister of Defence John G. Cobbe. In these meetings, the parties agreed that their military units should start training together, especially army and air force units.[76] In New Zealand at this time there was no Air Ministry and the RNZAF remained under army and navy control. For this reason, the group did not consider it practicable to maintain complete and up-to-date air units available to be sent abroad. In the case of New Zealand, the best form of cooperation would be individual pilots and crews assigned to British units.[77]

Throughout 1935, Britain and the Pacific Dominions continued to implement the defense programs initiated in 1934. Once again there were calls for the creation of an "Imperial Air Force" as a means of saving money, although this concept was not favored at the Air Ministry. The principles of liaison, cooperation, and conformity continued to be seen as the best for expanding imperial air defense.[78] The creation of the Dominions' air forces adequate for their own defense freed Britain from adding them to their defense responsibilities. Delays in producing aircraft hindered the Dominions' ability to provide for that defense. The twelve Vickers Vildebeests that New Zealand bought in February 1934 were not delivered until February 1935.[79] The difficulty both Dominions experienced in obtaining aircraft hampered their expansion efforts. For the RAF, the lack of personnel also held back their expansion plans. To address this problem, the British government in March 1935 approved a plan for the RAF to recruit pilots and technical crews in both Australia and New Zealand.[80]

Australia's goal in 1935 was completing Part I of the Salmond plan by the formation of new units, increasing personnel, and updating equipment and infrastructure. In all £708,536 was budgeted to the RAAF to increase its personnel from 126 to 178 officers, 946 to 1,476 airmen, and to set a target of training sixty new pilots annually. Fifteen of these new pilots were to be assigned to five years of service with the RAF.[81] Realizing that the most likely form of attack on Australia would come from highly trained "first-line (regular)" Japanese naval air units; the RAAF's leadership now recognized the limited effectiveness of the Citizen Air Force (CAF) units. RAAF officers who returned to Australia following service in the RAF concluded that the skills of CAF pilots "compare[d] very unfavorably with RAF pilots [and] this includes formation flying, fighting tactics, bombing and gunnery, reconnaissance, photography and artillery co-operation."[82] The Australian Air Staff determined that:

> [The CAF] are never likely to approach the R.A.F. standard and cannot be considered as ready to take the field until they have completed a period of intense collective training, depending on equipment and other facilities available. These remarks apply equally to skilled ground personnel of the units.[83]

Probably for these reasons the Australian government did not include any money for the expansion of the CAF in the 1935–1936 budget even though the CAF had been touted throughout as the most reasonable and inexpensive means for Australia's aerial defenses.[84]

In June 1935, a complete transformation of the National government to Conservative control took place when Ramsay MacDonald stepped down as prime minister and Stanley Baldwin returned to power. As part of Baldwin's cabinet restructuring on June 7, he replaced Londonderry with Philip Cunliffe-Lister (raised to the peerage as Lord Swinton in November 1935) as air minister. Described as one of Baldwin's best appointments, Cunliffe-Lister, a strong proponent of rearmament, oversaw the RAF expansion programs for the next three years.[85] His appointment could not have been timelier; the demands upon Britain's resources by air force expansion plans throughout the empire proliferated. Early in his tenure, Cunliffe-Lister with assistance from former air minister William Douglas Weir established the shadow factory system. This system included the construction of new aircraft factories with government funds. In addition, the Air Ministry directed that each of the fifteen major airframe and five engine manufacturers produce only one or two types of aircraft or engines, enabling the manufacturers to concentrate their efforts.[86] Although the production numbers were initially disappointing, these actions in mid-1935 placed British aviation in a wartime mode and by 1940 British aircraft production outpaced German production.

The pending technological conversion had critical implications for imperial defense. Whatever designs were adopted by the Royal Air Force, the British manufacturers would have produced enough aircraft to reequip the existing forty-two squadrons as well as produce planes for new units. The imperial policy adopted in 1918 held that all of the Dominions' air forces should be equipped, trained, and organized like the RAF, the intention being to allow the smooth transfer, cooperation, and operation of all of the empire's air forces. This required the British manufacturers to provide aircraft for twelve RAAF and Australian CAF squadrons and also to equip five squadrons of the RNZAF and New Zealand Territorial Air Force (NZTAF) units. There were also Canadian, South African, Rhodesian, and Indian squadrons to consider as well. In addition to military needs, the growing civil and commercial aviation sector required more aircraft. Because it would not be an easy task for the depressed British aircraft manufacturers to expand production levels rapidly, the Dominions' air forces faced the prospect that their squadrons would receive a lower priority than the demands of the RAF.

The specter of a simultaneous European and Far Eastern war became a growing concern for the British chiefs of staff in 1935. The Defence Requirements Committee Report argued that 1936 would be a dangerous year in the Far East, with Japan reaching the potential for hostile action. Japan was spending over 47 percent of the nation's budget on the military.[87] By 1936, Japan would have almost completed the modernization of its capital ships and expanded its air force, including the carrier-borne units.[88] These additions to Japan's air strength meant the British faced a force of considerable size and effectiveness. The British determined that Japan's Naval Air Service had 389 aircraft with 158 flying from aircraft carriers and the Army Air Force strength stood at 402 aircraft with 198 stationed in Japan, 141 in Manchukuo, and 41 in Korea.[89] By 1937–1938, Japanese naval authorities announced the expansion of their frontline strength to 384 shipborne aircraft and 424 shore-based aircraft.[90] The British also assumed that the Japanese Army Air Force would likely expand to 603 first-line aircraft.[91] Even though the British military recognized the threat posed by the growth of Japan's military aviation capabilities, they seriously underestimated Japanese competence in the area of design and construction of aircraft:

> At the present time the Japanese aircraft industry relies almost entirely on airframes and engines of foreign design which are purchased abroad and then laboriously copied in Japan and given Japanese names. So long as this state of affairs continues, Japanese aircraft will always be two or three years behind modern air powers in design and performance.[92]

Britain would pay dearly for this mistake when war broke out.

The British chiefs were most concerned about a Japanese threat to Singapore. Though the greater part of Japanese land-based aircraft were stationed in Japan, their air routes had been organized so that the squadrons could move rapidly south to Formosa, placing them within striking distance of Singapore and Hong Kong.[93] Moreover, Japan's increased carrier forces provided an even more effective means to attack Singapore.

For these reasons, the chiefs feared the "possibility of a sudden military action against ourselves" and that "European complications would be Japan's opportunity."[94] Thus, a "bolt from the blue" could not be disregarded and was not "inconsistent with the Japanese conduct on previous occasions."[95] The Air Staff therefore recommended doubling the RAF's strength at Singapore by assigning six land-based attack squadrons and three seaplane reconnaissance squadrons to the base. Additionally, one squadron should be posted to the Far East exclusive of Singapore.[96] Air Marshal Ellington hoped that Australia and New Zealand would also provide additional squadrons or other reinforcements since Singapore was critical for their security.[97] The new proposals to station permanent squadrons in the Far East ran counter to the RAF's claims for strategic mobility so highly touted throughout the interwar period. Even though the Air Ministry approved plans to build a chain of airfields in the Far East in 1926, the chain was not completed to Singapore until 1937.[98] In addition, the British still depended upon permission from the Netherlands to attain access through the Dutch East Indies on the final legs to Australia.

Ellington was advised by one of his officers, "If we now ask for squadrons to be permanently located at all these places it is possible that our claims regarding the mobility of air forces may be quoted against us."[99] The number of squadrons at Singapore remained capped at three land-based and two seaplane squadrons until adequate runways and facilities were built in 1938 to accommodate the proposed expansion.[100] The British Committee of Imperial Defence remained convinced that the focus of any Japanese attack in the Pacific would be Singapore, and that as long as the base remained operational the only aerial threat to Australia and New Zealand would be light raids launched from cruisers or raiders, not aircraft carriers.[101]

Britain's position was not reassuring to Australian defense secretary Sir Robert Parkhill, who asked for a complete reassessment from the Committee of Imperial Defence in light of Japan's growing number of aircraft carriers and naval aircraft.[102] For Parkhill, such a force constituted a serious danger to Australia. The appearance of inaction by the Australian government on air defense led to a sharp public criticism by Australia's chief of the Air Staff, Richard Williams, who argued that "it should not be beyond the resources of Australia to provide itself with an Air Force strong enough, when operating from its own bases, to repel an enemy invasion."[103] Williams's criticisms brought a swift and pointed rebuke from Parkhill: "The inference to be drawn from the competitive claims made by the Chief of the Air Staff is that the Government's Policy and Programme are unsoundly based. If the report is correct, such criticisms cannot be tolerated."[104]

Although Williams was not reprimanded for these comments, it was another instance in his long career of antagonizing his superiors. It is probable that such comments by Williams would contribute to his removal as the chief of the Air Staff in 1938. Contrary to Williams's assessment, the lack of progress in the Commonwealth's military expansion did concern Parkhill, who, according to E. V. Crutchley, "realized that the provision of adequate defence organisation necessitated the expenditure of large sums of money, but such was the important necessity of a sound defence policy that the Government felt its duty was to find the funds required."[105] By the end of 1935, Parkhill concluded that for an adequate air defense, Australia needed to reestablish its own aircraft industry. Such a move to "improve the present position of reliance on oversea sources of supply which may not be available in war" was an "important step towards further national self sufficiency."[106] The late delivery of the Hawker Demons earlier in the year was just the first warning that RAF expansion would interfere with the RAAF's development. In January 1936, the RAF announced its plan to have 1,750 frontline aircraft, train 2,500 new pilots and 22,000 airmen, and assign them among 123 operational squadrons by 1938.[107] Parkhill noted that for Australia, this meant that "[o]wing to the enormous expansion in Air Forces in Great Britain it is becoming increasingly difficult to obtain delivery of equipment and in times of emergency it would probably be quite impossible."[108]

As a result of perceived difficulties in buying equipment from Britain, the Commonwealth Aircraft Corporation was established in October 1936 to begin constructing aircraft for the RAAF. Australia's decision to manufacture aircraft produced a shift in the relationship between the Commonwealth and the United Kingdom. One debate concerned the type of aircraft to build—the British Westland A.39/34 Lysander or the American North American Type 16. The Australian Air Board was under great pressure to select Westland's aircraft. The board recognized that aircraft development was proceeding at an extraordinary pace and that in many ways it had surpassed the performance levels existing at the outset of the Three Year Programme.[109] The Lysander was an ungainly aircraft with a high parasol fabric-covered wing supported by two large struts and fabric-covered steel and aluminum tube fuselage. In addition, the aircraft's fixed undercarriage further reduced its performance. Poorly armed with two forward and one rear flexible mounted .303 Browning machine guns, the aircraft had little combat value beyond its role of artillery spotting and liaison duties. Ultimately, the board concluded that the Westland was already an obsolete design and that it "would make no contribution whatever to the development of the modern stressed skin type, nor give employees any experience in this direction."[110]

For this reason the Australians rejected the British model and decided to start manufacturing the North American Type 16. Unlike the Westland Lysander, even though the aircraft was considered an advanced trainer, it incorporated the latest all-metal monoplane construction and retractable landing gear. The 1923 assumption that the Dominions' air forces would exclusively use British equipment was thus abandoned. The Australian decision was not well received in Britain

Figure 9.2. In 1936 with the formation of the Commonwealth Aircraft Corporation, CAC reached a licensing agreement with North American Aviation to produce the NA-16 advance trainer. The CAC Wirraway and Boomerang were derivative designs of this aircraft. (Photograph courtesy of the Australian War Memorial)

where the British High Commissioner in Australia protested strongly to Lyons's government:

> My Government have instructed me to state that it was a fundamental condition of their agreement to give all possible support to the establishment of the new aircraft factory in Australia and that there should be uniformity of service type between the two countries, and it was on this understanding that the Royal Air Force undertook to co-operate fully in supplying secret technical information. The proposal set out in the Prime Minister's telegram to which I have referred runs completely counter to this understanding; and, in view of the explicit assurances given by the Commonwealth Government at every stage of the recent discussion that only British types

of service aircraft would be manufactured, its adoption would be received by my Government with surprise and dismay, and would necessarily involve the reconsideration of the whole question.[111]

British concerns about using American designs for Australian-made aircraft continued until the outbreak of the war. Yet the inability of British manufacturers to supply both the needs of the RAF and those of Australia also remained. Winston Churchill was particularly critical of Baldwin's government and the growing disparity between British and German armaments and called for the creation of a central ministry to oversee British production.[112] As a result, Baldwin created the cabinet position of minister for the coordination of defence to oversee all aspects of British defense production. Many expected Baldwin to appoint Churchill as the new minister. Churchill later wrote that he would have "gladly" accepted the post. Two days following Germany's reoccupation of the Rhineland, on March 13, 1936, Baldwin, influenced by Chamberlain, appointed Sir Thomas Inskip to head the new ministry.[113] Inskip was described as one of Baldwin's worst appointments, a thoroughly incompetent minister, and one of the most astonishing political appointments since "Caligula made his horse consul."[114] Churchill described him as having "the advantages of being little known and knowing nothing about military subjects."[115] In Inskip's defense, he had little chance to succeed even if he had had a stronger personality; his new ministry had "no real powers and little staff."[116] Throughout 1936, the new ministry had no effect on the aircraft supply problem, which confirmed the Australians' decision to turn to the United States for new aircraft and assistance in the formation of their aircraft manufacturing capability. In addition, the Australians viewed the expansion of the RAAF and the completion of Air Marshal Salmond's recommendations critical for Australian self-defense.

In New Zealand, a fundamental political shift took place with the election of that Dominion's first Labour government led by Michael J. Savage on December 5, 1935. In defense matters, the accession of Labour to power was met with some trepidation by New Zealand's military leaders. The chief of staff, General William Sinclair-Burgess, wrote to Maurice Hankey regarding the inexperience of the new leadership:

> Their present knowledge and experience of defense matters is not very extensive as this is their first period of office, but I believe they are anxious to learn ... [and] at present have very little appreciation of the necessity for Imperial cohesion and do not realize that the protection and progress of New Zealand is bound up with that of England.[117]

Although Savage's government shifted the Dominion's defense assumptions, Burgess's concern was overstated, and Savage continued to look upon the relationship with Britain as fundamental. Unlike its neighbor, New Zealand did not stray from traditional ties to Britain by inviting the United States to assist with aircraft purchases or production. In 1936, Savage completely reorganized the Dominion's defense establishment and shifted its focus from a predominantly naval orientation to a policy emphasizing the third option—air power. In June the Savage government advised its service chiefs that, "In view of the imperative need for an extension of air defence, [they must] re-organise their whole defence estimate entailing a reduction in their naval commitments, in order to ensure the maximum expansion in the air."[118] Doubts about the "Singapore Strategy" motivated this shift in policy. The "grave situation" in the Mediterranean due to developing tensions with Italy made it seem problematic that the British fleet could be sent to Singapore in the event of hostilities with Japan.[119] The New Zealanders nevertheless turned to Britain for assistance in the new strategy based on increased air power.

The new position taken by New Zealand naturally pleased the Air Staff in London. Recognizing that the 1928 Salmond recommendations no longer applied to conditions in 1936, the Air Staff deemed a reevaluation of New Zealand's aerial defense needs was necessary. The Air Staff advised that two new torpedo bombing squadrons and two flying boat reconnaissance squadrons should form the core of New Zealand's aerial defenses.[120] The staff continued to believe that the Dominion might be subject to light raids by the Japanese, the best protection against which was early warning. To achieve this, New Zealand was advised to annex the island groups north of the Dominion, which provided "almost unlimited opportunities for extending the radius of the action of flying boats."[121] Having addressed local defense needs, the Air Staff suggested that New Zealand could then assist against the "increasing air threat to the heart of the Empire" by contributing aircraft, pilots, and complete squadrons.[122]

To maintain and promote the imperial ties, Wing Commander Ralph Cochrane was sent out in October 1936 to work with New Zealand's Air Staff.[123] After meetings with New Zealand's chiefs and inspecting the few existing RNZAF squadrons, Cochrane submitted a five-point plan to enhance New Zealand's air defenses over a three-year period. These proposals expanded upon the Air Staff's suggestions made in June. Foremost for Cochrane was that New Zealand needed to create an Air Board within the Ministry of Defence and remove all vestiges of army and navy control over the air force.[124] He recommended the formation of two "permanent" squadrons of twenty-four medium bombers, together with reserve aircraft and repair facilities.[125] In addition to these squadrons, more reserve personnel should be trained to operate within these two new squadrons as well as an army cooperation squadron. The Dominion should also continue to encourage civil air transport as a "valuable backing to the regular Air Force" and subsidize the aero club training "so that the results conform more closely to defense requirements."[126] Finally, Cochrane wanted to make sure that the British remained directly involved in the Dominion's defense plans: "The government of the United Kingdom [should] be invited to co-operate in developing facilities to enable aircraft to operate in the areas of the Pacific islands." Cochrane estimated that the cost of the proposals would be approximately £1,100,000 with an annual maintenance cost of £435,000.[127]

Cochrane's five-point plan replaced Salmond's 1928 recommendations and became the basis of New Zealand's air defense until war broke out in 1939. Cochrane's proposals, like Britain's Air Scheme "A," would be subject to constant modifications over the next few years as the international situation grew more threatening.

Figure 9.3. In October 1936, Wing Commander Ralph Cochrane arrived in New Zealand to help revitalize the air force and make it independent from the army. On April 1, 1937, he was appointed as the first chief of the New Zealand Air Staff. (Photograph courtesy of the National Library of New Zealand)

The three years from the beginning of 1934 to the end of 1936 were a transitional period when British leadership began to prepare the national economy for war. Although they continued to express hopes for peace, disarmament, and reconciliation, behind this façade there was deep alarm about the lapse of the nation's defense capability and the rapidly developing threat of war both in Europe and the Pacific. In response, they began in earnest to rearm the nation, especially its aerial defense. The aviation manufacturing sector, weakened by lack of demand during the 1920s and devastated by the Depression, needed to be revitalized if it was to meet the demand for air force expansion. Although the process was initially slow, the industry began to recuperate during this period with new and innovative designs as well as increased production. Unfortunately for the Dominions, the British aviation industry was still incapable of supplying their needs as well as those of the Royal Air Force. The priority given in British strategic planning to Germany over Japan and the consequent difficulty in obtaining British aircraft became a serious concern for the armed forces and defense planning in Australia and New Zealand. The Dominions' self-interests and desire for self-preservation now took precedence over the unity of the empire.

CHAPTER 10

THE FINAL PREPARATIONS, 1937–1940

> *People sometimes speak of Australia and New Zealand as two isolated nations looking for help from the outside. . . . But in truth . . . they themselves are nations which can contribute at great deal to the security of the Pacific itself from their own strength.*[1]
>
> —*Lord Philip Henry Kerr*

Germany's and Italy's aggressive policies during 1935 and 1936, such as German rearmament, reoccupation of the Rhineland, abandonment of the Locarno Treaty, and the annexation of Abyssinia, as well as both powers assisting General Francisco Franco's forces in the Spanish Civil War, convinced the British chiefs of staff by 1937 that Britain and France would be engaged in a war with these two powers "within the next few years."[2] On this assumption Great Britain began converting its industrial resources to a war footing. The international situation also focused the discussions at the 1937 Imperial Conference, the last such meeting before the war, on the British Empire's global defense needs. A new emphasis by the British on air defense benefited the Royal Air

Force. But while the RAF received a greater share of the nation's industrial resources than the other services, there was uncertainty concerning its strategy. Air strategists debated whether to build an offensive/deterrent bomber force, or to place most resources in a defensive fighter force. A rapid succession of new defense schemes followed. In the years just before the outbreak of the war, the members of the British Empire attempted to resolve some lingering problems surrounding imperial security, especially aerial defense.

By early 1937, Sir Thomas Inskip, minister for coordination of defense, reported to the cabinet that the Royal Air Force's recruiting, training, and engine delivery programs were proceeding satisfactorily, but he felt that airframe production was "disappointing," particularly bombers.[3] Inskip remained optimistic that the production figures would increase since the Shadow Factory Scheme had yet to come into effect.[4] This new production scheme regulated production to a limited number of aircraft types and dispersed construction of aircraft components to nonaircraft manufacturers to augment the production of the traditional aircraft factories. In Parliament, Air Minister Sir Philip Sassoon confirmed Inskip's assessment and blamed the delays on overly optimistic schedules and forecasts by the manufacturers.[5] Inskip soon came to the conclusion that it was not possible to attain parity with the Germans in offensive bomber forces; he decided to concentrate British efforts on fighter production. For Inskip, "the role of our Air Force is not an early knock-out blow . . . but to prevent the Germans from knocking us out."[6] Although there was optimism about an increase in the aircraft available to the Dominions in the near future, the preponderance of aircraft built by British industry remained in Britain to the detriment of those nations who were also in desperate need of aircraft for their rearmament programs.

The 1930 and 1937 Imperial Conferences both met at times of crisis. Facing dire economic collapse, the conference addressed fiscal matters at the 1930 discussions, and defense topics were secondary. In contrast, the delegates to the 1937 conference confronted a deteriorating international situation; foreign affairs and defense were their primary focus at the meetings and discussions. Prime Minister Baldwin summarized expansion of armaments and the danger of aggressive powers in his opening statement: "We, in this country, have decided that it is our duty to put our own defences in order, at a cost the magnitude of which you know."[7] Baldwin did not exaggerate the sheer size of the cost; from February 1936 to January 1937, his government increased the RAF's budget from £118,000,000 to £177,000,000.[8]

On May 28, 1937, two weeks after the Imperial Conference opened, Baldwin retired and Neville Chamberlain became prime minister. Many of the defense policies that he had shaped as chancellor of the exchequer were continued, in particular the priority given to RAF expansion over the development of a large continental army. In addition, the British chiefs of staff and Chamberlain reaffirmed earlier strategic assumptions: Germany was still regarded as the principal threat to peace and stability, Italy now menaced vital British imperial communications and trade through the Mediterranean, and finally, the security of India, Australia, and New Zealand from Japanese aggression hinged upon the Singapore Naval Base.[9] The British chiefs were skeptical of the motivation behind the formation of the Anti-Comintern Pact signed by these three powers on November 25, 1936. Although touted as a unified league against the expansion of communism, the pact looked more like an alliance to the British that increased the risk of Britain being involved in a war simultaneously in Europe and the Far East.[10]

The British chiefs considered Japan their third defense priority and believed that Japanese military action in the Pacific was more likely if war broke out in Europe. The chiefs thought that the only solution to Japan's need for raw materials and its expanding population was to create a more self-sufficient empire.[11] They held that Japan had two strategies to consider: a policy centered on the Asian mainland favored by their army, or the southern strategy to capture the rubber and oil reserves in the Dutch East Indies preferred by their navy. Japanese aggression in the Far East began much earlier than the British chiefs had anticipated.

In July 1937, while the Imperial Conference met, the Japanese army began a new land offensive in China. At this time, the Imperial Japanese Navy was not prepared to execute the southern attacks because its naval expansion program, which included the modernization of a number of battleships as well as completing the super battleships *Yamato* and *Musashi*, would not be completed for another two years.[12] Until the Japanese launched attacks against the Western powers in December 1941, there were numerous and constant incidents between Japan and Western military and commercial interests throughout China. The most notable were the Japanese air attacks on the British gunboats *Scarab* and *Cricket*, and the sinking of the American gunboat *Panay*. Not in a position to fight both Britain and the United States, the Japanese apologized for these attacks, while both the British and Americans were similarly reluctant to become entangled in open war over China at this time.[13]

Despite increased tensions in Asia over the Japanese aggression in China, no steps were taken to reinforce the RAF in the region. The chiefs noted that reinforcements of Britain's Far Eastern air defense could come only from the "Metropolitan Air Force," and any reduction to these RAF units "would leave the United Kingdom dangerously inferior in the air to Germany."[14] The underlying message to the Pacific Dominions was that they could not count upon any additional support from Britain. In fact, Australia and New Zealand were pressed to provide air units for Singapore's defense.

Chamberlain agreed with the chiefs' strategic priorities relative to Germany, Italy, and Japan. He felt that "there were limits to our resources, both physical and financial and it was vain to contemplate fighting single-handed the three strongest powers in combination."[15] To this end, Chamberlain thought that "we ought to direct our foreign policy so that we did not quarrel with Germany."[16] By maintaining peace with Germany, Britain might reduce the danger from both Italy and Japan, but he still recognized that "we should regard Germany as our greatest potential danger and should give first priority to defence preparation against that country."[17] Defense preparations against Italy and Japan were considered secondary and tertiary. With additional funds provided for construction at Singapore in the earlier 1934–1935 budget, preparation of the base's defense and support facilities were considered completed by the British at the beginning of 1938. Except for some minor work on the fifteen-inch gun emplacements, "the Singapore naval base," according to one historian, "appeared to be in a state of readiness and adequately defended."[18]

To the British, Australia and New Zealand seemed to be avoiding commitments to the empire's overall security. With Chamberlain's emphasis on Germany and only scant interest in the Pacific, an independent course by Australia and New Zealand was predictable. The third option of air power was one of the key elements in their divergence from Britain. The British were particularly concerned about the emergent influence of the United States in Australia's aviation industry and in furnishing American aircraft to Royal Australian Air Force (RAAF) squadrons.

The RAAF's switch from British to American types of aircraft was driven by practical reasons. Australia's minister of defense, Sir Robert Parkhill, deemed that the construction of aircraft was "the most substantial and important step in Australia's self-sufficiency and the provision of local security that has taken place."[19] Parkhill preferred the North American Type 16 for its use of the latest stress skin construction methods, and he noted that no aircraft used by the Royal Air Force at that time was built in this manner.[20] In addition, the latest British fighters, particularly the Hawker Hurricane, were designed primarily for the defense of

London with limited range and could not fly from Melbourne to Sydney, a distance of 600 miles, without refueling. In justifying the selection of American aircraft, Sir Alexander Gore, the Australian high commissioner, informed the British Air Ministry that the "reason for choosing American machines is that defence of the United States, with its great distance and long coastline, correspond with those of Australia."[21] Gore noted, moreover, that the Australians were not abandoning the use of British aircraft and intended to manufacture them as soon as a suitable type was available.[22] Parkhill became increasingly frustrated with the British Air Ministry's objections to American aircraft. A telegram by the British high commissioner, Sir Geoffrey Whiskard, to the Dominion Office quoted Parkhill's statement to the press about the situation:

> The present position has been forced upon the Commonwealth Government by the inability to obtain full facilities for manufacture of a satisfactory up to date type from England embodying latest methods of construction. To wait for such facilities would be to involve considerable delay. The British aviation companies had the same opportunity as General Motors Corporation, designers and builders of [the North American] N.A. 16, to collaborate with the Commonwealth Aircraft Corporation in manufacture of aeroplanes and engines in Australia. They had, in fact, been given special time to co-operate with the Federal Government but were unwilling to do so. They have the same opportunity but none of them was prepared to invest any money.[23]

Whiskard felt that Parkhill should not be allowed to "get away with statements of this nature, without official remonstrance from us."[24] In his reply from the Dominion Office, Under-Secretary Sir Harry Batterbee agreed with Whiskard's view but cautioned, "if possible we should not allow ourselves to be dragged further into the dispute until we have had an opportunity of a full talk with Casey."²⁵ Richard G. Casey, Australian treasurer and minister for supply and development, was scheduled to visit London in March 1937 in preparation for the Imperial Conference and to discuss the delivery of military supplies to Australia. Regardless of the British concerns, if the Australian plans to expand the RAAF were to proceed, the only solution from their perspective was to have American aircraft augment their squadrons.

The Australians recognized the considerable pressure Britain faced with the RAF expansion, but in early 1937, a series of newspaper reports pointed out that "big warplane orders are being carried out by British firms for more than one foreign government," and that the companies had bypassed the requirements and orders made by the Dominions.²⁶ Apparently several shipments of fighters had been sent to Scandinavia with a particularly large order going to Finland. Squadron Leader Thomas A. Swinbourne, assistant to Chief of the Air Staff Williams, conveyed Australian frustration to the British in preparation for the Imperial Conference:²⁷

> We feel very strongly here that whilst the Dominion Governments are anxious to buy military aircraft in British factories then these orders should be fulfilled and preference given over any order from a foreign country. In this respect it is thought that we should have exactly the same standing as the Royal Air Force and receive our initial equipment aircraft immediately after the Royal Air Force initial equipment aircraft; and that whilst we are endeavouring to bring our defence up to date orders should not be accepted from foreign countries which might delay the equipment of our own forces.²⁸

Swinbourne also preempted any discussions at the conference about the manufacture of American aircraft types by informing the Air Ministry that "there's nothing much [more] to say about this."²⁹ Swinbourne confirmed Gore's earlier statement with the Air Ministry that the Australians were willing to produce British aircraft as soon as a suitable design for Australian conditions became available.³⁰

The British gave way to Australia on both the production of American aircraft and on the question of priority of delivery of aircraft to the Dominions over foreign governments. Secretary of State for Air Lord Philip Swinton, in a public address, observed that Australian aircraft production represented a "valuable addition" to the Commonwealth's munitions supply and also satisfied the British goal of decentralizing aircraft production.³¹ Finally, on the subject of aircraft deliveries, an agreement was reached between the Dominions and the Air Ministry that preference would be given to the empire's requirements once Britain discharged existing obligations.³² A number of British manufacturers already had extensive overseas contracts. Between November 1937 and April 1939 Gloster delivered 245 Gladiator fighters to Lithuania, Norway, Sweden, Finland, Belgium, China, Ireland, Greece, Portugal, Egypt, and Iraq.³³ Between 1937 and November 1939, Bristol Aircraft sold seventy-four Blenheim bombers to Finland, Turkey, Yugoslavia, and Romania. Thirteen Blenheims were also sold to Romania in an ineffective attempt to dissuade them from joining the Axis.³⁴ Between January and May 1939, Hawker Aircraft broke the agreement reached with the Australians and New Zealanders not to sell aircraft to foreign powers by signing contracts to sell Hurricanes to Poland, Yugoslavia, Belgium, Finland, Turkey, and Romania.³⁵

By the time the Imperial Conference opened in May, Australian prime minister Joseph Lyons had announced the further expansion of the RAAF. He noted that Australia had just completed Part I of the 1928 Salmond Scheme for eight combat squadrons, but he also announced his intention to double the RAAF to seventeen squadrons comprising 194 frontline aircraft by 1939.³⁶

In New Zealand, Prime Minister Savage's government seriously considered abandoning the operation of the Dominion's cruisers HMS *Achilles and HMS Leander* in favor of an investment in aircraft. In a Committee of Imperial Defence meeting in early 1937 prior to the opening of the Imperial Conference, New Zealand's finance minister and representative Walter Nash's announcement shocked the attendees, especially the Royal Navy's Admiral Sir Ernle Chatfield. Nash reported that New Zealand's government was committed to three principles of defense: the defense of New Zealand's territory, the defense of communications in the Pacific, and the general defense of the interests of the whole Commonwealth. These principles were not new, but Nash informed the committee that New Zealand intended to achieve these goals exclusively upon the recommendations provided by Wing Commander Ralph Cochrane who had recently been appointed as New Zealand's chief of the Air Staff on April 1, 1937.[37] Cochrane firmly believed that aircraft could supplant naval ships and coastal guns and that aircraft could become the key component to New Zealand's defense. From Nash's fiscal perspective, the initial capital outlay of £1,124,000 and the £435,000 annual expenditures for the Royal New Zealand Air Force's (RNZAF) expansion were considerable for New Zealand, considering that the Dominion's total annual defense budget at that time amounted to £1 million. Constrained by limited funds, New Zealand concluded that the maintenance of naval forces was probably not the best approach to defending their shores. The cruisers, HMS *Leander* and HMS *Achilles*, could do little to defend New Zealand's territory, especially if raiding forces of any size came into their waters. In addition, New Zealand's government fully accepted Cochrane's conclusions that aircraft "would be a better protection against such raids than would cruisers."[38]

Stunned by the announcement, Admiral Chatfield tried to convince Nash that the cruisers were of vital importance to communications in the Pacific and that the two squadrons of twenty-four aircraft designated to replace them provided "purely local protection and would not help in obtaining general superiority in the Pacific." Nash indicated, to Chatfield, that these aircraft could reinforce Singapore but even though New Zealand recognized its imperial commitments, "nevertheless she wished first to concentrate on her own local defence." Likely pleased with the direction of the meeting's discussion, Air Marshal Edward Ellington, asked if he had anything to contribute, said that "Mr. Nash had argued the air problem very completely and from the point of view of [my] own service, [and I have] little to add."[39] Hankey and Inskip held that New Zealand's decision was a complete departure from the defense principles established at the 1923, 1926, and 1930 Imperial Conferences and argued forcibly that the Dominion should continue its obligation to imperial defense by the continued maintenance of the cruisers.

Discussions about the cruisers continued throughout the conference. By September 1937, the British convinced the Savage government to keep its commitment and retain the two cruisers. Savage also decided to continue New Zealand's efforts to expand its air force to the levels recommend by Cochrane. Following these parallel paths was not insignificant for New Zealand, which had to nearly double its annual defense budget to £1.9 million.[40] If New Zealand ceased to pay for the cruisers, the ships would not have been scrapped and they certainly would have remained within the Royal Navy's force structure. It was a matter of who provided the money for the cruisers' operation, maintenance, and crews. Chatfield recognized that if New Zealand did not pay for the cruisers, this responsibility would fall upon Britain.[41]

Following extensive discussions at the Imperial Conference on European matters, the talks turned to Far Eastern defense. Admiral Chatfield informed the Dominions' representatives, Parkhill and Nash, that if war broke out with Japan, they could not count on the British "being able to support anything more than a defensive policy in the Far East" until the issue was settled with Germany.[42]

As usual, the importance of Singapore dominated the discussions. The British Air Staff attempted to persuade the Australians that it was in their best interests to provide for or cooperate in the defense of Singapore. The staff proposed that a visit of an RAAF squadron should be arranged, which they hoped could lead to locating an Australian squadron there permanently.[43] In addition, they offered to appoint an Australian officer to the Staff Headquarters, Royal Air Force, Far East. In early January 1938, the recently appointed chief of the British Air Staff, Sir Cyril Newall, wrote to his Australian counterpart, Air Marshal Williams, appealing for Australia to send a liaison officer to Singapore as a "step toward general cooperation."[44] Williams did not respond to Newall's request for two months, and when he finally did his reply was unenthusiastic:

> I fully appreciate the value of such an appointment, but try as I will I cannot see my way to make such an officer available at the moment. We are very short of officers with any sort of experience not only for staff duties but also for command of the units, and I cannot see any possibility of making an officer available for this appointment for some time.
>
> However, I will keep the matter in mind and should it become possible to do so I will let you know. I'm sorry.[45]

Only in March 1939 was an RAAF liaison officer posted to Singapore, the critical fortress in the Pacific upon which the defense of the Pacific Dominions and other British territories depended.[46]

Both Australia's and New Zealand's delegations at the Imperial Conference were more concerned about their defenses closer to home. Chatfield dismissed the Dominions' concerns. He still believed that a Japanese invasion of Australia was unlikely, although he suggested that Australia could be subject to "raids." He observed that "it was difficult to define the size of a raid—it might be anything from a few men landing in a boat to destroy a wireless station to a landing of much greater strength as a diversion to draw off forces from elsewhere. In any case it would have no real effect other than an annoyance."[47] To create a buffer to protect the Dominions from such attack, Parkhill insisted that steps be taken to secure the northern island groups because of their "considered value from an air point of view."[48]

The British Air Staff studied the problem on behalf of Australia and made a number of recommendations to make sure that the RAAF could effectively operate from the islands. First, Australian pilots needed to be trained and equipped to operate over distances up to 1,500 miles.[49] They required the establishment of a number of landing grounds or seaplane bases with "adequate stocks of fuel, bombs, ammunition, and maintenance spares," and this necessitated the assistance and cooperation of the British.[50] Most importantly, the Air Staff had reason to believe "that the necessary facilities could be provided without undue expense in a sufficient number of islands." Based upon the Air Staff's assessment, Ellington agreed with Parkhill on the need to utilize the islands and find suitable and economical locations to develop seaplane bases.[51] The conference adopted the proposal by Australia and New Zealand to begin the establishment of stations throughout these island groups. Australia soon began to bolster the defenses at Port Moresby and Rabaul. In addition, New Zealand began construction of a small station at Fiji.

By 1938, Britain's priority of rearming the Royal Air Force continued to strain the relationship with the Pacific Dominions and particularly frustrated some of the leaders in Australia. Deliveries of combat aircraft were unfulfilled or canceled outright. Plans to cooperate in the air defense of Singapore began to unravel as well. In a speech on March 8, 1938, outlining Britain's defense priorities, Neville Chamberlain stated that Great Britain "might not be able to defend her overseas possessions." This created grave misgivings in Australia.⁵² Chamberlain confirmed the essence of the speech and informed Australian prime minister Joseph Lyons that "our first main effort must have two main objectives: we must protect this country and we must preserve trade routes upon which we depend for our food and raw material."⁵³ Chamberlain attempted to reassure Lyons that Britain was not abandoning Australia's defense, although it was essential that Britain's defense was his first priority:

> We are merely doing what every other country is compelled to do, and, while strengthening our defenses as a whole and adopting a general system of priorities which provides first for our most threatened and most essential points, but is applied with care and discrimination. The idea that in the event of war we may not (depend on the defenses of) [handwritten correction, "be able to defend"] our overseas possession is entirely false.⁵⁴

Despite Chamberlain's reassurances, there now was a growing concern within the Australian government—accentuated by the lagging supply of aircraft—about Britain's commitment to Australia's defense.

The former prime minister and now minister for external affairs, Billy Hughes, raised the issue in the Australian Council of Defence in February. For Hughes the situation was "serious and required immediate action."⁵⁵ Hughes urged the council to buy combat aircraft from the United States to meet the gap unmet by the British.⁵⁶ The newly appointed minister of defense, Harold Thorby, felt the expansion of the production program at the Commonwealth Aircraft Factory could bridge the gap and meet the RAAF's needs by the end of June 1939.⁵⁷ Never known to understate a situation, Hughes replied, "There [is] little doubt that if Hitler were in command of the situation in Australia he would take immediate steps to rectify the situation."⁵⁸

Air Vice Marshal Williams felt that Australia was already close to achieving its goal of 200 first-line aircraft and reserves to protect Australia based on their "Raid Policy." Hughes asked Williams what would happen if Japan attacked Australia with an aircraft carrier, to which Williams replied that "there was very little danger of a carrier coming into Australian waters with a raiding force."[59] It appears that Williams accepted the British strategic assumption that the Japanese would not risk sending their valuable carriers on such a long mission. Neither the British nor Williams had any empirical evidence to support this assumption (proved wrong when four Japanese aircraft carriers attacked Darwin on February 19, 1942). Lyons then asked Williams if it were practicable for the air force to expand beyond seventeen squadrons within a reasonable time as he publicly announced at the Imperial Conference. Williams felt that it was possible, but it would take all of Australia's efforts to meet their seventeen-squadron goal within three years.[60] The seventeen-squadron plan became a stated goal for the Australians, but to achieve this would require support from American manufacturers.

By the summer of 1938, the failure of the British industry to deliver aircraft to the Dominions remained unresolved. The inability to obtain delivery prompted Lyons to appeal directly to Chamberlain. Lyons informed Chamberlain that:

> It is very disturbing to find that after the expenditures of millions of pounds much of it is ineffective from a defense point of view through inability to obtain the essential needs which have been on order for long periods. Special mention is made of the perspective delay in delivery of twin-engined aircraft the type of which has been changed and delivery of which is reported not to be possible for two years.[61]

Chamberlain appreciated the frustration that the Australians were experiencing but informed Lyons that "your difficulties in obtaining supplies are to a great extent similar to difficulties which we ourselves have experienced in meeting our own requirements."[62] The new Bristol Beaufort, a twin-engine attack bomber, was just starting to come off the production lines. Of the first 100 aircraft off Bristol's production line, the second 50 were promised to the RAAF. Unfortunately, the earliest anticipated delivery date was not until the summer of 1939.[63] The only aircraft that the British were able to deliver on a regular basis was the Avro Anson, a light liaison/trainer twin-engine, which was worthless as a combat aircraft.[64]

Unable to form many of the new squadrons in their expansion plans because of the delayed aircraft deliveries, the RAAF decided to form several new squadrons equipped with Ansons. It was better to have these squadrons operational even with inadequate aircraft rather than to wait to form them later when more advanced aircraft were available. Eventually the Ansons would be replaced with American Lockheed Hudsons and British Bristol Beauforts. The Australian Council of Defence thought that it was "extremely doubtful" that the British would allow aircraft to leave Britain in the middle of a European crisis and decided to ensure an alternative supply of aircraft by buying the American aircraft from Lockheed Aircraft Company.[65] Lockheed promised the Australians that they could deliver fifty of their twin-engine Hudsons between July and December 1938. The British Bristol Aircraft Company expected to deliver fifty twin-engine Beauforts attack aircraft between July and August 1939, with an additional forty promised by the summer of 1940.[66] The council also anticipated the delivery of 100 Wirraways (the Australian production version of the NA Type 16) from the Commonwealth Aircraft Corporation by February 1939.[67]

Figure 10.1. Newly arrived Lockheed Hudsons being assembled at Richmond. The inability to obtain aircraft from the British forced the RAAF to purchase modern aircraft types from the United States. (Photograph courtesy of the Australian War Memorial)

Even with expansion plans in place, there was growing concern in the Australian parliament about the government's actions and decisions. Labor MP France M. Baker pointed out that the British clearly were not providing the necessary materials for defense and that Australia was becoming more and more isolated. In addition, Baker correctly pointed out that the RAAF was "furnished with obsolete machines" and provided with "machines of less power than those of countries such as Portugal." He accused the government of trusting "to luck that it will be able to muddle through. 'Muddling through' may serve for a time, but it cannot be regarded as a satisfactory permanent policy."[68]

As the pace of the RAAF's expansion intensified, a troubling series of fatal crashes took place. Facing questions in the press and in Parliament,

Prime Minister Lyons requested that Britain send someone to investigate these accidents and determine if the RAAF's training and operational procedures were the root cause of the problem.[69] The British delegation was led by none other than Chief of the Air Staff Sir Edward Ellington. Ellington's inspection did not bode well for the Australian CAS, Richard Williams. Williams later wrote that he found out about the inspection through a newspaper report. When he confronted the newly appointed minister of defense, Frederick Shedden, about why he had not been informed of the visit, Shedden replied that "in his view, the [inspection was] something of which the Chief of the Air Staff need not be informed."[70] This is an extraordinary statement since the inspection focused on the very service that Williams commanded. Ellington issued a broad report on RAAF's strategic assumptions, training methods, equipment, and the underlying reasons for the accidents. Ellington's findings determined that poor design or inadequate maintenance of the aircraft played no role in the increase of the RAAF's accident rate. To Ellington, the root cause of the problem was "due to disobedience of orders or bad flying discipline" and pointed to "a need for strict enforcement of the regulations."[71]

In general, Ellington considered the composition and distribution of the RAAF and planned expansion suitable to meet the needs of the Dominion's air defense, but he felt that the service was not independent enough and too willing to subordinate itself to the needs of Australia's army and navy.[72] During his tour of the RAAF establishments, Williams took Ellington to the Commonwealth Aircraft Corporation to show him the Wirraway production line. According to Williams's account of the visit, Ellington refused even to watch the demonstration of the aircraft that was arranged for him.[73] Ellington was highly critical of the Wirraway, dismissing it as too slow and nothing more than an armed trainer and informing the Australians that it should be regarded only as a "temporary expedient."[74] Williams pointed out to him that the Wirraway had a better performance than the Hawker Demon biplane that was

Figure 10.2. The wreckage of an RAAF Hawker Demon at Laverton, Victoria, in 1938. During the expansion of the service in 1937–1938, it appeared that there was a severe spike in training accidents. PM Joseph Lyons was so concerned that he invited the RAF's chief of the Air Staff, Sir Edward Ellington, to Australia to assess the root causes. (Photograph courtesy of the Australian War Memorial)

currently Australia's frontline fighter and was obsolete by this time.[75] The Air Board also took exception to Ellington's comments about the Wirraway, noting that every aircraft could be considered a "temporary expedient" or for "interim use" until a better aircraft became available.[76] The cabinet also dismissed Ellington's criticism with the assertion that the Wirraway was "still the best aircraft in existence for the work required of [the] single-engine two-seater [reconnaissance and army cooperation] squadrons."[77] Ellington's assessment about the Wirraway being nothing more than a "trainer" was essentially correct, but the British did not provide or could not offer the Australians a more advanced aircraft design.

The principal purpose for Ellington's visit was to discover the underlying causes of the RAAF's accidents and not to assess Australia's aircraft industry. A primary element of his analysis was a review of pilot training and maintenance to determine if Australian procedures were wanting. Ellington evaluated the initial training of pilots at the Flying Training School at Point Cook and that of other ranks at Leverton and considered them to be methodically carried out, but thought that there was considerable room for improvement in advanced training, especially that relating to aerial gunnery.[78] The Australian Air Board sharply rebutted this criticism by placing the blame on the British:

Figure 10.3. Sir Edward L. Ellington. In 1938, CAS Sir Edward Ellington traveled to Australia to assess the underlying causes of the RAAF's increased accident rate during the force's expansion. Ellington believed that these training accidents were due to disobedience of orders, bad flying discipline, and the lack of strict enforcement of the regulations. In reality, the increased accident rate was proportional to the increased rate of flying hours. (Photograph courtesy of the National Portrait Gallery, London)

Advance training of pilots and crews in the application of flying to war obviously cannot precede [sic] without the necessary guns, bombsights, bomb racks, instruments etc. and of these there has been, and still are great shortages. On 1st July the value of equipment ordered from England over the last two years and remaining undelivered approximated £1,900,000.[79]

The Australian cabinet also noted that training had been interfered with because aircraft and engines were "unserviceable owing to the non-arrival of spare parts on order in England and training in gunnery was hindered by mechanical troubles experienced with new machine guns produced at the Small Arms Factory."[80]

Ellington pointed out that another inherent limitation to the air force was the unsatisfactory development of new flight instructors, which he considered an "urgent matter."[81] These additional instructors were needed for the RAAF's Flying Training School, cadre squadrons, and to supervise instruction at Australia's civil aviation schools. There were not enough instructors to keep up with the demands required to expand the ranks with new pilots. Again, the Air Board sharply disagreed and were "surprised" by Ellington's observations. In the board's opinion, the numbers were adequate for the current rate of expansion and the training facilities and aircraft available.[82]

After examining the reports on the flying accidents, Ellington concluded that even though the RAAF was a smaller force, the number of accidents per flying hour was higher than that of the RAF. The solution to Australia's problem, according to Ellington, was "strict enforcement of the regulations."[83] The Air Board contended that Ellington had used erroneous figures to compare the accident rates of the RAAF to the RAF and felt that considering all the factors surrounding the accidents, the RAAF's rate was "actually better" than that of the RAF.[84] The cabinet was not as dismissive of Ellington's suppositions as the Air Board and believed that "great weight must be attached to his conclusions."[85] The ultimate result of the Ellington Report came on January 16, 1939, when Prime Minister Lyons declared in Parliament that:

> The Air Board cannot be absolved from the blame for these criticisms and that the main responsibility rests on the Chief of the Air Staff.
>
> By arrangement with the Air Ministry, Air Vice-Marshal Williams is being sent abroad for two years, during which period he will be attached in the first instance to the Chief

of the Air Staff, Royal Air Force. Later, the Air Ministry proposes that he should assume the appointment of officer in charge of administration of the Coastal Command and subsequently executive command of an operational group.[86]

Once again, Air Marshal Williams learned of events through the newspaper. When Williams confronted the prime minister about his removal as Chief of the Air Staff and transfer to Britain, he reported that Lyons had informed him that:

> The Government, having been criticised in regard to accidents and having got a man of the standing of Sir Edward Ellington out here to report on the Service, cannot, just accept his report and say, "Thank you." It must do something. It is politically expedient for the Government to send you to England at the present time.[87]

It appears from the evidence that there was more behind Ellington's inspection than just determining the cause of the RAAF's flying accidents. The accident numbers seem to have corresponded proportionally with the increase in flying hours brought on by the air force expansion, and an investigation at this level did not require the direct involvement of the chief of staff of the Royal Air Force. It is probable that the Australian government was looking for a way to remove Air Marshal Williams. There is little doubt that Williams was a thorn in the government's side. His public criticisms of its policies in the press such as the ones made in 1935 (for which he received a severe rebuke from Minister of Defence Parkhill) exemplify his inclination to operate outside the chain of command. For Prime Minister Lyons to remove a man of Williams's standing and experience in the middle of an international crisis required an outsider and someone of Air Marshal Ellington's stature.

For all of the planning and discussions that took place on Pacific defense throughout the interwar period, direct exchanges between Australia and New Zealand were woefully lacking; in fact, they were almost nonexistent. This lack of communication between the two Dominions was appalling considering their proximity and mutual interests. In July 1938, New Zealand's military chiefs, Major General John E. Duigan, Group Captain Ralph Cochrane, and Commodore Henry Edward Horan, informed New Zealand's cabinet that "liaison with the United Kingdom is completely satisfactory, the liaison with Australia is very incomplete in everything except a few matters" and recommended that steps should be immediately taken to exchange defense information with Australia.[88] Ironically, New Zealanders found out about Australian defense activities through copies of Committee of Imperial Defence papers received from London.[89] To correct the omission, on September 23, 1938, Savage sent a letter to Lyons suggesting that "the Pacific Dominions should meet to discuss questions relating to defense and strategic cooperation between Australia and New Zealand."[90] In January 1939, Savage proposed several broad topics for discussion at the meeting, including: the potential threats to the empire's Pacific interests; measures to take to defend these interests; coordination of defense policies of the two Dominions, finding additional sources of military supply after the outbreak of war; commercial and military transpacific air routes; and U.S. Pacific defense policies.[91]

The Pacific Defence Conference met in Wellington from April 14 to 26, 1939. A week before the opening session, Lyons suffered a fatal heart attack, which placed the Australian government in a state of flux. For twenty days, Earle Page, leader of the conservative Country Party, took over as prime minister until Lyons's larger coalition party, the United Australia Party, elected its new leader, Robert Menzies. Because Page was only in temporary custody of the government, a low-level Australian delegation was sent to Wellington headed by Admiral

Sir Ragnar Colvin, a British Royal Navy officer recently appointed as Australia's chief of the Naval Staff. Colvin also served as Britain's naval representative at the conference.[92]

Many of the old discussions such as Singapore, the potential threat of Japanese raids, and the overseas commitment of Australia's and New Zealand's air, ground, and naval forces were repeated. In addition, the return of Germany's former Pacific colonies, the exchange of military staff officers between the two Dominions, defense responsibilities relating to the regional island groups, as well as the growing influence of the United States' transpacific air routes were discussed. Overall, no new initiatives came out of the conference; the attendees only confirmed strategic agreements already made at earlier Imperial Conferences. Colvin, without a single Australian political representative in his delegation, was not in a position to speak for the Australian government on any new initiatives. The only joint accord made at the conference was the agreement to establish preliminary aerial reconnaissance routes and the division of the defense of the island groups that surrounded the two Dominions. The conference designated the Australian sector as New Guinea, the Solomons, and New Hebrides, while New Zealand would cover the area from Fiji to Tonga.[93] This was not a difficult decision because each Dominion's geographical proximity determined this division. Concerning New Zealand, the conference attendees determined that Prime Minister Savage's desire to train 1,000 pilots annually was overly ambitious and scaled the plan back to 650 pilots.[94] Savage's 1,000-pilot plan highlighted the critical problem of training the empire's aircrews. It is surprising that for all of the discussions during the interwar period, there was no definitive plan for training pilots and aircrews even though this was a goal stated as early as 1920 by Air Marshal Trenchard. Not until the months immediately preceding and after the outbreak of the war in September 1939 were steps taken to solve the problem. Throughout the interwar period the two Pacific Dominions deemed it necessary to maintain independent control of their military forces and viewed an Imperial Air Force as an infringement on this independent control. With the British declaration of war on September 3, this attitude began to change.

On September 26, 1939, Secretary of State for Dominion Affairs Anthony Eden approached Australia's Prime Minister Menzies and asked if the Australians would participate in a joint training effort for imperial aircrews. Eden passed the same request along to the Canadian prime minister, Mackenzie King, and New Zealand's John Savage. Eden proposed that this training should be centered in Canada because of its immunity from attack and proximity both to the United Kingdom and to the "vast resources of the United States of America."[95] On October 4, 1939, a British commission of Lord Arthur Balfour, Air Marshal Robert Brooke-Popham, and Frank T. Hearle, managing director of de Havilland Aircraft, was sent to Ottawa to work out the details to coordinate imperial air training. The preliminary meetings of this commission began with the arrival of the Canadians, but full discussions did not take place until after the Australian delegation arrived on November 1 and the New Zealanders on November 3.[96] The British felt that the preponderance of training both financially and in personnel would fall upon Canada. Both Australia and New Zealand wanted the training of their citizens to take place in their respective Dominions, a concession that they would be granted.[97] In addition, the two Dominions also felt that their share of the scheme was too large relative to their populations and resources.[98] After extensive discussion about the cost and distribution of the training scheme, the conference agreed to divide it in proportion to their participation: United Kingdom, C$218,000,000; Canada, C$313,000,000; Australia, C$97,400,000; and New Zealand, C$21,500,000.[99] In addition, Britain would pay for all of the freight charges to transport the aircraft and engines to the respective training stations. The final agreements at Ottawa became the foundation of the Empire Air Training Scheme (EATS).

The EATS received mixed reviews for its success and contribution to the Dominions' and Allies' war effort. One historian called the EATS "one of the most brilliant pieces of imaginative organization ever conceived."[100] By 1943, 333 flight training schools were operational, instructing the pilots, crews, and mechanics essential for the RAF's wartime expansion.[101] It was agreed at Ottawa that the Dominion crews trained in the EATS would serve in Royal Air Force squadrons rather than in Dominion units. By the end of the war 27,899 (10,998 pilots) Australians had been trained in the EATS. The Australians who went through EATS training became the Dominion's single largest commitment to the war in Europe because no Australian army units served in western Europe during the war. Another historian critical of the EATS considered it

> [t]o be the source of the R.A.A.F.'s greatest disappointment, through the unwillingness of the Australian government to insist on senior command appointments in Europe for their airmen, a failure which, it could be argued, reduced the R.A.A.F.'s contribution to that of cannon fodder.[102]

Even before the creation of the EATS, the Savage government in New Zealand had already committed to the expansion of its air training program by building additional and enlarging existing flight schools.[103] To realize these plans, New Zealand required more than 250 training aircraft.[104] In March 1939, New Zealand reached an accord with the de Havilland Aircraft Company to begin the production of Tiger Moth primary trainers, the first of which were finally delivered to the RNZAF in January 1940.[105] During the war, New Zealand sent 2,743 pilots overseas to serve in Royal Air Force squadrons.[106] In fact, the RAF's first ace of the war was a New Zealander, Pilot Officer Edgar James ("Cobber") Kain.[107]

Within hours of Great Britain's declaring war on Germany on September 3, 1939, Australia and New Zealand once again followed Britain into war. The prediction of a war with Germany in 1939 or 1940 made by the British chiefs of staff in 1934 had become a reality, although Japan's attacks on China in 1937 had challenged Chamberlain's assessment that Germany was the greatest threat to peace. As long as this conflict remained isolated on the Asian mainland, however, the British were willing to tolerate occasional incidents to prevent the outbreak of a general war in Asia. Germany continued to be viewed as a direct threat to Britain. Like the French view of security behind the Maginot Line, the British saw their defense of the Far East secure behind the completed Singapore naval base.

Figure 10.4. A formation of RAAF 1 Squadron Lockheed Hudsons and a CAC Wirraway over Singapore in April 1941. This image demonstrates the RAF's growing dependence on the Dominions' air forces and their willingness to utilize aircraft other than those of British manufacture and design for imperial defense. (Photograph courtesy of the Australian War Memorial)

By March 1939, the Shadow Factory Scheme began to pay dividends, and aircraft production in Britain exceeded expectations.[108] These deliveries were still not enough to fill the needs of the RAF and Dominion air forces. Earlier criticisms of the Dominions for ordering American aircraft were forgotten when the British themselves turned to the United States and bought more than 400 aircraft from American manufacturers.[109] The Dominions' defense was still closely associated with the needs of empire, although they soon developed a regional perspective. The Pacific Dominions attempted to continue unity within the imperial structure, but the inability to obtain equipment forced them to turn to the United States. In addition, their perceived defense needs did not necessarily correspond with the view coming from Whitehall, and self-interest regarding their own defense seemed to demonstrate growing cracks in imperial unity. These were cracks, not gaping fissures. Even though the New Zealanders wanted to cease operation of the cruisers HMS *Leander* and HMS *Achilles* in favor of an expanded air force, they bowed to British pressure to pay for the ships' operation, although it meant doubling the Dominion's defense budget. Military leadership ties remained strong with British officers such as Wing Commander Ralph Cochrane leading the RNZAF and Admiral Sir Ragnar Colvin heading the Royal Australian Navy. Cochrane's suggestions to New Zealand's air defense were as influential to the Dominion's policy as Air Marshal John Salmond's had been to Australia's a decade earlier. In addition, when a perceived problem with accidents and the leadership of the RAAF materialized, the Australians turned to the British, who sent Chief of the British Air Staff Edward Ellington to lead the investigation. Finally, throughout the interwar period, the Dominions attempted to exercise independent control over their respective militaries. The creation of the Empire Air Training Scheme taught Dominion aircrews who served almost exclusively in the Royal Air Force. Though there were cracks in the foundation, defense ties with Britain still remained paramount.

EPILOGUE

With gratitude for the past and confidence in the future we range ourselves without fear beside Britain. Where she goes, we go; where she stands, we stand. We are only a small and young nation, but we march with a union of hearts and souls to a common destiny.[1]

—Michael Savage

In the predawn hours of September 1, 1939, Germany launched an all-out assault on Poland. A massive artillery barrage, soon followed by massive formations of armored fighting vehicles, broke the quiet morning hours. Unlike the slow-moving behemoths of the First World War, these new German panzers moved across the country at rapid speeds. In addition, formations of bombing aircraft supported the advance of the armor by disrupting the movement of Polish forces behind the front lines and destroying their air force on the ground. The prediction of a war with Germany in 1939 or 1940 made by the British chiefs of staff in 1934 had become a reality. The British and French prime ministers, Neville Chamberlain and Edouard Daladier, who both had hoped to delay the conflict, now had to act. They forwarded to the German government an ultimatum to withdraw their forces from Polish territory. Both men had to have known that this was a futile gesture. Hitler now had the war he had long desired. At this point, Chamberlain hoped that the war would remain concentrated in Europe. Even though Japan's attacks on China in 1937 had challenged this assessment, he understood that Germany was an immediate threat to Britain. As long as the Asian conflict remained isolated on the Chinese mainland, the British were willing to tolerate occasional incidents to prevent the outbreak of a general war in Asia. Like the French view of security behind the fortresses of the Maginot Line, the British saw their defense of the Far East secure behind the fortified Singapore naval base. Both were colossal strategic miscalculations.

Within minutes of the British and French declaration of war on Germany on September 3, the two most distant nations from the European conflict, Australia and New Zealand, affirmed their support for Britain and were the first countries to join the new Allied cause. Both the Australian and New Zealand prime ministers, Robert Menzies and Michael Savage, received near unanimous approval from their respective parliaments. If there were any questions regarding the Dominions' support for the empire, they hinged upon specific military responsibilities. The Menzies government favored a local or regional defense policy, the position also backed by the opposition Labor Party. For Menzies, any thought of sending troops out of Australia would be "widely condemned," but sustaining traditional imperial commitments overrode this preference.[2] Prime Minister Savage immediately offered New Zealand's full military assistance to the British cause without restriction. In November 1939, Richard G. Casey, Australia's representative in London, forwarded a request that Australia send the 6th Infantry Division to the Middle East along with both naval and air force units, a request the Australians fulfilled in early 1940.

Within a week of the declaration, British foreign secretary Anthony Eden sent the Pacific Dominions the British strategic judgment of the war and the needs for both Britain's and the empire's defense. Imperial air strategists revived the prewar plans but interwar theory was now replaced by the new reality of war. In the opinion of the secretary, the Dominions' greatest defense asset was their vast distance from the European combat theater. In the opinion of the Royal Navy, the only real threat to the Pacific Dominions were potential German surface raiders.

The German merchant raiders *Orion* and *Komet*'s operations throughout the Pacific and Indian Oceans from the summer of 1940 through the end of 1941 proved the Royal Navy's assessment correct. They sank a number of Allied merchant ships and temporarily closed Wellington and Lyttleton harbors by laying minefields.

In respect to the Dominion air forces, Eden informed the Dominion governments that the greatest need was to reduce the disparity between British and German air strength.[3] There were three ways the Dominions could assist: have them dispatch complete units to Great Britain, substitute British overseas squadrons with Dominion units, and finally supply aircraft, materiel, and most importantly, personnel.[4] The imperial leadership immediately adopted all three points.

Days prior to the German invasion of Poland, on August 26, the New Zealand government offered to attach its personnel and aircraft that were in the United Kingdom at Marham to the RAF. In addition, they agreed to fully participate in any training scheme agreed upon by imperial leadership.[5] Likewise, the Australians in Britain found themselves swept up by events on the continent.

The war forced the Dominions to participate in the empire's defense in ways that they had meant to avoid during the interwar period. This was particularly the case concerning air forces. In anticipation of hostilities, the RAAF started the hurried expansion of their forces. RAAF 10 Squadron formed at Point Cook in July 1939. Its primary function was to provide for maritime patrol and reconnaissance around Australia. Initially, the unit was not a squadron but a mere flight of three aircraft, equipped with two antiquated Supermarine Seagull flying boats and a de Havilland Moth fitted with pontoons. Early that summer the Australian government purchased Shorts Sunderland flying boats to equip 10 Squadron. The Shorts aircraft with its long range and heavy armament was an excellent choice for patrolling the coastal waters off Australia. In August, the pilots and officers made their way to Britain by empire flying boat to retrieve and train on their new aircraft while the squadron's enlisted personnel traveled by passenger ship.[6] Little did they know when they landed in Britain that they would not see their homes for the next six years.

Within days of their arrival, the Australians found themselves in the middle of the war. Their training took on a new urgency and by the beginning of October 1939, 10 Squadron was making their first combat air patrols. RAF Coastal Command was woefully short of both aircraft and personnel at the outbreak of the war and found it exceedingly difficult to release the squadron from an active war zone to the relative quiet of the Pacific. On October 7, the Australian government approved the British request and ordered that the squadron remain in service with Coastal Command. These Australians pilots and aircrews served with distinction with six confirmed U-boats sunk and conducted endless hours of combat patrols covering the convoys coming into the British Isles. The squadron would finally return to Australia when it was disbanded on October 7, 1945, six years to the day the government ordered them to remain in Europe.[7]

RAAF 3 fighter squadron also joined the Australian 6th Infantry Division in reinforcing British positions in the Middle East. Like No. 10 Squadron, No. 3 Squadron did not return to Australia for the remainder of the war and continued to serve in the Mediterranean Theater even after the Australian government recalled the rest of the Australian ground units from North Africa to the Pacific to reinforce Allied positions at the end of 1942. From September 1939 until the Japanese attack in December 1941, the commitment of Dominions forces in supporting the British actions overseas absorbed a significant proportion of their military resources, thus jeopardizing the Dominions' local defenses.

Like the Australians, New Zealanders of what would become 75 (NZ) Squadron confronted an almost identical situation as RAAF 10 Squadron. In 1938, the New Zealand government ordered thirty twin-engine Vickers Wellington bombers, the most advanced prewar bomber in the RAF's inventory. The plan was for the New Zealanders to train and then fly their aircraft back to the home for local defense needs. Again, RAF's dire need for aircraft and crews in Europe necessitated that the squadron remain in Britain. In August 1939, the New Zealand government agreed to keep the personnel in Britain. In April 1940, the RAF designated the unit 75 (NZ) Squadron. It became the first Commonwealth squadron formed during the war and it too served throughout the war with distinction. The squadron flew numerous missions as part of Bomber Command's earliest operations. One of its members, Sgt. Pilot James A. Ward, became the first member of the RNZAF to win the Victoria Cross during the war.

During a mission over Munster on July 7, 1941, the Wellington on which Ward served as copilot was attacked by a Me-110 fighter over the Zeider Zee. The damaged fuel lines to the starboard engine caught fire and threatened the survival of the aircraft. After several unsuccessful attempts to put out the fire, Ward crawled out of the astro-hatch on the top of the aircraft and proceeded across the aircraft wing by punching holes into the fabric covering of the aircraft wings for hand and foot holds. Ward hoped to smother the fire with the use of the aircraft's canvas engine covering. Just as Ward reached the fire, the aircraft's powerful slipstream tore the cover from his grasp. Exhausted by the crawl, Ward did manage to make his way back into the aircraft with the assistance of the navigator pulling him back in with the rope tied around his waist. Astonishingly, the fire went out on its own and the crew manage to fly back to England. The aircraft was a total loss from the extensive damage. Ward never received his Victoria Cross, however; he was killed on a mission over Hamburg on September 15.

The personnel of RAAF 10 Squadron and RNZAF 75 (NZ) Squadron became the unintentional first crews to help fill the squadrons of the RAF during the war. In addition, New Zealander Air Vice Marshal Keith Park, the commander of RAF Fighter Command's 11 Group, played a critical role in the RAF's victory over the Luftwaffe during the Battle of Britain.

Chamberlain's government has been severely criticized for Britain not being prepared for war in 1939. However, it was the very decisions made by his government prior to the war that enabled victory during the Battle of Britain in 1940. Almost £5 million was spent on the Chain Home Radio Detection/Finding System or radar. These radio towers that covered the southern coast and eastern coastline enabled the tracking of incoming bomber raids on the British Isles and their pinpoint interception by Fighter Command's squadrons.[8] In addition, the Chamberlain government insisted upon an aircraft construction program focused on the single-seat Hawker Hurricane and Supermarine Spitfire fighter aircraft. This was in direct opposition to the leadership of the RAF who wanted to build expensive offensive bomber aircraft.

Just as the Battle of Britain was starting to intensify in the summer of 1940, questions arose concerning Japanese intentions in the Far East and how they would affect Britain's strategic position. The Dominions' defenses were still closely associated with the needs of empire, but from Winston Churchill's perspective, the ultimate the security of the empire depended upon a secure Britain. With the growing aggression from Japan, the Australians' and New Zealanders' regional outlook and their perceived defense needs did not correspond with the view coming from Whitehall. Their rising self-interest demonstrated growing but not irreparable cracks in imperial unity.

Following the initial agreements at the Pacific Defence Conference, New Zealand in July 1940 begin the process of reinforcing the Fiji Islands. The island group is strategically placed almost halfway between New Zealand and the Marshall Islands group that was mandated to Japan at the Versailles Conference in 1919. The initial focus of defense was to transfer an army brigade and install naval defense artillery at the entrances of Suva and Lautoka Harbours. In September, the RNZAF also contributed to the island defenses by stationing two long-range flying boats and four land-based patrol aircraft. These aircraft's patrol duties also included the New Hebrides and Tonga. In the opinion of the New Zealand chiefs of staff, they would work in conjunction with the RAAF patrols in the Solomon Islands and New Guinea. Their intention was to create a reconnaissance zone that would cover an arc over 2,500 miles. Although it was a sound plan in theory, the two Dominions were woefully short of aircraft to patrol such a vast area.

By far the largest aerial obligation made by both Dominions prior to Japanese attacks in the Pacific was the air defense of Singapore. This commitment had disastrous results for these Dominion units. Throughout the interwar period the RAF's strategists wanted the Pacific Dominions to take over the fortress's air defenses. With the outbreak of war in Europe, the Australians offered to send four light bomber squadrons equipped with American-built Lockheed Hudsons and two fighter squadrons equipped with Australian-built C.A.C. Wirraways to Singapore in late September 1939. The Australians later reduced this commitment by two light bomber squadrons; the pilots and crews did not arrive at the island until the middle of July 1940. The fighter squadrons traded their Wirraways for American-made Brewster Buffalos already stationed in Singapore. The Australians and New Zealanders replaced the RAF pilots in Singapore who then returned to England and fought in the Battle of Britain. When the personnel from RAAF

Nos. 21 and 453 squadrons and RNZAF No. 488 squadron arrived in Singapore, over 170 Brewster Buffalo fighters awaited their use.

In the winter of 1940, the RAF gave up on the interwar notion of exclusive use of British types. Facing dire shortages of combat aircraft, in January, the British established the Direct Purchase Commission in the United States to obtain American aircraft to help supplement domestic production. Part of this purchase included these fighters. When the Buffalos began to arrive in England in the summer of 1940, the British determined that the ungainly, underpowered, and lightly armed aircraft was inadequate in combat versus the Germans' Bf 109 and Bf 110 fighters. Dismissive of the reports regarding the quality of Japanese aircraft and the skill of Japanese pilots, they decided to ship all of the aircraft to Malaya. The use of the Buffalos left in Singapore resulted in dire consequences for the Dominion pilots.

When Japan attacked Malaya on December 8, 1941, the more experienced Japanese pilots flying the superlative Mitsubishi A6M Zero fighters outclassed Australians and New Zealanders. The Commonwealth forces found themselves in an attrition battle where they suffered heavy losses of aircraft on the ground and in aerial combat. Approximately sixty aircraft were shot down, forty destroyed on the ground, and twenty more destroyed in operational accidents within the first few days of the war in the Pacific. Only ten aircraft managed to reach India and the Dutch East Indies.[9] Like the Dominion air forces in Singapore, the Royal Navy suffered a similar disaster. On December 10, the battlecruiser HMS *Repulse* and battleship *Prince of Wales*, sailing without air cover, were sunk by Japanese aircraft. Within four weeks, even though British imperial ground forces outnumbered the Japanese army, Lt. Gen. Arthur Percival surrendered the 138,000-man Singapore garrison.

The loss of the Singapore fortress and the *Repulse* and *Prince of Wales* represented the failure of Admiral Jellicoe's Fleet to Singapore strategy formulated in 1919. The British military strategist became fixated on Singapore and its role in the overall defense of the Pacific. Even if the Royal Navy sent a fleet as originally envisioned by Jellicoe, it was questionable if it were sizable enough to challenge the entire Japanese Imperial Navy. Likewise, the British Army's leaders considered the fortress so valuable that they placed the Australian 8th Infantry and the 9th and 11th Indian Infantry Divisions in Malaya for Singapore's defense. Similarly, the Royal Air Force also concentrated its squadrons in Singapore. Like the navy, the fate of these imperial air forces represented the failure of the series of interwar air policies devised by Group Captain Arthur Bettington, and Air Vice Marshal John Salmond, and Wing Commander Ralph Cochrane. They too were blinded by the value of the Singapore fortress as the key to the defense of the Pacific. The desire to concentrate these forces here by the RAF seems even more peculiar since air strategists touted air mobility as the cornerstone of RAF policy throughout the 1920s and 1930s. The most serious failure of the policy was miscalculating Japan's military abilities. This ultimately resulted in providing inadequate forces to counter the Japanese threat.

Like all of the allied forces, the RAAF and RNZAF grew to a force strength unimaginable during the interwar period. The RAAF by the end of the war operated sixty-three combat squadrons in the Pacific that included all types of fighter, light and heavy bombers, and transport aircraft. In addition, seventeen RAAF-designated squadrons flew with the RAF Bomber Command, and their crews became the largest contingent of Australians serving in the Northern European Theater during war. Likewise, the RNZAF had thirty-one operational combat squadrons in the Pacific as well as nine RNZAF-designated squadrons in Bomber Command.

The RAF designed their interwar air strategies to help maintain the long-established British foreign policy goals of a balance of power on the European continent and protection of the vital trade routes throughout the empire. The RAF's leaders viewed the broad imperial defense as their best opportunity to expand the service's responsibilities. Britain's military planners had to devise their policies to compensate for the dire economic conditions that Britain and the Dominions experienced throughout the interwar period. Self-imposed economic restrictions created by the Geddes Axe or external influences, particularly relating to the economic dislocation created by the Depression, were the principal economic factors that left very little money to provide any significant funding for the empire's respective militaries. The air services spent the entire interwar period attempting to create a strategy in the face of these considerable restrictions. British air power advocates, such as Trenchard, contended that the new technology of the airplane could provide effective defense economically. But there was little empirical data to support their claims.

The necessity to economize manifested itself in many ways throughout the interwar years. The pursuit of "imperial" standards concerning equipment, pilot training, and aerial tactics became the principal means to achieve these economies. The earliest example was the gift of 100 aircraft to the Dominions. Although these aircraft did not realistically contribute to the defense of the Dominions in 1919, the intention of the gift was to dispose of a glut of military aircraft and encourage Australia and New Zealand to maintain an air force with British equipment.

Another key component of imperial air strategy was the assertion of "air mobility." Parties within the Air Ministry and industry believed that the RAF's involvement in commercial endeavors would improve the air defense of the empire. The intention of this public and private partnership was to establish strategic and commercial air routes as an aerial network to move military assets throughout the empire. The other benefit of this partnership was that the commercial airlines would make available a cadre of pilots and mechanics during times of international crisis. But this, like so many plans espoused by the air advocates, simply did not work. The early airlines could not afford the resources to construct these airports. Also, as time went on, the military and commercial interests directly competed for the few experienced pilots, and the demand for large and modern commercial aircraft absorbed some of the limited manufacturing capacity, thus restricting production of military aircraft.

Successful RAF operations throughout the Middle East from 1919 to 1924 encouraged the Air Ministry assertions that air mobility offered an economical imperial defense. By 1928, air mobility became the cornerstone of Air Marshal Salmond's imperial defense plans. The scheme meddled with the established responsibilities of the British Army for port defense and the Royal Navy for protecting the British Isles and trade routes. Salmond declared that airplanes could cope with these requirements and promoted this strategic model as a means to achieve defense economies while providing protection of the vast empire. Salmond's goals could not be met. The air mobility strategy required an extensive network of strategic airbases that did not exist and the British could not afford to build. In addition, abundant stocks of bombs and ammunition were necessary to have on site to make the aircraft a viable strike force once they arrived on station. Again, these resources did not exist. Finally, the aircraft needed by the RAF were not available and additional money to purchase them was unlikely.

By the end of the 1920s, it was clear that the Geddes economies were having a detrimental impact upon the operational capabilities of the RAF. Even if increased funding were committed to the service, it likely would not have improved its condition. Throughout the interwar period, military service remained unpopular and service in the RAF did not appeal to the public. In Britain and the Dominions, the establishment of a part-time Auxiliary Air Force in Britain and the Citizens Air Force attempted to solve this manpower shortage in an economic manner. As shown, both programs met with only limited success.

As long as the international situation remained calm, the military economies did not seem detrimental to the security of the empire. As Germany, Italy, and Japan began their military preparation and expansions in the 1930s, the effects of economizing and disarmament became evident. The British armed forces were woefully unprepared. The British government understood the danger that these three powers presented but feared the effect of rearmament upon the delicate British economy. By 1934, a new program of rearmament and expansion of the military industrial infrastructure began, but in a more restricted approach than that of the three Axis powers. As they became more aggressive, the British abandoned this restricted approach and intensified their own rearmament program. The government directed preponderance of these resources to the RAF that were seen more as a deterrent rather than an offensive force.

There were unfortunate consequences that resulted from the late emergence of British rearmament. Despite the acceptance of the aerial "Third Option," the British aircraft industry was barely capable of supplying the Royal Air Force. In addition, the focus on European affairs over the Pacific resulted in the two Dominions receiving a lower priority. This was the penalty paid for their desire for greater independence within the imperial system throughout the interwar period. Their continued but unsuccessful efforts to acquire British aircraft and manufacturing capabilities required them to seek the assistance of the United States.

Central to the story of the Royal Air Force during the interwar period is how this infant military service had to fight to maintain its independence and its very existence. The Air Force created by the unification of the Royal Flying Corps and Royal Naval Air Service during the First World War faced a battle against the two senior services to reclaim their air assets. An even more significant challenge to the RAF's future existence was the Exchequer's Office. A constant desire for budget savings made the military and the RAF a favorite target for the budget axe. Air defense of the empire gave the justification for continued independence. The defense of Australia and New Zealand, Britain's most distant imperial partners, was the most daunting test for the fledgling service. To survive, the empire's military air services presented themselves as a viable and economical third option in the defense of Britain's global empire. The imperial air forces had to navigate the political and economic difficulties of the interwar period that forced their leaders to muddle through. During the war they achieved great victories and suffered humiliating defeats, but by the end of the war they were larger and stronger than any prewar strategist could have imagined.

NOTES

Introduction

1. C. D. Coulthard-Clark, *The Third Brother: The Royal Australian Air Force 1921–1939* (Sydney: Allen & Unwin, 1991), 469.
2. http://www.defence.gov.au/RAAF/raafmuseum (accessed 15 March 2007).
3. Leonard Bridgman, ed., *Jane's All the World's Aircraft, 1945–1946* (London: Janes Defence Group, 1946), 43a-44a.
4. Peter Liddle, John Bourne, and Ian Whitehead, eds., *The Great World War, 1914–1945* (New York: HarperCollins, 2001), 207.
5. Ibid., 202.

Chapter 1

1. Baron William Douglas Weir, "Memorandum. On the Postwar Functions of the Air Ministry and Postwar Strengths of the Royal Air Force," 12 December 1918, 1, G.T. 6478, CAB 24/71 (London: Swift, 1979).
2. Winston S. Churchill, "British Military Liabilities," 11 June 1920, p. 2, C.P. 1467, CAB 24/107 (London: Swift, 1979).
3. Air Staff, "Air Staff Memorandum on the World Situation, May 1920, and the Immediate Need for an Air Force Reserve," 15 June 1920, C.P. 1469, CAB 24/107 (London: Swift, 1979).
4. Sir Hugh Trenchard, "Memorandum by the Chief of the Air Staff on Air Power Requirements of the Empire," p. 7, 15 December 1918, G.T. 6477, CAB 24/71 (London: Swift, 1979).

5. Hon. William Hughes, "Australian Monroe Doctrine Speech by the Right Hon. W. Hughes," 1 June 1918, MP1049/1 1918/9/0477, National Archives Australia (hereafter referred to as NAA).
6. Imperial War Cabinet Vol. 47, no. 30 (London: HMSO, December 1918), pp. 6–7.
7. *State Department Papers Relating to the Foreign Relations of the United States* vol. 117 (Washington, DC: U.S. Government Printing Office, 1947), pp. 20–22.
8. L. F. Fitzhardings, "W. M. Hughes and the Treaty of Versailles," *Journal of Commonwealth Political Studies* 5 (July 1967), 136.
9. Peter Spartalis, *The Diplomatic Battles of Billy Hughes* (Sydney, Australia: Hale and Iremongen, 1983), 128.
10. Arthur Berriedale Keith, ed., *Speeches and Documents on the British Dominions 1918–1931* (London: Oxford University Press, 1948), pp. 28–29.
11. M. P. Lissington, *New Zealand and Japan, 1900–1941* (Wellington: New Zealand: P. D. Hasselberg Government Printer, 1972), 38.
12. Monroe Furguson, "Telegram: Commonwealth of Australia to Secretary of State for Colonies," 26 May 1920, C.P. 1339, CAB 24/106 (London: Swift, 1979).
13. Weir, "On the Postwar Functions," 1.
14. Trenchard, "Air Power Requirements of the Empire," 1.
15. Ibid., 4.
16. Ibid.
17. Ibid., 7.
18. Weir, "On the Postwar Functions," 2.
19. Trenchard, "Air Power Requirements of the Empire," 3–10.
20. Ibid., 8–9.
21. "Commercial Aviation in the Light of War Experience," *Flight* 11 (16 January 1919): 84.
22. Major Clive L. Baillieu, "Air Service for Australia—Establishment and Administration of Proposals of Defence Department," 14 January 1919, MP1049/1 1919/0146, NAA.
23. "Council of Defence Meetings," p. 2, 4 November 1918, A9787 2, NAA.
24. Council of Defence, "Minutes of Meetings of Council of Defence, Minutes of Special Meeting (11th) of the Council of Defence," 12 April 1920, MP1049/1 1919/0106, NAA.
25. "Conference Senior Naval, Military, Air Commanders," 18 February 1920, A5954 1209/4, NAA.
26. Ibid.
27. *Flight* 11 (24 April 1919): 548.
28. "Conference Senior Naval, Military, Air Commanders."
29. Trenchard, "Air Power Requirements of the Empire," 3.
30. Captain Arthur V. Bettington, p. 2, June 1919, "Bettington Report," AIR 103 1, Archives New Zealand (hereafter referred to as ANZ).

31. Ibid., 3.
32. Ibid., 2.
33. Ibid., 4.
34. Ibid., 12.
35. Ibid., 3.
36. Ibid., 2.
37. Ibid., 18.
38. Ibid., 19.
39. Ibid., 20.
40. John Edward Bernard Seely, 21 May 1919, "Memoranda: Proposed Transfer of Aeroplanes of the Royal Air Force to Dominion Governments," G.T. 7332, CAB 24/80 (London: Swift, 1979).
41. War Cabinet, 4 June 1919, "Gift of Surplus Aeroplanes and Subsidiary Equipment to Colonial and Dominion Governments," War Cabinet Minute 573, MUN 4/5980, National Archives (hereafter referred to as NA).
42. Council of Defence, 21 June 1919, "Aviation Gift of Aeroplanes: Gift to Australia of 100 Aeroplanes by the British Air Ministry," MP367/1 415/1/1214, NAA.
43. Ibid.
44. Ibid.
45. Ibid.
46. Ibid.
47. Acting Minister of Defence, Russell, Letter to Minister for the Navy, 24 September 1919, "Gift Aeroplanes Presented by British Government," MP1049/1 1919/0190, NAA.
48. Aeroplane Construction Committee, 1918, "Establishment, to Supervise Construction of Aircraft in Australia for Navy and Defence Depts," MP1049/1 1918/0554, NAA.
49. Bettington, "Bettington Report," 19.
50. Ibid.
51. *Flight* 11 (June 19, 1919), 792.
52. Bettington, "Bettington Report," 19.
53. Ibid.
54. Ibid.

Chapter 2

1. Air Staff, Memorandum, the Part of the Air Force of the Future of Imperial Defence, February 1921, "Plans Archives vol. 12, Air Power and Imperial Defence," AIR 9/15, NA.

2. Air Staff, Notes on the Air Forces Required for the Defence of the British Empire and the Estimated Annual Cost, February 1921, "Plans Archives vol. 12, Air Power and Imperial Defence," AIR 9/15, NA.
3. Ibid.
4. Ibid.
5. C. D. Coulthard-Clark, *The Third Brother: The Royal Australian Air Force, 1921–1939* (Sydney, Australia: Allen & Unwin, 1991), 4–7.
6. Air Council, 31 March 1921, "Memorandum for the Prime Minister on the Royal Australian Air Force and the Australian Air Force Policy," A5954 10/5, NAA.
7. Ibid.
8. Ibid.
9. Defence Council, 1922, "Government's Statement in Relation to Defence Policy," MP367/1 549/4/395, NAA.
10. Ibid.
11. Air Staff, "Notes," February 1921.
12. Ibid.
13. Air Board, 21 August 1921, "Copies of Air Board Minutes Nos. 1 to 28," AIR 21 1, ANZ.
14. Ibid.
15. Ibid.
16. British Air Staff, Air Defence and Suggested Lines of Development for Dominion Air Forces, 1921, "Department of Defence Munitions Supply Board," B197/0 1821/1/124, NAA.
17. Ibid.
18. Ibid.
19. Ibid.
20. Ibid.
21. Ibid.
22. "Imperial Meetings 1921: Minutes of Meetings of the Sub-Committees," 5 July 1921, Part II, AIR 8/38, NA.
23. Peter Spartalis, *The Diplomatic Battles of Billy Hughes* (Sydney, Australia: Hale and Iremongen, 1983), 222.
24. Stephen Roskill, *Naval Policy Between the Wars: The Period of Anglo-American Antagonism, 1919–1929* (New York: Walker, 1968), 22.
25. Wm. Roger Louis, *British Strategy in the Far East, 1919–1939* (London: Oxford University Press, 1971), 29.
26. Ibid.
27. Lovell Clark, ed., *Documents on Canadian External Relations* (Ottawa, Canada: Queens Printer, 1967–1980), vol. 3, pp. 162–163.

28. Louis, *British Strategy*, 55.
29. "Imperial Meetings 1921: Notes of Meetings E.1 to E.34, June 20 to August 5, 1921," Part I, AIR 8/38, NA.
30. Ibid.
31. Arthur Berriedale Keith, ed., *Speeches and Documents on the British Dominions, 1918–1931* (London: Oxford University Press, 1948), 56–57.
32. Arthur James, Lord Balfour, Cable to David Lloyd George, 3 December 1921, "Washington Conference on Limitation of Armaments," AIR 5/478, NA; see also Sally Marks, *The Illusion of Peace: International Relations in Europe, 1918–1933* (New York: St. Martin's Press, 1976), 40–42.
33. Eugene Miller, *Strategy at Singapore* (New York: Macmillan, 1942), 8.
34. M. P. Lissington, *New Zealand and Japan, 1900–1941* (Wellington, New Zealand: P. D. Hasselberg Government Printer, 1972), 53.
35. Robert Thorton, "The Semblance of Security: Australia and the Washington Conference, 1921–1922," *Australian Outlook* 32 (April 1978): 83.
36. Ian Nish, *The Anglo-Japanese Alienation 1919–1952* (London: Cambridge University Press, 1982), 8.
37. Air Staff, Cable to Air Marshal Higgins, 3 December 1921, "Washington Conference on Limitation of Armaments," AIR 5/478, NA.
38. Aviation Sub-Committee, Minutes, 14 December 1921, "Washington Conference on Limitation of Armaments," AIR 5/478, NA.
39. Ibid.
40. Arthur James Lord Balfour, Dispatch to David Lloyd George, n.d., "Washington Conference on Limitation of Armaments," AIR 5/478, NA.
41. Aviation Sub-Committee, Minutes.
42. Ibid.
43. Ibid.
44. Air Staff, Memorandum, 16 September 1921, "Dispatch of Royal Air Force Drafts to the East," C.P. 3322, CAB 24/128 (London: Swift, 1979).
45. Air Marshal Hugh Trenchard, Letter to Eric Geddes, "Committee of Expenditure (Geddes) 1921 Memoranda, Cabinet Committee (Churchill) on 'Geddes Report' Notes on the Development of Mechanical Warfare in Relation to Manpower," AIR 8/42, NA.
46. Robert Rhodes James, *The British Revolution: 1880–1939* (New York: Alfred Knopf, 1977), 438–439
47. Andrew MacDonald, "The Geddes Committee and the Formulation of Public Expenditure Policy, 1921–1922," *Historical Journal* 32 (June 1989): 643–674.

Chapter 3

1. Winston S. Churchill, "Committee of National Expenditure (Geddes) 1921: Memoranda, Churchill Report, Air Ministry Comments," AIR 8/42, NA.
2. Committee of Expenditure (Geddes), 1921 Memoranda, "Observations by Committee of National Expenditure," AIR 8/42, NA.
3. Ibid.
4. Winston S. Churchill, "Cabinet Committee Memorandum," "Committee of Expenditure (Geddes) 1921 Memoranda," AIR 8/42, NA.
5. David Chandler, ed., *The Oxford History of the British Army* (Oxford: Oxford University Press, 1994), 263; and Paul Kennedy, *The Rise and Fall of British Naval Mastery* (London: Ashfield Press, 1983), 274.
6. Ibid.
7. Membership of the Air Council: Secretary of State for Air Winston Churchill, Chief of the Air Staff, Sir Hugh Trenchard, Controller General for Civil Aviation, Maj. Gen. Frederick Sykes, Director General for Science and Research, Air Vice Marshal E. L. Ellington, Additional Members, Sir James Stevenson and Rear Admiral Sir C. F. Lambert and Secretary of the Air Ministry, W. F. Nicholson, from H. Montgomery Hyde, *British Air Policy Between the Wars, 1919–1939* (London: Heinemann, 1976), 511.
8. Churchill, "Cabinet Committee Memorandum."
9. Cabinet Committee, February 1922, "Appendices to Report of Cabinet Committee Appointed to Examine Part I of Report of the Geddes Committee on National Expenditure," C.P. 3692A, CAB 24/132 (London: Swift, 1979).
10. Churchill, "Cabinet Committee Memorandum."
11. Ibid.
12. Ibid.
13. Ibid.
14. Cabinet Committee, "Appendices to Report of Cabinet."
15. Cabinet Committee, February 1922, "Report of Committee Appointed to Examine the Report of the Geddes Committee," C.P. 3692, CAB 24/132 (London: Swift, 1979).
16. "The Geddes Report and Air Economies," *Flight* 14 (16 February 1922): 107.
17. Ibid.
18. Ibid.
19. Ibid.
20. Committee of National Expenditure, 63, December 1921, "Interim Report of Committee of National Expenditure," C.P. 3570, CAB 24/131 (London: Swift, 1979).
21. Ibid.

22. Sir David Beatty, 2 February 1922, "Relations between the Navy and the Air Force," C.P. 3700, CAB 24/132 (London: Swift, 1979).
23. Sir Henry Wilson, 10 January 1922, "Expenditure Interim Report: Memorandum by the Secretary of State for War," C.P. 3619, CAB 24/132 (London: Swift, 1979).
24. Ibid.
25. Admiralty, 6 February 1922, "Relations between the Navy and the Air Force, Memorandum by the Admiralty," C.P. 3700, CAB 24/132 (London: Swift, 1979).
26. Ibid.
27. Secretary of State for War Sir Laming Worthington-Evans, 4 February 1922, "Expenditure Interim Report: Alternative to a Ministry of Defence," C.P. 3681, CAB 24/132 (London, Swift, 1979).
28. Admiralty, "Relations between the Navy and the Air Force."
29. Ibid.
30. Committee of Expenditure, 1921 Memoranda.
31. Ibid.
32. Secretary of State for Air Frederick Guest, 11 February 1922, "Reply to Relations between the Navy and the Air Force," C.P. 3736, CAB 24/133 (London: Swift, 1979).
33. Ibid.
34. Ibid.
35. Winston S. Churchill, February 1922, "Report of Committee Appointed to Examine the Report of the Geddes Committee," C.P. 3692, CAB 24/132 (London: Swift, 1979).
36. Ibid.
37. *Flight* 14 (16 February 1922): 110.
38. Royal Australian Air Force Headquarters, 4, 6 April 1922, "Policy Royal Australian Air Force," MP153/20, NAA.
39. Ibid.
40. Ibid.
41. Ibid.
42. Ibid.
43. Tami Davis Biddle, *Rhetoric and Reality in Air Warfare: The Evolution of British and American Ideas about Strategic Bombing, 1914–1945* (Princeton, NJ: Princeton University Press, 2002), 69–128.
44. Eric M. Bergerud, *The Sky on Fire: The Air War in the South Pacific* (Boulder, CO: Westview Press, 2000), 49–93.
45. "In Parliament, Air Power," *Flight* 14 (29 June 1922): 376.
46. *Flight* 14 (7 September 1922): 506.
47. Angus Ross, "Reluctant Dominion or Dutiful Daughter? New Zealand and the Commonwealth in the Inter-War Years," *Journal of Commonwealth Political Studies* 10 (March 1972): 32.

48. Peter M. Sales, "W. M. Hughes and the Chanak Crisis of 1922," *Australian Journal of Politics and History* 17 (December 1971): 393–397.
49. *Flight* 15 (8 February 1923), 74.
50. Ibid.
51. "Air Estimates, 1923–1924," *Flight* 23 (15 March 1923): 146.
52. Committee of Imperial Defence, Ad Hoc Sub-Committee, Minutes, Memoranda and Reports, "Minutes 6 July 1923 Meeting Committee of Imperial Defence Sub Committee of National and Imperial Defence," CAB 16/46 , NA.
53. Ibid.
54. Ibid.
55. "Imperial Conference 1923: Memoranda and Papers," Series Nos. 4 October 1923, E.57 to E.94, E.70, AIR 8/64, NA.
56. "Imperial Conference 1923: Memoranda and Papers," October 1923, E Series Nos. E.57 to E.94, E.70, AIR 5/334, NA.
57. Ibid.
58. John McCarthy, *Australia and Imperial Defence, 1918–1939: A Study in Land, Air, and Sea Power* (St. Lucia, Queensland: University of Queensland Press, 1976), 65.
59. Alan Stephens, *The Royal Australian Air Force* (Melbourne: Oxford University Press, 2001), 36.
60. Ibid.
61. Ibid.
62. "Imperial Conference 1923," AIR 8/64.
63. Ibid.
64. "Imperial Conference 1923," AIR 5/334
65. Ross Ewing and Ross MacPherson, *The History of New Zealand Aviation* (Auckland, New Zealand: Heinemann, 1986), 74–75.
66. Rear Admiral Alan Hotham, November 1923, "Co-operation between Air Forces of Great Britain and New Zealand," AIR 5/597, NA.
67. Air Commodore Steel, 7 November 1923, "Co-operation between Air Forces of Great Britain and New Zealand," AIR 5/597, NA.
68. Hotham, "Co-operation between Air Forces."
69. Ibid.

Chapter 4

1. C. G. Grey, *A History of the Air Ministry* (London: George Allen & Unwin, 1940), 88.
2. Civil Air Transport Committee, p. 1, 1 December 1918, "Reports of the Civil Aerial Transport Committee," box 365, B-10-f, RG38, National Archives and Records Administration (hereafter referred to as NARA).

3. Ibid., 7.
4. Ibid., 17.
5. Ibid., 63.
6. Ibid., 47.
7. Ibid.
8. Hugh Trenchard, Memorandum by the Chief of the Air Staff on Air Power Requirements of the Empire, 9 December 1918, "Committee of Imperial Defence, Separate Air Force, Air Defence, Air Expansion, Cabinet Papers and Notes ca. 1921–1922," AIR 8/6, NA.
9. Civil Air Transport Committee, "Reports," 47.
10. Ibid., 63.
11. Baron William Douglas Weir, 12 December 1918, "Memorandum. On the Postwar Functions of the Air Ministry and Postwar Strength of the Royal Air Force," G.T. 6478, CAB 24/71 (London: Swift, 1979).
12. John Stroud, *Annals of British and Commonwealth Air Transport: 1919–1960* (London: Putnam, 1962), 23.
13. *Flight* 11 (16 January 1919): 63.
14. Sir Frederick Sykes, *From Many Angles: An Autobiography* (London: George Harrap, 1942), 274.
15. Stroud, *Annals*, 25.
16. *Flight* 11 (20 February 1919): 250.
17. Hilary St. George Saunder, *Per Ardua: The Rise of British Air Power, 1911–1939* (New York: Arno, 1962), 297.
18. Sir Ross Smith, *14,000 Miles by Air* (London: Macmillan, 1922), 1.
19. Mead, Under-Secretary of State, Colonial Office to the Secretary of the Air Council, 14 November 1920, "Air Ministry Communiqué No. 418 and Letter," AIR 2/119, NA.
20. *Flight* 12 (1 January 1920): 20.
21. Baron William Douglas Weir, pp. 3–4, 19 April 1920, "Report on Government Assistance for the Development of Civil Aviation," CAB 24/105 (London: Swift, 1979).
22. Ibid., 10.
23. Ibid.
24. "Air Conference Minutes of Proceedings," 13, October 1920, box 98, A-1-q, RG38, NARA.
25. Ibid., 15.
26. Ibid., 15–16.
27. Ibid., 16.
28. Ibid., 28.
29. Ibid., 26.
30. Ibid., 27.

31. Ibid., 98–99.
32. Ibid., 104.
33. Ibid., 106.
34. Sir Frederick Sykes, 1, 14 March 1920, "Aviation and Air Transport," box 103, A-1-q, RG38, NARA.
35. Ibid., 2.
36. Ibid., 6.
37. Civil Air Transport Committee, "Reports," 47.
38. Civil Aviation Advisory Board, 4, "Civil Aviation Advisory Board First Report," box 365, B-10-f, RG38, NARA.
39. Ibid.
40. Ibid.
41. *The West Australian*, August 27, 1926, p. 8.
42. *Imperial Conference 1926 Summary of Proceedings*, National Library of New Zealand, p. 25.
43. CAB 24/249/29, "Scheme for the Carriage of First-Class Mails by Air," National Archives.
44. Leigh Edmonds, "Australia, Britain and the Empire Air Mail Scheme, 1934–1938, *Journal of Transport History*, p. 94.
45. *Flight*, November 8, 1934, p. 1164.
46. Ibid.

Chapter 5

1. "The Commercial Future of Airships," *Flight* 12 (22 April 1920): 455.
2. "Work Done by British and French Airships," 2 September 1918, G.T. 5589, CAB 24/62 (London: Swift, 1979).
3. *Flight* 11 (10 January 1919): 86.
4. James A. Sinclair, *Airships in Peace and War* (London: Rich & Cowan, 1934), 171–174.
5. *Flight* 11 (10 January 1919): 86.
6. Sir Hugh Trenchard, 15 December 1918, Memorandum, "Airpower Requirements of the Empire," G.T. 6477, CAB 24/71 (London: Swift, 1979).
7. Ibid.
8. Ibid.
9. "Transfer of Airship Programme from the Admiralty to the Air Ministry," May 14, 1919, AIR 2/127, NA.
10. Patrick Abbott, *Airship: The Story of the R.34 and the First East-West Crossing of the Atlantic by Air* (New York: Charles Scribner's Sons, 1973), 67–125; see also Ian Bunyan, *R.34: Twice across the Atlantic* (Edinburgh: National Museums of Scotland, 1989).

11. *Flight* 11 (31 July 1919;) 1020.
12. Ibid.
13. Admiralty, 22 August 1919, Memorandum, "Transfer of Airship Programme from the Admiralty to the Air Ministry," AUR 2.127, NA.
14. Christoper Birdwood Thomson, Memorandum: Airship Development, "Airships. Burney Scheme, 1922-1924," Appendix I, AIR 8/60, NA.
15. Admiralty, Memorandum, 22 August 1919.
16. Robin D. S. Higham, *The British Rigid Airship, 1908–1931: A Study in Weapons Policy* (Westport, CT: Greenwood Press, 1975), 188–198.
17. Minutes, September 8, 1919, "Transfer of Airship Programme from the Admiralty to the Air Ministry," AIR 2/127, NA.
18. Ibid.
19. Ibid.
20. Ibid.
21. Commodore E. M. Maitland, "The Commercial Future of Airships," *Flight* 12 (22 April 1920): 455.
22. Thomson, Memorandum, Appendix I.
23. C. G. Grey, *A History of the Air Ministry* (London: George Allen & Unwin, 1940), 91.
24. Winston S. Churchill, 26 June 19, "Disposal of Rigid Airships," C.P. 1565, CAB 24/108 (London: Swift, 1979).
25. Ibid.
26. Ibid.
27. W. F. Nicholson, Letter: Air Council to Admiralty, 20 November 1920, "Policy Regarding Development of Airships 1919," AIR 5/301, NA.
28. W. J. Evans, Letter: Admiralty to Air Ministry, 23 November 1920, "Policy Regarding Development of Airships 1919," AIR 5/301, NA.
29. Ibid.
30. *Flight* 13 (10 March 1921): 164; *Flight* 13 (2 June 1921): 367–368.
31. A. H. Ashbolt, Letter to Australian House of Lords, 20 April 1920, "Papers of the Imperial Communications Committee Regarding Airships," AIR 8/44, NA.
32. Air Ministry, Development of Civil Air Communications within the Empire, "Papers of the Imperial Communications Committee Regarding Airships," AIR 8/44, NA.
33. Ibid.
34. Sinclair, *Airships*, 178–192.
35. Air Ministry, Development.
36. Sir Frederick Sykes, June 1921, "Aviation and Air Transport," box 103, A-1-q, RG38, NARA.
37. Air Ministry, Development.

38. Ibid.
39. Minutes, "Imperial Meetings 1921: Minutes of Meetings of Sub-Committees, Meeting 7," Part II, AIR 8/38, NA.
40. Ibid.
41. Ibid.
42. Higham, *British Rigid Airship*, 210–225.
43. *Flight* 13 (25 August 1921): 566–567.
44. *Flight* 13 (15 December 1921): 822.
45. *Flight* 14 (16 February 1922): 110.
46. Group Captain C. R. Samson, December 1919, "Policy Regarding Development of Airships 1919," AIR 5/301, NA.
47. Ibid.
48. Higham, *British Rigid Airship*, 236–242.
49. Commander C. Dennis Burney, Proposal to Air Ministry, 27 March 1922, "Airships, Burney Scheme, 1922–1924," AIR 8/60, NA.
50. Ibid.
51. Ibid.
52. Robert Stevenson Horne, 12 June 1922, "Commander Burney's Scheme," C.P. 4023, CAB 24/137 (London: Swift, 1979).
53. Winston S. Churchill, 21 June 1922 "The Burney Airship Scheme," C.P. 4053, CAB 24/137 (London: Swift, 1979).
54. Ibid.
55. Sir Frederick Guest, "Memorandum: Scheme for the Development of a Commercial Airship Service, Commander Burney's Proposals for Commercial Airship Service in Relation to the Continental Air Menace," 22 June 1921, AIR 5/574, NA.
56. Ibid.
57. *Flight* 14 (27 July 1922), 429.
58. Sir Hugh Trenchard, Letter to Secretary of State for Air, 8 November 1922, "Airships, Burney Scheme, 1922–1924," AIR 8/60, NA.
59. Sir Hugh Trenchard, Letter to Secretary of State for Air, n.d., "Policy Regarding Development of Airships 1919," AIR 5/301, NA.
60. Admiralty, Memorandum, 10 July 1923, "The Financial Aspect of Schemes for the Development of a Commercial Airship Service," C.P. 436-B, CAB 24/161 (London: Swift, 1979).
61. Sir Samuel Hoare, Memorandum, 10 July 1923, "The Financial Aspect of Schemes for the Development of a Commercial Airship Service," C.P. 436-B, CAB 24/161 (London: Swift, 1979).
62. Sir Samuel Hoare, Memorandum, 2 August 1923, "Papers of the Imperial Communications Committee Regarding Airships," AIR 8/44, NA.
63. *Flight* 15 (25 October 1923): 659.
64. Ramsay MacDonald, Letter, 22 February 1924, box 366, B-10-f, RG38, NARA.

65. Christopher B. Thomson, Memorandum, 11 February 1924, "Airship Development," C.P. 104, CAB 24/165 (London: Swift, 1979).
66. Ibid.
67. *Flight* 16 (22 May 1924): 295.
68. *Flight* 16 (29 May 1924): 348.
69. Sir Samuel Hoare, Memorandum, 11 February 1925, "Airship Development," C.P. 84, CAB 24/171 (London: Swift, 1979).
70. Sir Hugh Trenchard, Note, 15 October 1925, "Questions Arising Out of Lord Haldane's Committee on Airships," AIR 5/381, NA.
71. Admiralty, Memoranda, 18 October 1925, "Questions Arising Out of Lord Haldane's Committee on Airships," AIR 5/381, NA.
72. Sir Hugh Trenchard, Note, AIR 5/381.
73. Ibid.
74. Ibid.
75. Directory of Airship Development, Letter to Group Captain P. F. M. Fellowes, 12 May 1927, "Airship Mission to the Dominions," AIR 5/1053, NA.
76. Ibid.
77. Group Captain P. F. M. Fellowes, "Report of Visit of Airship Mission to Australia," 15 May 1927, AIR 2/305, NA.
78. Ibid.
79. Stanley Bruce, Letter to Group Captain P. F. M. Fellowes, 21 May 1927, "Report of Visit of Airship Mission to Australia," AIR 2/305, NA.
80. Group Captain P. F. M. Fellowes, June 1927, "Report of Visit of Airship Mission to New Zealand," AIR 2/305, NA.
81. Joseph Gordon Coates, Letter to Group Captain P. F. M. Fellowes, 17 June 1927, "Report of Visit of Airship Mission to New Zealand," AIR 2/305, NA.
82. *Flight* 18 (4 March 1926): 130.
83. *Flight* 18 (25 February 1926): 115.
84. John Duggan and Henry Cord Meyer, *Airships in International Affairs, 1890–1940* (New York: Palgrave, 2001), 195–199.
85. Lord Christopher Birdwood Thomson, Letter, 2 October 1930, "Disaster to Airship R.101: Investigation by Sir Bernard Spilsbury," AIR 2/1247, NA.
86. Higham, *British Ridged Airship*, 300–310; also Robert Jackson, *Airships: A Popular History of Dirigibles, Zeppelins, and Blimps* (New York: Doubleday, 1973), 167–178.

Chapter 6

1. *Flight* 17 (19 March 1925): 167.
2. General Earl Cavan, Chief of the Imperial General Staff, 17 January 1924, "Annex I," CAB 53/1, NA.

3. Charles L. Mowat, *Britain between the Wars: 1918–1940* (Chicago: University of Chicago Press, 1955), 178–179.
4. Hilary St. George Saunders, *Per Ardua: The Rise of British Air Power, 1911–1939* (New York: Arno Press, 1972), 311.
5. Air Staff, December 1923, Memorandum on Limitation of Air Armament, "Comments on Proposed Air Staff Memoranda on the Limitation of Armaments," AIR 5/360, NA.
6. Ibid.
7. Ibid.
8. Ibid.
9. Air Vice Marshal Henry Brook-Popham, 6 March 1924, Memorandum to the Secretary, Air Ministry, "Comments on Proposed Air Staff Memoranda on the Limitation of Armaments," AIR 5/360, NA.
10. Air Attaché Report, 18 March 1924, "British Air Force Policy," file 906, box 98, A-1-v, RG38, NARA.
11. *Flight* 16 (28 February 1924): 124.
12. Air Attaché Report, "British Air Force Policy."
13. *Flight* 16 (28 February 1924): 125.
14. Air Attaché Report, "British Air Force Policy."
15. Ibid.
16. Ibid.
17. Ibid.
18. "Air Estimates," *Flight* 16 (13 March 1924): 125.
19. "The Auxiliary Air Force and Air Force Reserve," *Flight* 16 (27 March 1924): 182.
20. Ibid.
21. Secretary of State for the Colonies James Henry Thomas, 14 March 1924, "Memoranda from the Sec. State for Colonies to Dominion PMs," C.P. 187, CAB 24/165 (London: Swift, 1979).
22. Sir Henry William Forster, 14 March 1924, Telegram to Secretary of State for the Colonies James Henry Thomas, "Telegrams from the Dominion Governments," C.P. 178, CAB 24/165 (London: Swift, 1979).
23. Adm. John Jellicoe, 14 March 1924, Telegram to Secretary of State for the Colonies James Henry Thomas, "Telegrams from the Dominion Governments," C.P. 178, CAB 24/165 (London: Swift, 1979).
24. "The British Aviation Mission to the Imperial Japanese Navy," *Flight* 16 (10 April 1924): 209–213.
25. United States Naval Attaché's Office, "Australian Defence Policy, 1924," box 111, A-1-q, RG38, NARA.
26. Air Staff, Australia, Scale of Air Attack on Ports, ca. 1925, "Plans Archive, Dominions' Air Defence and Air Forces: 1925–1939, vol. 26," AIR 9/56, NA.
27. Ibid.

28. Air Staff, Note on Employment of New Zealand Air Force, ca. 1925, "Plans Archive, Dominions' Air Defence and Air Forces: 1925–1939, vol. 26," AIR 9/56, NA.
29. Council of Defence Meeting, Minutes, March 21, 1924, A5954 762/12, NAA.
30. Ibid.
31. United States Naval Attaché's Office, "Australian Defence Policy."
32. *Melbourne Evening Sun*, April 29, 1924, 5.
33. Council of Defence Meeting, March 21, 1924, Minutes.
34. Air Board, June 1924, "RAAF Statement, 1924," A5954 877/8, NAA.
35. Ibid.
36. Ibid.
37. Air Board, December 1924, "Memorandum: Prime Minister on the R.A.A.F.," A5954 10/5, NAA.
38. J. H. Thomas, 30 September 1924, Letter to Air Ministry, "Co-operation between the Air Forces of Great Britain and New Zealand," AIR 5/597, NA.
39. Charles Fergusson, 16 December 1924, Letter to Leo Amery, Secretary of State for the Colonies, "Co-operation between the Air Forces of Great Britain and New Zealand," AIR 5/597, NA.
40. *Flight* 17 (15 January 1925): 28.
41. Stanley Baldwin, 3 April 1925, Annex I: Conclusions of the Committee of Imperial Defence, "Note by the Prime Minister, Naval Policy," C.P. 196, CAB 24/172 (London: Swift, 1979).
42. Austin Chamberlain, 5 January 1925, "Political Outlook in the Far East," C.P. 120, CAB 24/172 (London: Swift, 1979).
43. *Flight* 17 (26 February 1925): 113–115.
44. "Our Air Policy," *Flight* 17 (5 March 1925): 130–131.
45. H. Montgomery Hyde, *British Air Policy between the Wars: 1919–1939* (London: Heinemann Press, 1976), 170.
46. David E. Omissi, *Airpower and Colonial Control: The Royal Air Force 1919–1939* (Manchester, England: Manchester University Press, 1990), 18–38.
47. "Our Air Policy," *Flight* 17 (5 March 1925): 130–131.
48. *Flight* 17 (19 March 1925): 166.
49. Minutes, "16th Meeting, Committee of Imperial Defence, Chiefs of Staff Sub-Committee," National Archives, CAB 53/1, 24 February 1925.
50. Ibid.
51. Ibid.
52. Ibid.
53. Sir Hugh Trenchard, "The Air Defences of Great Britain," *Flight* 17 (7 May 1925): 273–275.
54. Minutes, 3 July 1925, "21st Meeting, Committee of Imperial Defence, Chiefs of Staff Sub-Committee," CAB 53/1, NA.

55. Ibid.
56. Minutes, 23 June 1925, "20th Meeting, Committee of Imperial Defence, Chiefs of Staff Sub-Committee," CAB 53/1, NA.
57. Ibid.
58. Ibid.
59. Minutes, 1 July 1925, "21st Meeting, Committee of Imperial Defence, Chiefs of Staff Sub-Committee," CAB 53/1, NA.
60. Ibid.
61. Air Marshal Sir Hugh Trenchard, 18 September 1925, The Defence of Australia, "Plans Archive, Dominions' Air Defence and Air Forces: 1925–1939, vol. 26," AIR 9/56, NA.
62. Ibid.
63. Ibid.
64. Air Board, 1 July 1925, "Memorandum: Prime Minister on the R.A.A.F.," A5954 10/5, NAA.
65. Chief of the Air Staff Group Captain Richard Williams, 30 November 1925, "Training Pilots for the Citizen Air Force," A705 209/1/25, NAA.
66. Alan Stephens, *The Australian Centenary History of Defence: The Royal Australian Air Force* (Melbourne: Oxford University Press, 2001), 35–36.
67. *Flight* 18 (2 September 1926): 543–544.
68. Air Staff, 11 October 1926, Australia, "Imperial Conference 1926: Notes on Dominion Air Forces," AIR 9/54, NA.
69. Air Staff, 11 October 1926, New Zealand, "Imperial Conference 1926: Notes on Dominion Air Forces," AIR 9/54, NA.
70. Air Marshal Sir Hugh Trenchard, 16 November 1925, Review of Defence Requirements for the Chiefs of Staff Committee, "Plans Archive: Air Power and Imperial Defence vol. 12," AIR 9/15, NA.
71. "Air Estimates 1926–1927," *Flight* 18 (23 February 1926): 112–115.
72. Ibid.
73. Ibid.
74. "Samuel Hoare's Speech," *Flight* 18 (6 May 1926): 276.
75. "Samuel Hoare's Speech," *Flight* 18 (17 June 1926): 374.
76. Maurice Hankey, March 1926, "Report: Imperial Conference (Agenda) Committee," C.P. 124, CAB 24/98 (London: Swift, 1979).
77. Air Marshal Sir Hugh Trenchard, 2 November 1926, "Memorandum: Air Power and Imperial Defence," AIR 8/81, NA.
78. Air Board, "Memorandum: Prime Minister on the R.A.A.F."
79. Committee of Imperial Defence, ca. 1926, "Air Policy: Outline of Questions of Air Policy for Discussion at the Imperial Conference, 1926, Memorandum by the Air Ministry," A5954 1702/16, NAA.

Chapter 7

1. Maj. F. A. de V. Robertson, "Air Defences of the Empire," *Flight* 19 (10 March 1927): 130.
2. "Air Estimates," *Flight* 19 (10 March 1927): 125–126.
3. Ibid.
4. Ibid.
5. Ibid.
6. Ibid.
7. Samuel Hoare, 18 February 1927, "Certain Aspects of the Indian Flight," C.P. 62, CAB 24/185 (London: Swift, 1979).
8. Ibid.
9. Committee of Imperial Defence Overseas Sub-Committee, 12 March 1927, Some General Principles of Imperial Defence, "Imperial Defence General Principles Affecting the Overseas Dominions and Colonies," CAB 21/315, NA.
10. Ibid.
11. Ibid.
12. Ibid.
13. Ibid.
14. Ibid.
15. Air Staff, January 1927, Note, Scale of Ammunitions, Bombs, and Torpedoes Recommended to Maintain for Local Defence in the Dominions, Colonies, and Protectorates, "Plans Archives vol. 12, Air Power and Imperial Defence," AIR 9/15, NA.
16. Ibid.
17. Leo Amery, Secretary of State Colonial Office, April 1927, Letter, "Plans Archives vol. 12, Air Power and Imperial Defence," AIR 9/15, NA.
18. Air Service, ca. 1927, "Memorandum Regarding Air Defence of Australia," A5954 1083/2, NAA.
19. Ibid.
20. Ibid.
21. Anthony J. Watts, *Japanese Warships of World War II* (London: Ian Allan, 1974), 37–40; see also Mark R. Peattie, *Sunburst: The Rise of Japanese Naval Air Power, 1909–1941* (Annapolis, MD: Naval Institute Press, 2001), 228–232.
22. H. T. Lenton, *Navies of the Second World War: British Battleships and Aircraft Carriers* (Garden City, NY: Doubleday, 1972), 92–101.
23. Air Service, "Memorandum."
24. Ibid.
25. Ibid.

26. Chief of the Air Staff (Cochrane), January 1932, Note, "Plans Archives vol. 26, Dominions' Air and Air Forces 1926–1939," AIR 9/56, NA.
27. Gordon Coates, 23 August 1927, Singapore and Naval Defence, "Singapore Defence General File 1923–1927," AIR 455/7/1, ANZ.
28. Anonymous, 23 August 1927, The Singapore Base, "Singapore Defence General File 1923–1927," AIR 455/7/1, ANZ.
29. Sir Samuel Hoare, 17 October 1927, "The Great Cruise," C.P. 246, CAB 24/188 (London: Swift., 1979).
30. "The Great Flying-Boat Cruise," *Flight* 19 (20 October 1927): 730–734.
31. Andrew Boyle, *Trenchard* (London: Collins, 1962), 552.
32. General Staff, 3 November 1927, "The Respective Roles of Aircraft and Fixed Defences in Coast Defence," MP197 1855/1/76, NAA.
33. Ibid.
34. Ibid.
35. Air Staff Map, November 1926, British Air and Trade Routes, Showing Sphere of Potential Influence of Foreign Aircraft, "Memorandum: Air Power and Imperial Defence," AIR 8/81, NA.
36. Mobilization Committee, 29 February 1924, Conclusions of the 4th Meeting of the Committee to Consider Mobilization Requirements, "Departmental Committee to Investigate Problems Regarding Mobilization," AIR 2/229, NA.
37. Minutes, 23 January 1928, "Committee of Imperial Defence, Chiefs of Staff Sub-Committee 64th Meeting," CAB 53/2, NA.
38. Ibid.
39. Ibid.
40. Committee of Imperial Defence, Chiefs of Staff Sub-Committee, 7 March 1928, "Singapore: Scale of Attack and Scale of Defence," C.P. 113, CAB 24/194 (London: Swift, 1979).
41. Ibid.
42. Ibid.
43. Committee of Imperial Defence, 25 June 1928, Imperial Defence Policy 900-B, "Imperial Defence Policy," vol. 2508 RG 25, National Archives of Canada (hereafter referred to as NAC).
44. Ibid.
45. Ibid.
46. Ibid.
47. Minutes, 6 July 1928, "Committee of Imperial Defense, Chiefs of Staff Sub-Committee 73rd Meeting," CAB 53/2, NA.
48. Committee of Imperial Defence, 30 November 1928, "The Defences and Development of the Singapore Naval Base, 329-C," vol. 2508, Series E-7-C, RG25, NAC.
49. Ibid.

50. Defence Committee, 9 August 1928, Naval Board, "Appreciation of War in the Pacific," MP1185/8 1846/4/363, NAA.
51. Ibid.
52. Ibid.
53. Charles G. Grey, *A History of the Air Ministry* (London: George Allen & Unwin, 1940), 203.
54. Air Marshal Sir John M. Salmond, 20 September 1928, "Salmond Report: The Organization, Administration, Training, and General Policy of the Royal Australian Air Force, Part I," MP153/18 NN, NAA.
55. Ibid.
56. Ibid.
57. Ibid.
58. Ibid.
59. Air Marshal Sir John M. Salmond, 20 September 1928, "Salmond Report: The Employment of the Royal Australian Air Force in the Defence of the Commonwealth, Part II," MP153/18 NN, NAA.
60. Ibid.
61. Ibid.
62. Minutes, 13 April 1928, Council of Defence Meeting, "Salmond Report," MP153/18 NN, NAA.
63. Ibid.
64. Ibid.
65. Jeffery Grey, *A Military History of Australia* (Melbourne: Cambridge University Press, 1999), 267–270.
66. Major George Maxted, 6 December 1928, Remarks of Military Board by Air Marshal Sir John M. Salmond, "Salmond Report Parts I and II," MP153/18 NN, NAA.
67. Ibid.
68. Ibid.
69. Ibid.
70. Leo White, *Wingspread: The Pioneering of Aviation in New Zealand* (Auckland, New Zealand: Unity Press, 1941), 179.
71. Air Marshal Sir John Salmond, 17 October 1928, "Report: The Organization, Administration, Training, and General Policy of Development of the New Zealand Air Force, Part I," AIR 103 2, ANZ.
72. Ibid.
73. Ibid.
74. Ibid.
75. Ibid.
76. Ibid.
77. Ibid.

78. Air Marshal Sir John Salmond, 17 October 1928, "Report: The Organization, Administration, Training, and General Policy of Development of the New Zealand Air Force, Part II," AIR 103 2, NAA.
79. Ibid.
80. Ibid.
81. Sir Samuel Hoare, 14 January 1929, "Air Estimates and the Course of Air Expenditure in This Country and Abroad," C.P.4, CAB 24/201 (London: Swift, 1979).
82. Ibid.
83. Minutes, 8 July 1929, "General Meeting of the Council of Defence," A5954 762/18, NAA.
84. Ibid.
85. Ibid.
86. Ibid.
87. John McCarthy, *Australia and Imperial Defence: A Study in Air and Sea Power, 1918–1939* (St. Lucia, Queensland: University of Queensland Press, 1976), 38.
88. Secretary of State for Dominion Affairs Sir Sidney Webb, 11 November 1929, Cablegram, "Royal Australian Air Force General File," A461 C337/1/6 Part 1, NAA.
89. Minutes, 12 November 1929, "General Meeting of the Council of Defence," A5954 908/4, NAA.
90. Air Marshal Sir Hugh Trenchard, November 1929, "Fuller Employment of Air Power in Imperial Defence," AIR 2/1560, NA.
91. Ibid.
92. Ibid.
93. Thomas Shaw, 7 December 1929, "The Fuller Employment of Air Power in Imperial Defence, Note by the Secretary of State for War," C.P. 356, CAB 24/207 (London: Swift, 1979).
94. Ibid.
95. Christopher Birdwood Thomson, 7 December 1929, "The Fuller Employment of Air Power in Imperial Defence, Memorandum by the Secretary of State for Air," C.P. 365, CAB 24/207 (London: Swift, 1979).
96. Ibid.
97. Albert Victor Alexander, 20 December 1929, "The Fuller Employment of Air Power in Imperial Defence, Memorandum by the Secretary of State for Air," C.P. 369, CAB 24/207 (London: Swift, 1979).

Chapter 8

1. Field Marshal Sir George F. Milne, Admiral Frederick L. Field, and Air Marshal John M. Salmond, 29 October 1930, Memoranda to Prime Minister, "Annual Reviews of Imperial Defence Policies," CAB 21/368, NA.
2. Christopher Birdwood Thomson, 5 December 1929, "Proposal to Postpone the Completion of the Royal Air Force Scheme of Expansion for Home Defence Until 1938," C.P. 355, CAB 24/207 (London: Swift, 1979).
3. Ibid.
4. John Laffin, *Swifter Than Eagles: The Biography of Marshal of the Royal Air Force, Sir John Maitland Salmond* (Edinburgh and London: William Blackwood & Sons, 1964), 217.
5. Air Marshal John Salmond, 20 March 1930, "The Disarmament Convention and the Dominions' Sub-Committee of Imperial Defence Set Up to Study Land and Air Disarmament," AIR 2/1571, NA.
6. Minutes, 7 January 1930, "Minutes First Meeting the Committee of Imperial Defence Sub-Committee on the Reduction in Limitation of Armaments," AIR 2/1570, NA.
7. Minutes, 17 January 1930, "Minutes Third Meeting the Committee of Imperial Defence Sub-Committee on the Reduction in Limitation of Armaments," AIR 2/1570, NA.
8. Christopher Birdwood Thomson, 27 March 1930, Letter Secretary of State for Air to Lord Passfield Dominion Office, "Sub Committee of Imperial Defence Set Up to Study Land and Air Disarmament," AIR 2/1571, NA.
9. Ibid.
10. A. E. Green, 4 February 1930, "Memorandum the Minister of Defence Regarding the Determination of the Principles of National Defence and the Relation of the Question to the Imperial Conference, 1930," A5954 841/23, NAA.
11. Ibid.
12. Ibid.
13. "The Scullin Government's Defence Policy," March 1930, A5954 764/33, NAA.
14. Alan Stephens, *The Royal Australian Air Force* (Melbourne. Oxford University Press, 2001), 49.
15. Jeffery Grey, *A Military History of Australia* (Melbourne: Cambridge University Press, 1999), 130.
16. Major General R. Young, Commander N.Z. Military Forces, 1 June 1930, Defence Forces of New Zealand, "Subject Files Papers New Zealand, February 1929 to October 1930," AIR 80 3, ANZ.

17. Flt. Lt. S. Wallingford, "Western Samoa Operations, 1930: Air Report," *Royal Air Force Quarterly* 3, no. 3 (July 1930).
18. Expenditure Charts, October 1930, "Subject Files Papers New Zealand, February 1929 to October 1930," AIR 80 3, ANZ.
19. Wing Commander S. Grant Dalton, Director Air Services, October 1930, Imperial Conference, Appendix 1, "Subject Files Papers New Zealand, February 1929 to October 1930," AIR 80 3, ANZ.
20. Ibid.
21. Ibid.
22. Wing Commander S. Grant Dalton, Director Air Services, "Copies Air Liaison Records," 3 September 1930, AIR 80 7, ANZ.
23. Chief of the Imperial General Staff Sir George Milne, First Sea Lord Admiral Sir Frederick Field, Air Chief Marshal John Salmond, 11 March 1931, "C.I.D., Imperial Defence as Affecting New Zealand," CAB 53/22, NA.
24. Ibid.
25. Flt. Lt. A. Nevill, 3 September 1930, General HQ, New Zealand Military Forces Memorandum for New Zealand Air Liaison Officer London and Air Ministry, "Copies Air Liaison Records," AIR 80 7, ANZ.
26. "Cooperation with the R.N.Z.A.F.," 13 July 1931, A705 208/1/1221, NAA.
27. Field Marshal George Milne, Admiral Frederick Field, and Air Chief John Salmond, Memoranda, 29 October 1930, For the Personal Information of the Prime Minister, "C.I.D. Chiefs of Staff Sub-Committee 94th Meeting," CAB 53/3, NA.
28. Ibid.
29. Philip Snowden, J. H. Scullin, and George W. Forbes, November 1930, Report of a Committee to the Imperial Conference 1930, "The Singapore Base," Series E-7-C, RG25, NAC.
30. Col. C. G. Liddell, War Office, Capt. J. H. D. Cunningham, RN, W.Cdm. R. H. Peck Air Ministry, "Minutes 41st Meeting, Committee of Imperial Defence, Joint Planning Sub-Committee of the Chiefs of Staff Committee," 12 November 1930, CAB 55/1, NA.
31. Snowden et al., Report of a Committee to the Imperial Conference 1930.
32. Ibid.
33. Air Staff, ca. 1930, Notes on Singapore, "Department of Defence Imperial Defence Co-operation. Singapore—the Need for an Imperial Naval Base, 1930," A5954 1024/20, NAA.
34. G. N. Macready, Secretary, 28 July 1930, Overseas Defence Committee, "British Solomon Islands Protectorate, Defence Scheme," A5954, 1739/3, NAA.
35. John Scullin, 1 March 1930, "Dispatch from Prime Minister, Commonwealth of Australia, to Secretary of State for Dominion Affairs," A5954 1739/3, NAA.

36. Ibid.
37. W. J. Hobson, *New Guinea Empire* (Melbourne: Cassell Australia, 1974), 3.
38. James S. Corum, *The Luftwaffe: Creating the Operational Air War, 1918–1940* (Lawrence, KS, University of Kansas Press, 1997), 115.
39. "Minutes Third Meeting the Committee of Imperial Defence Sub Committee on the Reduction in Limitation of Armaments," 17 January 1930, AIR 2/1570, NA.
40. Malcolm Smith, *British Air Strategy between the Wars, 1919–1939* (London: Oxford University Press, 1984), 116.
41. Air Staff, 9 April 1930, Memorandum on Difficulties of Budgetary Limitation, "Sub Committee of Imperial Defence Set Up to Study Land and Air Disarmament," AIR 2/1571, NA.
42. Committee of Imperial Defence, 16 January 1930, Draft Disarmament Convention, "Minutes Second Meeting the Committee of Imperial Defence Sub Committee on the Reduction in Limitation of Armaments," AIR 2/1570, NA.
43. John Davis, *A History of Britain: 1885–1939* (New York: St. Martin's Press, 1999), 195–203.
44. Smith, *British Air Strategy*, 119.
45. Air Staff, ca. 1931, "Air Disarmament," A5954 923/12, NAA.
46. Ibid.
47. S/L H. M. Wrigley, 9 July 1931, Memoranda to PM Scullin, "Draft Disarmament Convention: Air Force Information," A5954 923/4, NAA.
48. Joseph Lyons, pp. 25–26, 4 October 1933, "Budget Speech, 1933–34," A5954 2390/14, NAA.
49. "Minutes, Committee of Imperial Defence, Chiefs of Staff Sub-Committee 95th Meeting," 4 December 1930, CAB 53/3, NA.
50. Ibid.
51. Wm. Roger Louis, *British Strategy in the Far East, 1919–1939* (Oxford: Clarendon Press, 1971), 171–183.
52. Ibid.
53. Maurice Hankey, 25 February 1932, Note to Prime Minister Baldwin, "Annual Reviews of Imperial Defence Policies," CAB 21/368, NA.
54. M. P. Lissington, *New Zealand and Japan 1900–1941* (Wellington, New Zealand: A. R. Shearer, Govt. Printer, 1972), 107; and Bruce S. Bennett, *New Zealand's Moral Foreign Policy, 1935–1939: The Promotion of Collective Security Through the League of Nations* (Wellington, New Zealand: New Zealand Institute of International Affairs, 1988), 7.
55. Chief of the Imperial General Staff Sir George Milne, First Lord of the Admiralty Sir Frederick Field, Air Marshal Sir John Salmond, 30 August 1932, "The Defence of Australia," CAB 53/22, NA.

56. Ibid.
57. Air Staff, 28 May 1931, Notes for Inclusion in the Air Policy Section of the Annual Review of Imperial Defence, 1931, "Annual Reviews of Imperial Defence Policies," CAB 21/368, NA.
58. Ibid.
59. Minutes, 11 November 1931, "Deputy Chiefs of Staff Sub-Committee," CAB 55/3, NA.
60. Ibid.
61. Ibid.
62. Ibid.
63. Maurice Hankey, VAdm F. C. Dreyer, MGen. W. H. Bartholomew, AVM C. S. Burnett, 22 February 1932, "The Situation in the Far East," CAB 53/22, NA.
64. Ibid.
65. Summary, 23 February 1932, "Annual Reviews of Imperial Defence Policies," CAB 21/368, NA.
66. "Minutes, 103rd Meeting of Committee of Imperial Defence, Chiefs of Staff Sub Committee," 2 June 1932, CAB 53/22, NA.
67. Ibid.
68. William ("Billy") Hughes, "Imperial Defence, Military, Land, and Air Forces of British Overseas Dominions," Australia National Archives, A981 DEF340, 5 September 1933.

Chapter 9

1. Sir Philip Sassoon, Under-Secretary of State for Air, "The Air Estimates," *Flight* 26 (18 March 1934): 257.
2. Imperial Defence Policy: Memorandum by the Secretaries of State for War, Air and the First Lord of the Admiralty, 20 April 1934, "Ministerial Discussions on Defence Requirements, 1934, vol. 1," AIR 8/169, NA.
3. Keith Neilson, "The Defence Requirements Sub-Committee, British Strategic Foreign Policy, Neville Chamberlain and the Path to Appeasement," *English Historical Review* 118 (June 2003): 651–655; see also Lars Skalnes, "Grand Strategy and Foreign Economic Policy: British Grand Strategy in the 1930s," *World Politics* 50 (July 1998): 585.
4. Items from the Conclusions of a Meeting of the Cabinet, 30 April 1934, "Ministerial Discussions on Defence Requirements, 1934, vol. 1," AIR 8/169, NA.
5. Items from the Conclusions of a Meeting of the Cabinet, 19 March 1934, "Ministerial Discussions on Defence Requirements, 1934, vol. 1," AIR 8/169, NA.

6. Ibid.
7. Imperial Defence Policy: Memorandum by the Secretaries of State for War, Air and the First Lord of the Admiralty, 20 April 1934, "Ministerial Discussions on Defence Requirements, 1934, vol. 1," AIR 8/169, NA.
8. Ibid.
9. Ibid.
10. Items from the Conclusion of a Meeting of the Cabinet, 19 March 1934.
11. Ibid.
12. Peter Lewis, *The British Fighter since 1912* (London: Putnam, 1979), 224–237.
13. *Flight* 26 (6 December 1934): 1293.
14. Ministerial Committee, Minutes, 3 May 1934, Disarmament Conference 1932, "Ministerial Discussions on Defence, vol. 1," AIR 8/169, NA.
15. Ibid.
16. Ibid.
17. Ibid.
18. Richard Overy and Andrew Wheatcroft, *The Road to War: Origins of World War II* (London: Macmillan, 1989), 318.
19. Stanley Baldwin on Behalf of the Defence Requirements Committee, 27, 31 July 1934, "Defence Requirements Report," C.P. 205(34), CAB 24/250, (London: Swift, 1979).
20. Ministerial Committee, Minutes, 15 May 1934, Disarmament Conference 1932, "Ministerial Discussions on Defence, vol. 1," AIR 8/169, NA.
21. Ibid.
22. Ibid.
23. Ibid.
24. Neilson, Ibid., 663.
25. Summary Brief for the Deputy Chief of the Air Staff, September 1934, "Royal Air Force Expansion Scheme A," AIR 5/1370, NA.
26. Chief of the Air Staff Edward Ellington, Memorandum, Air Defence Requirements for Defence of Great Britain in Relation to German Air Developments, 29 May 1934, "Ministerial Discussions on Defence, vol. 1," AIR 8/169, NA.
27. Minutes, 3 May 1934, Disarmament Conference 1932, Ministerial Committee, "Ministerial Discussions on Defence, vol. 1," AIR 8/169, NA.
28. Ibid.
29. Cabinet, May 1934, Disarmament Conference 1932, Ministerial Committee, Defence Requirements Draft Report, "Ministerial Discussions on Defence, vol. 1," AIR 8/169, NA.
30. Ibid.
31. Ibid.
32. Minutes, 25 June 1934, Disarmament Conference 1932, Ministerial Committee, "Ministerial Discussions on Defence," AIR 8/175, NA.

33. Ibid.
34. Ibid.
35. Minutes, 26 June 1934, Disarmament Conference 1932, Ministerial Committee, "Ministerial Discussions on Defence," AIR 8/175, NA.
36. Minutes, 11 July 1934, Ministerial Committee, "Ministerial Discussions on Defence Requirements, 1934, vol. 2," AIR 8/175, NA.
37. Stanley Baldwin, 11 July 1934, Sub-Committee on the Allocation of Air Forces Report, "Ministerial Discussions on Defence Requirements, 1934, vol. 2," AIR 8/175, NA.
38. Neville Chamberlain, Chancellor of the Exchequer, Notes on the Report by the Defence Requirement Committee, 20 June 1934, "Ministerial Discussions on Defence," AIR 8/175, NA.
39. R. A. C. Parker, *Chamberlain and Appeasement: British Policy and the Coming of the Second World War* (New York: St. Martin's Press, 1993), 93–99.
40. Ibid.
41. Ibid.
42. "Ministerial Discussions on Defence," 25 June 1934.
43. Gen. Jan Smuts, 13 November 1934, British Policy Today, "Air Defence and Air Forces 1926–1939," AIR 9/56, NA.
44. Ibid.
45. P. G. Edwards, *Prime Ministers and Diplomats: The Making of Australian Foreign Policy, 1901–1949* (Melbourne: Oxford University Press, 1983), 90–91; also Itinerary, n.d., "Personal Papers of P.M. Lyons Correspondence 'L' [Sir John Latham]," CP30/3 53, NAA.
46. E. V. Crutchley to Sir Edward Harding, Dominion Office, 15 January 1934, "Defence of Australia," DO 35/182/6, NA.
47. Ibid.
48. Joseph Lyons, ca. 1935, "Speech on the International Outlook and Australian Defence," A5954 841/7, NAA.
49. Ibid.
50. Prime Minister Joseph Lyons, n.d., Extract from the Budget Speech by the Prime Minister of the Commonwealth of Australia, "Defence of Australia," CAB 21/397, NA.
51. Francis K. Mason, *Hawker Aircraft since 1920* (London: Putnam, 1961), 193–195.
52. *Hansards*, 31 July 1934, Australian House of Commons Debate, "Defence of Australia," CAB 21/397, NA.
53. Ibid.
54. Air Staff, 30 July 1934, Notes on the Royal Australian Air Force, "Dominions' Air Defence and Air Forces 1926–1939," AIR 9/56, NA.
55. Ibid.
56. Ibid.

57. Ibid.
58. Minutes, 24 July 1934, 132nd Meeting Chiefs of Staff Sub-Committee, "Committee of Imperial Defence," CAB 53/5, NA.
59. Ibid.
60. W. David McIntyre, *New Zealand Prepares for War* (Christchurch, New Zealand: University of Canterbury Press, 1988), 130–131.
61. "New Zealand Buys British," *Flight* 26 (7 February 1934): 150.
62. John G. Cobbe, Minister of Defence, "New Zealand Permanent Air Force Proposed Change for Designation," National Archives, DO35/325/14, 2 March 1934.
63. Air Staff, 30 July 1934, Notes on the Royal New Zealand Air Force, "Dominions' Air Defence and Air Forces 1926–1939," AIR 9/56, NA.
64. Ibid.
65. Ibid.
66. Ann Trotter, "The Dominions and Imperial Defence: Hankey's Tour in 1934," *Journal of Imperial and Commonwealth History* (2)3 (1974): 318–329.
67. Maurice Hankey, Letter to Archdale Parkhill, Minister of Defence, Australia, 18 November 1934, "Imperial Defence: Defence Schemes, Defences of Australia, Visit by Sir Maurice Hankey," CAB 21/386, NA.
68. Sir Maurice Hankey, 15 November 1934, Report by Sir Maurice Hankey on Certain Aspects of Australian Defence, "Imperial Defence: Defence Schemes Defences of Australia, Visit by Sir Maurice Hankey," CAB 21/386, NA.
69. Ibid.
70. Ibid.
71. Ibid.
72. Ibid.
73. Ibid.
74. Sir Robert Archdale Parkhill, 2 February 1935, "Memorandum for Cabinet by Minister of Defence," CRS A6006 Reel 9, NAA.
75. Sir Richard Williams, *These Air Facts: The Autobiography of Air Marshal Sir Richard Williams* (Canberra, Australia: The Australian War Memorial and the Australian Government Publishing Service, Canberra, 1977), 221.
76. Maurice Hankey, 14 January 1935, Letter to Ramsay MacDonald, "Discussion on Defence of New Zealand and Australia," PREM 1/174, NA.
77. Ibid.
78. Deputy Director Plans to D.C.A.S., 6 February 1935, An Imperial Air Force, "Air Power and Imperial Defence, Plans Archives vol. 12," AIR 9/15, NA.
79. Grey, *A Military History of Australia*, 130.
80. Ibid.
81. Department of Defence (Australia), ca. 1935, Estimates of Expenditure, 1935–36, "Imperial Defence Schemes," CAB 21/397, NA.

82. Air Staff, 27 May 1935, "R.A.A.F. Organisation," A5954 877/5, NAA.
83. Ibid.
84. Department of Defence (Australia), Estimates of Expenditure, 1935–36, "Imperial Defence Schemes."
85. Robert Rhodes James, *The British Revolution, 1880–1939* (New York: Knopf, 1977), 554.
86. W. J. Reader, *Architect of Air Power: The Life of the First Viscount Weir of Eastwood* (London: Collins, 1968), 207–220.
87. Adm. Ernle Chatfield, Gen. A. A. Montgomery Massinger, Air Vice Marshal E. L. Ellington, 29 April 1935, "Committee of Imperial Defence: Annual Review by the Chiefs of Staff Sub-Committee, 1935," vol. 2508, RG 25, NAC.
88. Ibid.
89. Defence Requirements Sub-Committee, 16 July 1935, Summary of Position of Japanese Air Services June 1935, "Chief of the Air Staff Archive, Defence Requirements Committee," AIR 8/195, NA.
90. Ibid.
91. Ibid.
92. Ibid.
93. Chatfield et al., "Annual Review."
94. Ibid.
95. Air Staff, 17 June 1935, Air Requirements for the Defence of Singapore, "Singapore: Second State Defence, Consideration of C.I.D. Joint Overseas and Home Defence Committee," AIR 2/2695, NA.
96. Joint Overseas and Home Defence Committee, 17 June 1935, Singapore Defences, "Singapore: Second State Defence, Consideration of C.I.D. Joint Overseas and Home Defence Committee," AIR 2/2695, NA.
97. Chief of the Air Staff Air Marshal E. L. Ellington, 2 October 1935, Royal Air Force Requirements Additional to the Approved Expansion of First Line Strength for Home Defence, "Chief of the Air Staff Archive, Defence Requirements Committee," AIR 8/195, NA.
98. Robin Higham, *Bases of Air Strategy, Building Airfields for the RAF, 1914–1945* (Shrewsbury, England: Airlife Publishing, 1998), 195.
99. Sqd. Ldr. A. P. W. Laudeip D.D. Plans, 27 June 1935, Note to Deputy Chief of the Air Staff, Revision of Defence Requirements—R.A.F. Needs Additional to Home Defence, "Revision of Defence Requirements, 1935, R.A.F. Requirements," AIR 2/1616, NA.
100. Ian Hamill, *The Strategic Illusion: The Singapore Strategy and Defence of Australia and New Zealand* (Singapore: Singapore University Press, 1981), 216.
101. F. G. Shedden, Secretary, Defence Committee, 19 July 1935, Referencing Committee of Imperial Defence Paper 2490 Paragraph 12 Part 1, "Minutes by Defence Committee Meeting," Reel 9, CRS A6006, NAA.

102. Sir Robert Archdale Parkhill, 4 September 1935, "Memorandum for Cabinet by Minister of Defence," Reel 9, CRS A6006, NAA.
103. *Argus*, 11 November 1935, 1; and *Herald*, 18 November 1935, 1.
104. Minister of Defence Robert A. Parkhill, 20 November 1935, Letter to Chief of Air Staff Richard Williams, "Air Force Policy," A5964 1027/17, NAA.
105. E. V. Crutchley, Letter to Sir Edward Harding, Dominion Office, 3 September 1935, "Defence of Australia," DO 35/182/6, NA.
106. Sir Robert Archdale Parkhill, the Minister for Defence, 2 December 1935, Statement of the Government's Policy Regarding the Defence of Australia, "Defence of Australia," DO 35/182/6, NA.
107. *Flight* 28 (5 March 1936): 266; and "Air Estimates," *Flight* 28 (12 March 1936): 285–287.
108. Archdale Parkhill, Minister for Defence, January 1936, Speech on Australian Civil Aviation, "Imperial Defence Schemes," CAB 21/397, NA.
109. Department of Defence, ca. 1936 Estimates of Expenditure 1936–1937, "Defence of Australia," DO 35/182/6, NA.
110. P. E. Coleman, Secretary to the Air Board, 16 October 1936, Manufacture of Aircraft in Australia, "First Lyons Ministry," Reel 10, CRS A6006, NAA.
111. Geoffrey Whiskard, Office of the High Commissioner for the United Kingdom, 1 October 1936, Letter to Earle Page, M.P., Deputy Prime Minister Cable to Secretary of State for Dominion Affairs, "First Lyons Ministry," Reel 10, CRS A6006, NAA,.
112. Winston Churchill, *The Gathering Storm* (Boston: Houghton Mifflin, 1948), 199–200.
113. Ibid., 200.
114. James, *The British Revolution, 1880 to 1939*, 572; and Charles L. Mowart, *Britain Between the Wars* (Chicago: University of Chicago Press, 1955), 570.
115. Ibid.
116. James, *The British Revolution, 1880 to 1939*, 571.
117. General W. L. H. Sinclair-Burgess, 11 February 1936, Letter to Sir Maurice Hankey, CAB 21/414, NA.
118. Col. Sir Ronald Adam, War Office, Capt. T. S. V. Phillips, R.N., Group Capt. A. T. Harris, Air Ministry, 16 June 1936, Meeting Minutes, "Minutes and Memoranda, Joint Planning Sub-Committee of the Chiefs of Staff Committee," CAB 55/2, NA.
119. Ibid.
120. Air Staff, June 1936, Formation of New Zealand's Air Forces, "Dominions' Air Defence and Air Forces 1926–1939," AIR 9/56, NA.
121. Ibid.
122. Air Staff, 26 November 1936, New Zealand and Imperial Defence, "Dominions' Air Defence and Air Forces 1926–1939 vol. 26," AIR 9/56, NA.

123. W. David McIntyre, *New Zealand Prepares for War* (Christchurch, New Zealand: University of Canterbury Press: 1988), 154–158; and John M. Ross, *Official History of New Zealand in the Second World War, 1939–1945: Royal New Zealand Air Force* (Wellington, New Zealand: R. E. Owen Government Printer, 1955), 24–27.
124. Wing Commander R. A. Cochrane, 26 November 1936, Air Aspects of the Defence Problems of New Zealand, "Report on Air Aspects of Defence Problems," AIR 100 1, NA.
125. Ibid.
126. Ibid.
127. Ibid.

Chapter 10

1. John W. Holmes, ed., *Australia and New Zealand at War* (Toronto: Oxford University Press, 1940), 40.
2. Adm. Ernle Chatfield, Air Marshal E. L. Ellington, Gen. C. J. Deverell, 9 February 1937, "Preparations for War of Great Britain in Relation to Other Powers," C.P. 58, CAB 24/268 (London: Swift, 1979).
3. Sir Thomas Inskip, 1 February 1937, "Progress in Defence Armaments," C.P. 40, CAB 24/267 (London: Swift, 1979).
4. Ibid.
5. "Largest Air Estimates Ever," *Flight* 29 (26 August 1937): 205.
6. Patrick Bishop, *The Fighter Boys: The Battle of Britain, 1940* (London: Penguin Press, 2004), 46–47.
7. Stanley Baldwin, 14 May 1937, Opening Statement, First Meeting, "Imperial Conference 1937 Series Papers E (37) 1-40," AIR 8/220, NA.
8. Sir John Simon, Chancellor of the Exchequer, 25 June 1937, "Defence Expenditure," C.P. 165, CAB 24/70 (London: Swift, 1979).
9. Chiefs of Staff (E. Chatfield, E. L. Ellington, C. J. Deverell), 22 February 1937, Review of Imperial Defence by the Chiefs of Staff Sub-Committee of the Committee of Imperial Defence, "Imperial Conference 1937 E(37) Series Memoranda No. 1-40," AIR 8/220, NA.
10. Ibid.
11. Ibid.
12. Anthony Clayton, *The British Empire as Superpower, 1919–1939* (Athens, GA: University of Georgia Press, 1986), 333–334.
13. Ibid.
14. Ibid.
15. Committee of Imperial Defence, 5 July 1937, "Minutes, the Mediterranean Assumptions to Govern Defensive Preparations," C.P. 183, CAB 24/270 (London: Swift, 1979).

16. Ibid.
17. Ibid.
18. Ian Hamill, *The Strategic Illusion: The Singapore Strategy and the Defence of Australia and New Zealand* (Singapore: Singapore University Press, 1981), 223–224.
19. "Plans for 40 Aircraft," *Sydney Morning Herald*, 9 January 1937.
20. "N.A. 16 Planes, Not Obsolete," *Sydney Morning Herald*, 14 January 1937.
21. Sir Alexander Gore, High Commissioner Australia, 13 January 1937, Telegram to Air Council, "Australian Aircraft Factory, Type of Service Aircraft to Manufacture," AIR 2/1893, NA.
22. Ibid.
23. Sir Geoffrey Whiskard, 21 January 1937, Cypher Message to Dominion Office, "Australian Aircraft Factory, Type of Service Aircraft to Manufacture," AIR 2/1893, NA.
24. Ibid.
25. Sir Harry Batterbee, 27 January 1937, Cypher Message to High Commissioner, "Australian Aircraft Factory, Type of Service Aircraft to Manufacture," AIR 2/1893, NA.
26. "Australia's U.S. Planes," *Daily Herald*, 25 January 1937.
27. Thomas Anthony Swinbourne, Record of Service, "Personnel File, Swinbourne, T. A.," A9300 2002/05090863, 1921–1940, NAA.
28. SqdLdr T. A. Swinbourne, R.A.A.F. Headquarters, 16 March 1937, Letter to Ulex E. Ewart, Australian Liaison Officer, Air Ministry, "Imperial Conference 1937: Preparation Papers by the Air Staff," AIR 2/1898, NA.
29. Ibid.
30. Ibid.
31. Sir Archdale Parkhill, ca. 1937, Speech, "The Imperial Conference 1937: Empire Civil Aviation and Aircraft Manufacture," A5954 860/7, NAA.
32. Ibid.
33. Derek N. James, *Gloster Aircraft since 1917* (London: Putnam, 1971), 218–225.
34. C. H. Barnes, *Bristol Aircraft since 1910* (London: Putnam, 1964), 267–270.
35. Francis K. Mason, *Hawker Aircraft since 1920* (London: Putnam, 1971), 337–340.
36. J. A. Lyons, Prime Minister Australia, 14 May 1937, Opening Statement, First Meeting, "Imperial Conference 1937 Series Papers E (37) 1-40," AIR 8/220, NA.
37. Committee of Imperial Defence, Chiefs of Staff Sub-Committee, 16 March 1937, "201st Meeting Minutes," CAB 53/7, NA.
38. Ibid.; see also Donald Cowie, "The Arming of Australia and New Zealand," *Pacific Affairs* 11 (September 1938): 342.
39. Ibid.

40. Ian C. McGibbon, *Blue Water Rationale: The Naval Defence of New Zealand, 1914–1942* (Wellington, New Zealand: P. D. Hasselberg Government Printer, 1981), 300.
41. W. David McIntyre, *New Zealand Prepares for War* (Christchurch, New Zealand: University of Canterbury Press, 1988), 158.
42. This "Germany First" strategy was later confirmed as Allied policy by the Arcadia Conference held in Washington, D.C. between December 22, 1941, and January 14, 1942. Committee of Imperial Defence, Chiefs of Staff Sub-Committee, 1 June 1937, "209th Meeting Minutes," CAB 53/7, NA.
43. Air Staff, 1 June 1937, Note, "Australian Co-operation in the Defence of Singapore and the Far East," AIR 2/2199, NA.
44. Air Chief Marshal Cyril Newall, 8 January 1938, Letter to AVM R. Williams, "Australian Co-Operation in the Defence of the Far East," AIR 2/2199, NA.
45. AVM R. Williams, 10 March 1938, Letter to Air Chief Marshal Cyril Newall, "Australian Co-Operation in the Defence of the Far East," AIR 2/2199, NA.
46. Air Chief Marshal Cyril Newall, 22 February 1939, Letter to AVM S. J. Goble, "Australian Co-Operation in the Defence of the Far East," AIR 2/2199, NA.
47. Ibid.
48. Committee of Imperial Defence, Chiefs of Staff Sub-Committee, 7 June 1937, "211th Meeting Minutes," CAB 53/7, NA.
49. Air Staff, 11 June 1937, Note for the Information of the Australian and New Zealand Delegations to the Imperial Conference 1937, "Committee of Imperial Defence, Chiefs of Imperial General Staff Minutes and Memoranda," CAB 53/32, NA.
50. Ibid.
51. Committee of Imperial Defence, "211th Meeting."
52. Joseph Lyons, 10 March 1938, Cablegram to Neville Chamberlain, "Imperial Defence," A5954 1023/1, NAA, also CAB 104/18 National Archives,.
53. Neville Chamberlain, 11 March 1938, Cablegram to Lyons, "Imperial Defence," A5954 1023/1, NAA.
54. Ibid.
55. Council of Defence, 24 February 1938, Extracts from Summary of Proceedings, "Estimates 1936/37 and New Programme Proposals," A5954 1029/5, NAA.
56. Ibid.
57. Ibid.
58. Ibid.
59. Council of Defence, 24 February 1938, "Council of Defence Meeting Minutes, 24 February 1938," A9791 21, NAA.

60. Ibid.
61. Joseph Lyons, 13 July 1938, Cablegram to Chamberlain 18 March 1938, "Council of Defence Agenda: Delays in Overseas Delivery of Aircraft, Armament, Ammunition, and Equipment," A9787 63, NAA.
62. Neville Chamberlain, 13 July 1938, Cablegram to Lyons 28 March 1938, "Council of Defence Agenda: Delays in Overseas Delivery of Aircraft, Armament, Ammunition, and Equipment," A9787 63, NAA.
63. Council of Defence, 11 July 1938, "Delays," NAA, A5954 914/8, NAA.
64. Council of Defence, 26 August 1938, Minutes, "Council of Defence Meeting," NAA, A9787 97, NAA.
65. Council of Defence, 31 December 1938, "Air Force Defence Development Programme, 1937/38–1940/41," A9787 102REF, NAA.
66. Ibid.
67. Ibid.
68. Australia, House of Representative Debates (Wednesday, 7 December 1938) Loan Bill (No. 2) 1938 (Mr. Baker).
69. Air Marshal Sir Edward Ellington, ca. 1938, "Report of Marshal of the Royal Air Force, Sir Edward Ellington and Air Board Comments: Australian Air Force," AIR 20/392, NA.
70. Sir Richard Williams, *These Are Facts: The Autobiography of Air Marshal Sir Richard Williams* (Canberra, Australia, Government Publishing Service, 1977), 235–236.
71. Ellington, "Report."
72. Ibid.
73. Williams, *These Are Facts*, 237.
74. Ellington, "Report."
75. Williams, *These Are Facts*, 236.
76. Air Board, ca. 1938, Reply, "Report of Marshal of the Royal Air Force, Sir Edward Ellington and Air Board Comments: Australian Air Force," MP392/11 764/501/60, NAA.
77. Cabinet, ca. 1938, Reply, "Report of Marshal of the Royal Air Force, Sir Edward Ellington and Air Board Comments: Australian Air Force," MP392/11 764/501/60, NAA.
78. Ellington, "Report."
79. Air Board, Reply.
80. Cabinet, Reply.
81. Ellington, "Report."
82. Air Board, Reply.
83. Ellington, "Report."
84. Air Board, Reply.
85. Cabinet, Reply.

86. Joseph Lyons, 16 January 1939, Appendix, "Report of Marshal of the Royal Air Force, Sir Edward Ellington and Air Board Comments: Australian Air Force," MP392/11 764/501/60, NAA.
87. Williams, *These Are Facts*, 244.
88. Maj. Gen. John E. Duigan, Group Captain Ralph Cochrane, and Commodore Henry E. Horan, 27 July 1938, Paper, "Liaison with Australia," Air 101 1 COS 13, ANZ.
89. Ibid.
90. R. G. Neale, ed., "Letter, Mr. M. J. Savage, N.Z. Prime Minister to Mr. J. A. Lyons, Prime Minister," *Documents on Australian Foreign Policy, 1937–1949, vol. 1* (Canberra, Australia: Australian Government Printing Service, 1975), 480.
91. Ibid., vol. 2, pp. 19–20.
92. Col. V. A. H. Sturdee of the Military Board, Wing Commander G. Jones of the Air Board, and Captain E. C. Johnson of the Civil Aviation Department accompanied Colvin. New Zealand's representatives included Prime Minister Savage, Minister of Finance Nash, Minister of Defence Jones, and the military chiefs of staff, Major-General J. E. Duigan, Commander H. E. Horan. British interests were represented by Sir Harry Batterbee, high commissioner of New Zealand, Sir Harry Luke, governor of Fiji and high commissioner of the Western Pacific, Major General P. J. Mackesy, War Office, Air Marshal Sir Arthur Longmore, Air Ministry, 13 April 1939, "Defence Conference Meeting, 1939," AD 1 220/3/14, box 1580, ANZ.
93. McIntyre, *New Zealand Prepares for War*, 212.
94. John M. Ross, *Official History of New Zealand in the Second World War, 1939–1945: Royal New Zealand Air Force* (Wellington, New Zealand: R. E. Owen Government Printer, 1955), 33.
95. R. G. Neale, "Cablegram, A. Eden to R. G. Menzies, 26 September 1939," *Documents on Australian Foreign Policy, 1937–1949, vol. 2, 1939* (Canberra, Australia: Australian Government Printing Service, 1976), 285.
96. Lord Riverdale, November 1939, Office Memorandum, Mission to Canada in Connection with the Dominion Air Training Scheme, "Air Training Scheme: Agreement between the Governments of United Kingdom, Canada, Australia, and New Zealand," AIR 20/340, NA.
97. Ibid.
98. Ibid.
99. Ibid.
100. Sir Maurice Dean quoted by John Terraine, *A Time for Courage: The Royal Air Force in the European War, 1939–1945* (New York: Macmillan, 1985), 257.
101. Ibid., 258.

102. Allen Stephens, *The Australian Centenary of Defence: The Royal Australian Air Force* (Melbourne: Oxford University Press, 2002), 60.
103. John Slessor, Director of Plans, 27 January 1939, Note to Chief of the Air Staff, "Imperial Defence, Additional Assistance by Australia and New Zealand," CAB 21/496, NA.
104. Ibid.
105. Ross, *Official History*, p. 33.
106. Ibid.
107. Tony Holmes, *Hurricane Aces, 1939–1940* (Oxford, England: Osprey, 2004), 6–8.
108. Charles L. Mowat, *Britain Between the Wars* (Chicago: University of Chicago Press, 1955), 627.
109. Ibid.

Epilogue

1. http://www.teara.govt.nz/en/speech/34551/new-zealand-declares-war-on-germany
2. R. G. Neale, ed., "Cablegram Mr. Menzies, Prime Minister to Mr. Bruce, High Commissioner London," *Documents on Australian Foreign Policy 1937–1949 vol. II* (Canberra: Australian Government Publishing Service, 1976), 232.
3. Neale, *Documents on Australian Foreign Policy 1937–1949 vol. II*, p. 251.
4. Ibid.
5. *Documents Relating to New Zealand's Participation in the Second World War 1939–45, Volume I*, "Negotiations Regarding Participation of New Zealand's Armed Forces," p. 19.
6. "RAAF Unit History sheets (Form A50) [Operations Record Book—Forms A50 and A51]) Number 10 Squadron," A9126, 25, NAA.
7. Ibid.; and Alan Stephens, *The Royal Australian Air Force* (Melbourne, Australia: Oxford University Press, 2001), 75–79.
8. David Edgerton, *Britain's War Machine: Weapons, Resources, and Experts in the Second World War* (Oxford, England: Oxford University Press, 2011), 39–40.
9. Owen Thetford, *Aircraft of the Royal Air Force* (London: Putnam, 1988), 129–130.

BIBLIOGRAPHY

Primary Source Documents

Archives of New Zealand

Air 21 Records of the Air Department
Air 80 Records of the Air Department
Air 103 Records of the Air Department
Air 455 Records of the Air Department

National Archives

Air 2 Air Ministry and Ministry of Defence: Registered Files
Air 5 Air Ministry: Air Historical Branch, Papers (Series II)
Air 8 Air Ministry and Ministry of Defence: Department of the Chief of the Air Staff, Registered Files
Air 9 Air Ministry: Directorate of Operations and Intelligence and Directorate of Plans, Registered Files
Cabinet Office CAB16 Committee of Imperial Defence, Ad Hoc Sub-Committees: Minutes, Memoranda and Reports
Cabinet Office CAB21 Cabinet Office and Predecessors: Registered Files (1916 to 1965)
Cabinet Office CAB24 Cabinet Office, Correspondence
Cabinet Office CAB53 Committee of Imperial Defence: Chiefs of Staff Committee, Minutes and Memoranda
Cabinet Office CAB55 Committee of Imperial Defence: Joint Planning Committee: Minutes and Memoranda

Dominion Office DO35 Dominions Office and Commonwealth Relations Office: Original Correspondence
Munitions MUN4 Records of the Ministry of Munitions and successors
Premier's Office PREM 1 Prime Minister's Office: Correspondence and Papers, 1916-1940

National Archives Australia

A461 Prime Minister's Correspondence Files
A705 Royal Australian Air Force Main Correspondence Files from 1922 to 1960
A981 Department of External Affairs Correspondence Files from 1927 to 1942
A9787 Council of Defence Minutes and Agenda Papers
A5954 Sir Frederick Shedden Collection. Records collected by Shedden during his career with the Department of Defence and in researching the history of Australian Defence Policy
A5964 Department of Aviation Registration and Movement Cards for Correspondence Files
A6006 Cabinet Papers
B197 Department of Defence Secret and Confidential Correspondence Files
MP153/20 Military Board Unregistered Papers Relating to Australian Defence
MP367/1 Department of Defence General Correspondence Files
MP1049/1 Navy Office Secret and Confidential Correspondence Files
MP1185/8 Navy Office, Secret and Confidential Correspondence Files

National Archives of Canada

Record Group 25

National Archives and Records Administration

Record Group 38 Office of Naval Intelligence
National Library of New Zealand, 1926 Imperial Conference, Summary of Proceedings

United States Government Printing Office

State Department Papers Relating to the Foreign Relations of the United States vol. 117, Washington, DC: U.S. Government Printing Office, 1947.

Secondary Sources

Books and Unpublished Manuscripts

Abbott, Patrick. *Airship: The Story of the R.34 and the First East-West Crossing of the Atlantic by Air.* New York: Charles Scribner's Sons, 1973.

Barnett, Correlli. *The Collapse of British Power.* New York: Morrow, 1972.

Bennett, John. *The Imperial Gift: British Aeroplanes Which Formed the RAAF in 1921.* Maryborough, Queensland: Banner Books, 1996.

Bergerud, Eric M. *The Sky on Fire: The Air War in the South Pacific.* Boulder, CO: Westview Press, 2000.

Biddle, Tami Davis. *Rhetoric and Reality in Air Warfare: The Evolution of British and American Ideas about Strategic Bombing, 1914–1945.* Princeton, NJ: Princeton University Press, 2002.

Bower, Chaz. *R.A.F. Operations 1918–1938.* London: William Kimber, 1988.

Boyle, Andrew. *Trenchard.* London: Collins, 1962.

Bunyan, Ian. *R34: Twice across the Atlantic.* Edinburgh, Scotland: National Museums of Scotland, 1989.

Chandler, David, ed. *The Oxford History of the British Army.* Oxford: Oxford University Press, 1994.

Clark, Lovell, ed., *Documents on Canadian External Relations.* Ottawa, Canada: Queens Printer, 1967–1980.

Collier, Basil. *A History of Air Power.* New York: Macmillan, 1974.

Coombs, L. F. E. *The Lion Has Wings: The Race to Prepare the R.A.F. for World War II, 1935–1940.* Shrewsbury, England: Airlife Publishing, 1997.

Coulthard-Clark, C. D. *Third Brother: The Royal Australian Air Force, 1921–1939.* Sydney, Australia: Allen & Unwin, 1991.

Cowling, Maurice. *The Impact of Hitler: British Politics and Policy, 1933–1940.* Chicago: University of Chicago Press, 1975.

Davis, John. *A History of Britain: 1885–1939.* New York: St. Martin's Press, 1999.

Duggan, John, and Henry Cord Meyer. *Airships in International Affairs, 1890–1940.* New York: Palgrave, 2001.

Edgerton, David. *Britain's War Machine.* London: Penguin Books, 2012.

Edwards, P. G. *Prime Ministers and Diplomats: The Making of Australian Foreign Policy, 1901–1949.* Melbourne: Oxford University Press, 1983.

Evans, Suzanne Jillian. *The Empire Air Training Scheme: Identity, Empire and Memory.* Melbourne: University of Melbourne Custom Book Centre, 2010.

Ewer, Peter. *Wounded Eagle: The Bombing of Darwin and Australia's Air Defence Scandal.* Sydney: New Holland Press, 2009.

Ewing, Ross, and Ross Macpherson. *The History of New Zealand Aviation.* Auckland, New Zealand: Heinemann, 1986.

Gething, Michael J. *Sky Guardians: Britain's Air Defence, 1918–1993*. London: Arms and Armour Press, 1993.
Golovine, Nicholai N. *Air Strategy*. London: Gale & Polden, 1936.
Golovine, Nicholai N. *Views on Air Defence*. London: Gale & Polden, 1938.
Grey, C. C. *A History of the Air Ministry*. London: George Allen & Unwin, 1940.
Grey, Jeffery. *A Military History of Australia*. Melbourne: Cambridge University Press, 1999.
Groves, Perry R. C. *Our Future in the Air*. London: Hutchinson, 1923.
Groves, Perry R. C. *Behind the Smoke Screen*. London: Faber and Faber, 1933.
Higham, Robin D. S. *The Military Intellectuals in Britain, 1918–1939*. New Brunswick, NJ: Rutgers University Press, 1966.
Higham, Robin D. S. *The British Rigid Airship, 1908–1931: A Study in Weapons Policy*. Westport, CT: Greenwood Press, 1975.
Higham, Robin D. S. *Bases of Air Strategy: Building Airfields for the R.A.F. 1914–1945*. Shrewsbury, England: Airlife Publishing, 1998.
Hoare, Sir Samuel. *Empire of the Air: The Advent of the Air Age, 1922–1929*. London: Collins, 1957.
Hobson, W. J. *New Guinea Empire*. Melbourne: Cassell Australia, 1974.
Hyde, H. Montgomery. *British Air Policy Between the Wars, 1919–1939*. London: Heinemann, 1976.
Jackson, Robert. *Airships: A Popular History of Dirigibles, Zeppelins, and Blimps*. New York: Doubleday, 1973.
James, Robert Rhodes. *The British Revolution: 1880–1939*. New York: Alfred Knopf, 1977.
Johnson, Franklyn Arthur. *Defence by Committee: The British Committee of Imperial Defence, 1885–1959*. London: Oxford University Press, 1960.
Keith, Arthur Berriedale, ed. *Speeches and Documents on the British Dominions 1918–1931*. London: Oxford University Press, 1948.
Kennedy, Paul. *The Rise and Fall of British Naval Mastery*. London: Ashfield Press, 1983.
Kier, Elizabeth. *Imagining War: French and British Military Doctrine Between the Wars*. Princeton, NJ: Princeton University Press, 1997.
Laffin, John. *Swifter Than Eagles: The Biography of Marshal of the Royal Air Force, Sir John Maitland Salmond*. Edinburgh and London: William Blackwood & Sons, 1964.
Lenton, H. T. *Navies of the Second World War: British Battleships and Aircraft Carriers*. Garden City, New York: Doubleday, 1972.
Lewis, Peter. *The British Fighter since 1912*. London: Putnam, 1979.
Lissington, M. P. *New Zealand and Japan, 1900–1941*. Wellington, New Zealand: P. D. Hasselberg Government Printer, 1972.
Louis, Wm. Roger. *British Strategy in the Far East, 1919–1939*. London: Oxford University Press, 1971.

Marks, Sally. *The Illusion of Peace: International Relations in Europe, 1918–1933*. New York: St. Martin's Press, 1976.

Mason, Francis K. *Hawker Aircraft since 1920*. London, Putnam, 1961.

McCarthy, John. *Australia and Imperial Defence, 1918–1939: A Study in Land, Air, and Sea Power*. St. Lucia, Queensland: University of Queensland Press, 1976.

McCarthy, John. *A Last Call of Empire: Australian Aircrew, Britain and the Empire Air Training Scheme*. Canberra, Australia: Australian War Memorial, 1988.

McIntyre, W. David. *New Zealand Prepares for War*. Christchurch, New Zealand: University of Canterbury Press, 1988.

Miller, Eugene. *Strategy at Singapore*. New York: Macmillan, 1942.

Mowat, Charles L. *Britain between the Wars: 1918–1940*. Chicago: University of Chicago Press, 1955.

Neale, R. G., ed. *Documents on Australian Foreign Policy 1937–1949*. Canberra, Australia: Australian Government Publishing Service, 1975.

Nish, Ian. *The Anglo-Japanese Alienation 1919–1952*. London: Cambridge University Press, 1982.

Odgers, George. *The Royal Australian Air Force*. Sydney: Ure Smith, 1965.

Omissi, David E. *Airpower and Colonial Control: The Royal Air Force 1919–1939*. Manchester, England: Manchester University Press, 1990.

Pirie, Gordon. *Air Empire: British Imperial Civil Aviation 1919–1939*. Manchester: Manchester University Press, 2009.

Pollard, Alfred O. *The Royal Air Force: A Concise History*. London: Hutchenson, 1934.

Reader, W. J. *Architect of Air Power: The Life of the First Viscount Weir of Eastwood, 1877–1959*. London: Collins Press, 1968.

Roskill, Stephen. *Naval Policy Between the Wars: The Period of Anglo-American Antagonism, 1919–1929*. New York: Walker, 1968.

Roskill, Stephen. *Hankey: Man of Secrets vol. 2: 1919–1931*. Annapolis, MD: Naval Institute Press, 1972.

Ross, John M. *Official History of New Zealand in the Second World War, 1939–1945: The Royal New Zealand Air Force*. Wellington, New Zealand: R. E. Owen Government Printer, 1955.

Saunders, Hilary St. George. *Per Ardua: The Rise of British Air Power, 1911–1939*. New York: Arno, 1962.

Sinclair, James A. *Airships in Peace and War*. London: Rich & Cowan, 1934.

Slessor, John C. *Air Power and Armies*. London: Oxford University Press, 1936.

Smith, Malcolm. *British Air Strategy between the Wars, 1919–1939*. London: Oxford University Press, 1984.

Smith, Sir Ross. *14,000 Miles by Air*. London: Macmillan, 1922.

Spartalis, Peter. *The Diplomatic Battles of Billy Hughes*. Sydney, Australia: Hale and Iremongen, 1983.

Spencer, Alex M. *A Third Option: Imperial Air Defense and the Pacific Dominions, 1918–1939*. Auburn, AL: Auburn University, 2008.
Stephens, Alan. *The Australian Centenary History of Defence: The Royal Australian Air Force*. Melbourne: Oxford University Press, 2001.
Stephens, Alan. *Power Plus Attitude: Ideas, Strategy and Doctrine of the Royal Australian Air Force, 1921–1991*. Canberra: Royal Australian Air Force Air Power Development Centre, 1992.
Stephens, Alan, ed. *The War in the Air, 1914–1994*. Canberra: Royal Australian Air Force Air Power Development Centre, 1992.
Stroud, John. *Annals of British and Commonwealth Air Transport: 1919–1960*. London: Putnam, 1962.
Sykes, Sir Frederick. *From Many Angles: An Autobiography*. London: George Harrap, 1942.
Sykes, Sir Frederick. *From Many Angles: An Autobiography*. London: George G. Harrap, 1943.
Sykes, Sir Frederick, and Brendan O'Loghlin, eds. *The Decisive Factor: Air Power Doctrine by Air Vice-Marshal H. N. Wrigley*. Canberra, Australia: Australian Government Printing Service, 1990.
Turner, Charles C. *Britain's Air Peril: The Danger of Neglect, Together with Considerations on the Role of the Air Force*. London: Sir Isaac Pitman & Sons, 1933.
Watts, Anthony J. *Japanese Warships of World War II*. London: Ian Allan, 1974.
White, Leo. *Wingspread: The Pioneering of Aviation in New Zealand*. Auckland, New Zealand: Unity Press, 1941.
Williams, Air Marshal Richard. *These Are Facts: The Autobiography of Air Marshal Sir Richard Williams*. Canberra, Australia: Australian War Memorial and Australian Government Publishing Service, 1977.

Journal Articles

Burchall, H. "The Politics of International Air Routes." *Royal Institute of International Affairs* 14, no. 1 (January–February 1935).
Casey, R. G. "Australia in World Affairs." *Royal Institute of International Affairs* 16, no. 5 (September 1937).
Charlton, L. E. O. "Air Power and the Principle of Parity." *Royal Institute of International Affairs* 17, no. 4 (July–August, 1938).
Coulthard-Clark, C. D. "'A Damnable Thing': The 1938 Ellington Report and the Sacking of Australia's Chief of the Air Staff." *Journal of Military History* 54, no. 3 (July 1990).
Cowie, Donald. "The Arming of Australia and New Zealand." *Pacific Affairs* 11, no. 3 (September 1938),

Cruickshank, A. A. "Changing Perspectives of New Zealand's Foreign Policy." *Pacific Affairs* 40, no. 1/2 (Spring–Summer 1967).

Darwin, John. "Imperialism in Decline? Tendencies in British Imperial Policy between the Wars." *Historical Journal* 23, no. 3 (September 1980).

Dinerstein, Herbert S. "The Impact of Air Power on the International Scene, 1933–1940." *Military Affairs* 19, no. 2 (Summer 1955).

Dunbabin, J. P. D. "British Rearmament in the 1930s: A Chronology and Review." *Historical Journal* 18, no. 3 (September 1975).

Edmonds, Leigh. "Australia, Britain and the Empire Air Mail Scheme, 1934–1938." *Journal of Transport History* 20, no. 2 (September 1999).

Eggleston, F. W. "Disarmament and the Pacific." *Pacific Affairs* 3, no. 12 (December 1930).

Ewer, Peter. "A Gentlemen's Club in the Clouds: Reassessing the Empire Air Mail Scheme, 1933–1939." *Journal of Transport History* 28, no. 1 (March 2007).

Ewer, Peter. "Servants of the National Interest? Conservatives and Aviation Policy-Making in the 1930s." *Australian Historical Studies* 38, no. 129 (September 2008).

Fitzhardings, L. F. "W. M. Hughes and the Treaty of Versailles." *Journal of Commonwealth Political Studies* 5, no. 2 (July 1967).

Grattan, C. Hartley. "The British Dominions and the Pacific." *Pacific Affairs* 16, no. 1 (March 1943).

Groves, P. R. C. "The Influence of Aviation on International Relations." *Journal of the Royal Institute of International Affairs* 6, no. 3 (May 1927).

Groves, P. R. C. "The Influence of Aviation on International Relations." *Journal of the Royal Institute of International Affairs* 8, no. 4 (July 1929).

Johnston, Iain E. "The British Commonwealth Air Training Plan and the Shaping of National Identities in the Second World War." *Journal of Imperial and Commonwealth History* 45, no. 5 (December 2014).

Lee, Asher. "Trends in Aerial Defense." *World Politics* 7, no. 2 (January 1955).

Lloyd, Lord George Ambrose. "The Need for the Re-Armament of Great Britain: Its Justification and Scope." *Royal Institute of International Affairs* 15, no. 1 (January–February 1936).

MacDonald, A. "The Geddes Committee and the Formulation of Public Expenditure Policy, 1921–1922." *Historical Journal* 32.

McAuley, James. "Defence and Development in Australian New Guinea." *Pacific Affairs* 23, no. 4 (December 1950).

McCarthy, John. "Air Power and Australian Defence, 1923–1939." *Victorian Historical Magazine* 42, no. 3 (August 1971).

McDonald, Andrew. "The Geddes Committee and the Formulation of Public Expenditure Policy, 1921–1922." *Historical Journal* 32, no. 3 (September 1989),

Menzies, R. G. "Australia's Place in the Empire." *Royal Institute of International Affairs* 14, no. 4 (July–August 1935).

Neilson, Keith. "The Defence Requirements Sub-Committee, British Strategic Foreign Policy, Neville Chamberlain and the Path to Appeasement." *English Historical Review* 118, no. 477 (June 2003).
Peden, G. C. "The Burden of Imperial Defence and the Continental Commitment Reconsidered." *Historical Journal* 27, no. 2 (June 1984).
Ross, Angus. "Reluctant Dominion or Dutiful Daughter? New Zealand and the Commonwealth in the Inter-War Years." *Journal of Commonwealth Political Studies* X, no. 1 (March 1972).
Sales, Peter M. "W. M. Hughes and the Chanak Crisis of 1922." *Australian Journal of Politics and History* XVII, no. 3 (December 1971).
Skalnes, Lars S. "Grand Strategy and Foreign Economic Policy: British Grand Strategy in the 1930s." *World Politics* 50, no. 4 (July 1998).
Soward, F. H. "The Imperial Conference of 1937." *Pacific Affairs* 10, no. 4 (December 1937).
Spencer, Alex M. "Britain's Airship Program: Royal Navy vs. the Royal Air Force after the First World War." *Centennial of Naval Aviation Forum*, American Institute of Aeronautics and Astronautics (September 2011).
Sutch, W. B. "New Zealand and World Affairs." *Royal Institute of International Affairs* 16, no. 5 (September 1937).
Thorton, Robert. "The Semblance of Security: Australia and the Washington Conference, 1921–1922." *Australian Outlook* 32, no. 1 (April 1978).
Trotter, Ann. "The Dominions and Imperial Defence: Hankey's Tour in 1934." *Journal of Imperial and Commonwealth History* 2, no. 3 (1974).
Wimperis, H. E. "Air Power." *Royal Institute of International Affairs* 18, no. 4. (July–August, 1939).

Newspapers and Periodicals

Argus
The Aeroplane
Flight Magazine
Herald
Melbourne Evening Sun
Royal Air Force Quarterly
The Times
The West Australian

INDEX

1 Squadron (Australia Flying Corps, Royal Australian Air Force), 79, 238
3 Squadron (RAAF), 244
8 Squadron, 77
10 Squadron (RAAF), 244-246
21 Squadron, 248
75 (NZ) Squadron, 245-246
120 Squadron, 77
453 Squadron, 246
488 Squadron, 248

Achilles, HMS, 221, 239
Adelaide, Australia, 38, 79, 143
Aerial Navigation Bill, 78
Admiralty, 54, 59-61, 74, 95, 97, 99, 108, 110-111, 161, 187
Air Board (Australian), 24, 32, 39, 126, 205, 230-232
Air Board (British), 74
Air Board (New Zealand), 41, 126, 155, 209
Air Conference (1923), 67
Air Congress, 81, 81, 85
Air Council (Australian), 24, 32, 39-40
Air Council (British), 17, 56, 59, 76-77, 98-99

Air Estimates
   1922, 55, 57
   1923, 67
   1924, 109, 120-121, 128
   1925, 127
   1926-27, 113, 134
   1927-28, 138, 144
   1930, 164
Air Liaison Office, London, 39, 170
Air Ministry, 18, 20, 27, 29, 39, 42-43, 54-55, 57, 60-62, 71-75, 77-79, 81, 83, 87, 95, 97-102, 104-114, 126, 129, 134-136, 138-140, 147-149, 155, 186, 188, 197, 199, 201, 203, 218-220, 232-233, 250-251
Air Service (Australian), 2, 13, 18-19, 21, 31, 253
Air Service (New Zealand), 2, 13, 18, 143, 253
Air Staff (Australian), 40, 142 143, 152, 172, 175, 200, 204
Air Staff (British), 17-19, 30, 37-39, 41-44, 49, 51, 57, 71, 98, 118-119, 123, 125, 128, 134, 136, 141, 143, 146-148, 159, 164, 172, 174-175, 178, 184, 195-196, 203, 209, 223-224

Air Staff (New Zealand), 209-210, 221
Aircraft
    Avro 504, 30-31, 34, 71, 167, 170
    Avro Anson, 227
    Avro Lancaster, 6
    Bristol Beaufort, 227
    Bristol Blenheim, 220
    Bristol F2B Fighter, 30, 34, 71, 155, 167
    Bristol Type 133, 186
    Brewster F2A Buffalo, 248
    Commonwealth Boomerang, 206
    Commonwealth Wirraway, 206, 226, 229-230, 238, 247
    De Havilland D.H. 4, 32, 71
    De Havilland D.H. 9, 30, 34, 71, 125
    De Havilland D.H. 60 Moth, 167, 169, 244
    Gloster Gladiator, 186, 220
    Gloster Grebe, 167
    Handley-Page Halifax, 6
    Hawker Demon, 194, 204, 229-230
    Hawker Fury, 186
    Hawker Hurricane, 186, 217, 220, 246
    Hawker Tomtit, 170
    Lockheed Hudson, 227-228, 238, 247
    Messerschmitt Bf 109, 248
    Messerschmitt Bf 110, 248
    Mitsubishi A6M Zero, 248
    North American NA 16, 205-206, 217-218, 227
    Parnall Panther, 105
    Royal Aircraft Factory S.E.5a, 30-31, 34
    Shorts Stirling, 6
    Shorts Sunderland, 244
    Sopwith Snipe, 30-31, 105
    Supermarine Seagull, 133, 194, 244
    Supermarine Southampton, 144-145
    Supermarine Spitfire, 186, 246
    Supermarine Type 224, 186
    Vickers Vimy, 30, 79-80
    Vickers Vildebeest, 196-197, 199
    Vickers Wellington, 245
    Westland Lysander, 205
    Westland P.V.4, 186
Airship Development Committee, 109
Airships
    Graf Zeppelin, 113
    L59, 94
    R.34, 95-97
    R.36, 98
    R.37, 98
    R.38, 97-98, 103, 105-106
    R.39, 98
    R.40, 98
    L.71, 105
    R.100, 111-114
    R.101, 89, 109, 111-114
Aircraft Construction Committee (Australian), 32
Akagi, IJN, 123-124, 143, 179
Albatross, HMAS, 133
Alexander, First Lord of the Admiralty Albert Victor, 161
Allen, New Zealand Defence Minister Sir James, 16, 24, 28, 33-34
Amagi, IJN, 123
Amery, Sir Leo, 67-68, 108, 141
Anglo-Japanese Naval Alliance, 13, 44-45, 47-48, 52, 183
Argus, HMS, 104
Ashbolt, Alfred H., 100
Auckland, New Zealand,

INDEX

Australia, 1, 4, 5, 7, 12, 13, 14, 15, 16, 19, 21, 22, 23, 24, 2527, 30, 33-34, 38-39, 43, 45-48, 63-65, 79-80, 90, 92, 97-98, 102-103, 105-106, 108, 111, 122, 124-126, 132-133, 135-137, 142-143, 145, 149, 151-153, 156-158, 160, 165-166, 171-173, 175, 179-181, 192-195, 197-200, 203-207, 211, 213, 215, 217-220, 223-226, 228-232, 234-236, 238-239, 242-244, 250, 253
Australia House, 97-98
Australian Army, 21-22, 237
Australian Flying Corps, 20, 79
Auxiliary Air Force (RAF), 121, 133, 1346, 251
Aviation Sub-Committee (Washington Conference), 48-50

Baillieu, Major Clive L., 20
Baldwin, Prime Minister Sir Stanley, 107-108, 110, 118, 126-127, 137, 184, 186, 190, 200, 207, 215
Balfour, Lord Arthur, 47-49
Barstow, George L., 99
Batterbee, Sir Harry, 173, 218
Battle of Britain, 6, 246-247
Beatty, Admiral Sir David, 59-60, 128, 130
Bettington, Group Captain Arthur, 6, 24-28, 33-34, 153, 156, 248
Blamey, Brigadier General, Thomas A., 30
Board of Trade, 74-75
Bockholt, Kapitanleutnant Ludwig, 94
Bomber Command (RAF), 6, 61, 245, 249
Bonar Law, Sir Andrew, 67, 107
Bowden, Eric K., 125
Brabazon, John T.H., 96

Brancker, Major-General Sir Sefton, 83-84, 113
Brisbane, Australia, 38-39, 143
British Army, 2, 7, 26, 56, 121, 135, 160, 249, 251
British Empire, 1, 3, 12, 16, 17, 19, 26, 27, 49, 73, 79, 80, 90-, 93, 94, 96, 108, 129, 135, 139, 160, 165, 181, 192, 213, 214
Brooke-Popham, Air Vice-Marshal Henry, 119
Brook-Popham, Air Marshal Robert, 5, 236
Bruce, Prime Minister Stanley, 48, 112, 125, 149, 152, 157-158
Burney Airship Scheme, 105-110
Burney, Commander C. Dennis, 105-108, 117, 121

Caroline Islands, 14, 16, 45
Casey, Richard G., 219, 242
Cave-Browne-Cave, Group Captain Henry M., 144
Cavendish, Sir Victor, 45
Cecil, Lord Robert, 165, 175
Chamberlain, Austin, 127
Chamberlain, Neville, 184, 186-192, 207, 215-217, 224-227, 238, 241-242, 246
Chanak, Turkey, 66
Chatfield, Admiral Ernle, 84, 184, 221-223
Chaytor, Major General Sir Edward, 41
Christchurch, New Zealand, 28, 112, 134, 153-154, 168
Churchill, Sir Winston, 12, 45, 53, 56-58, 62-63, 77-78, 81, 99, 207, 246
Citizen Air Force (CAF), 23-24, 133, 136, 150-151, 200-201

INDEX

Civil Aerial Transport Committee, 74-77
Civil Aviation Advisory Board, 87
Coates, Prime Minister Joseph Gordon, 112, 144, 155
Cobbe, John G., 199
Cobham, Capt. Alan, 88, 135
Cochrane, Wing Leader Ralph, 209-210, 221-222, 234, 239, 249
Colonial Office, 74
Colvin, Admiral Ragnar, 235, 239
Commercial Aerial Transport Committee, 85
Committee of Defence (Australian), 32
Committee of Imperial Defence (CID), 66, 82-83, 107-108, 111, 127, 134, 139-142, 156, 164, 173, 178, 183, 203, 221, 234
Committee of National Expenditure (Geddes Committee), 51, 54-61
Commonwealth Aircraft Corporation (CAC), 198, 205-206, 218, 225, 227, 229, 238
Conservative Government, 67, 72, 107-108, 121, 126-127, 136, 200
Conservative Party (Tory), 66, 175
Council of Defence (Australian), 21-23, 125, 157-159, 225, 227
Courageous, HMS, 143
Crutchley, E.V., 193, 204
Cunliffe-Lister, Philip, 192, 200-201
Cunningham, Captain Andrew, 178-179

Daimler Air Line, 83, 87
Daladier, Edouard, 241
Darwin, Australia, 1, 4, 18, 124, 143, 226
Davidson, Major General John, 128
Dawes Plan, 118
de Havilland Aircraft Company, 98, 236-237

Defence Committee (Australian), 39, 149, 166, 172
Defence Council (Australian) 40, 125, 152
Defence Requirements Committee (DRC), 184, 188-191, 201
Depression, 2, 157-158, 162-163, 181, 185, 194, 210, 250
Dominion Office, 173, 218
Dreadnought, HMS, 185
Duigan, Major General John E., 234
Dunedin, HMS, 167-168

Eden, Sir Anthony, 190, 236, 242-243
Egypt, 59, 67, 78-79, 82, 220
Ellington, Air Marshal Edward, 184, 188, 195, 203, 222, 224, 229-233, 239
Empire Air Mail Scheme (EAMS), 89-90
Empire Air Training Scheme (EATS), 34, 236-237, 239
Evans, W.J., 99

Fellowes, Group Captain Peregrine F.M., 111-112
Fiji, 234=235, 247
Fleet Air Arm, 62, 134, 186, 188
Fletcher, Sir Lionel, 97
Forbes, Prime Minister George W., 168,170, 176, 199
Forbes-Sempill, Sir John, 85, 123
Foreign Office, 52, 74, 131, 134, 177, 184
Forster, Sir Henry William, 122
Four Power Pact, 47-48
Francis, Josiah, 194
Furguson, Monroe, 16
Furkert, Engineer-in-Chief F.W., 41

INDEX

Gallipoli, 67
Geddes Axe, 54-56, 66-67, 72, 250
Geddes Committee (See Committee for National Expenditure)
Geddes, Sir Eric, 51, 54, 56-57, 59-60, 62, 67, 72, 89-90, 251
Geneva Conference, 164-165, 173-175, 177-178, 180-181, 191, 193
Germany, 2, 11, 13, 15, 47, 93, 117-118, 173, 181-184, 188-192, 197, 207, 211, 213, 215-217, 222, 235, 238, 241-242, 252
Glasgow, Sir William, 152, 157
Goble, Group Captain Stanley J., 157
Gore, Sir Alexander, 218, 220
"Great Cruise", 144-145, 147
Green, Albert, E., 166
Guest, Sir Frederick, 57, 62, 102-103, 108

Haldane, Lord Richard, 111
Hambling Committee, 88
Handley-Page Transport, 87
Hankey, Sir Maurice, 135, 177, 184-187, 195-199. 208, 222
Hawker Aircraft Company, 186, 194, 220
Harding, President Warren, 47
Higgins, Air Vice Marshal Sir John, 49
Hitler, Adolf, 183, 225, 241
Hoare, Sir Samuel, 67-68, 89, 108, 110-112, 119-121, 127-128, 134-135, 138-139, 144, 156, 187-188
Horan, Commodore Henry E., 234
Home Office, 74
Hong Kong, 62, 130-131, 147, 179, 202
Horne, Sir Robert, 54, 106
Hosho, IJN, 123
Hotham, Rear Admiral Alan, 71-72

Howden Air Station, 99
Hughes, Secretary of State Charles Evans, 47
Hughes, Prime Minister William "Billy", 13-15, 31-32, 44-47, 63, 79-80, 102-103, 158, 173, 181, 225-226

Illustrious, HMS, 143
Imperial Air Force, 19-20, 27, 29, 52, 199, 236, 249
Imperial Airways, 73, 87-91
Imperial Conferences
   1919, 51
   1921, 44-45, 100, 102-103
   1923, 54, 67, 69-70, 72, 108, 123, 126, 222
   1926, 89, 135-136, 142, 154, 222
   1930, 114, 164-165, 168, 170-171, 173, 214, 222
   1937, 213-216, 219-223, 226, 235
Imperial General Staff, 4, 19, 60, 117, 138, 145, 168
Imperial German Navy, 11, 13
Imperial Aircraft Gift, 29-34, 41, 125, 250
Imperial Japanese Navy, 1, 124, 216
Imperial War Cabinet, 14, 18, 29
India, 63, 67, 79, 82, 97, 104-106, 114, 131, 138-139, 144, 147-148, 156, 177, 181, 198, 215, 248
Inniskilling Fusiliers, 128
Inskip, Sir Thomas, 207, 214, 222
Institute of Transport, 101
Instone Air Lines, 83, 87
Instone, Samuel, 83
Iraq, 51, 67, 79, 86, 128, 141, 148-149, 156, 220
Italy, 2, 171, 174, 176, 181-182, 184, 191, 208, 213, 215-217, 252

INDEX

Japan, 2, 4, 11-14, 16, 18, 25-26, 37-38, 45-48, 62, 65, 123, 130-131, 134, 147, 149, 171-173, 177-183, 187-191, 193, 196, 202-203, 208, 211, 215-217, 222, 226, 238, 242, 247-249, 252
Japanese Army Air Force, 1, 202
Japanese Naval Air Service, 142, 200, 202
Jellicoe, Admiral John, 5-6, 16, 63, 122, 192, 248-249
Joynson-Hicks, Sir William, 66, 82-83

Kain, Pilot Officer Edgar James "Cobber", 237
Kaga, IJN, 123-124, 143, 179
Kellogg-Briand Pact, 137
Kenworthy, Joseph Montague, 96
Kerr, Rear Admiral William M., 158
Kohimarama Flying School, New Zealand, 29, 41

Labour Government, 72, 109-110, 117-121, 123, 126-127, 136, 162, 174, 181
Labor Party (Australia), 158, 166, 276-177, 228, 242
Labour Party, 96, 109, 118-121, 156, 163, 171, 175
Lambert, Lord Cavan Frederick Rudolph, 129-130
Latham, Sir John, 180, 193
Leach, William, 119-121
League of Nations, 15-16, 33, 118, 123, 134, 162, 164, 173, 177, 178, 183, 189, 193
Leander, HMS, 221, 239
Legge, Major General John G., 21
Lexington, USS, 143
Liberal Party, 109, 156, 163, 175

Liberal Party (New Zealand), 176
Lloyd George, Prime Minister David, 15, 31, 44, 47, 50-51, 54, 66, 74, 107
Locarno Pact (Treaty), 134, 137, 162, 213
Lockheed Aircraft Company, 227
London Naval Treaty, 171
Londonderry, Lord (Charles Vane-Tempest-Stewart), 175, 184-189, 200
Ludlow-Hewitt, Capt. Edgar, 61
Lyons, Prime Minister Joseph, 176, 193-194, 198, 206, 220, 225-227, 229-230, 232-234

MacDonald, Prime Minister Ramsey, 72, 109-110, 117-120, 122, 136, 162-163, 166, 171-172, 174-175, 184, 200
Macquire, Lieutenant Colonel H., 30-31
Manchurian Crisis, 172, 177-178, 180, 190
Mandates, 12, 15-16, 48, 167, 249
Marshall Islands, 14, 16, 45, 247
Massey, Prime Minister William Ferguson, 41, 45-46, 102
Meighen, Prime Minister Arthur, 46
Melbourne, Australia, 38-39, 64-65, 88, 112, 143, 196, 218
Menzies, Prime Minister Robert, 234, 236, 242
Mitchell, Reginald, 186
Mitchell, Gen. William "Billy", 42
Monash, Sir John, 158

Nationalist Party (Australia), 158, 176
Netherlands East Indies (Dutch), 90, 147, 203, 216, 248
New Guinea, 14, 16, 235, 247

INDEX

New Zealand, 1, 3-5, 7, 12-13, 16, 24-27, 29, 33-34, 41, 45, 47-48, 63, 65, 71-72, 79, 97, 102-104, 111-112, 122-126, 134, 142-144, 149, 153-156, 167-168, 170-171, 176, 179, 192, 195-197, 199, 203, 208-209, 211, 231, 215-217, 221-224, 234-239, 242, 245, 247, 250, 253

New Zealand Air Force (NZAF), 71, 156

New Zealand Permanent Air Force (NZPAF), 71, 151, 153, 155-156, 167-170, 176, 196

New Zealand Territorial Air Force (NZTAF), 201

Newall, Air Chief Marshal Cyril, 223

Nicholson, Walter F., 72, 99

No. 1 Flying Training School, 39

No. 1 Aircraft Depot, 39

No. 1 Composite Squadron (RAAF), 133

No. 3 Composite Squadron (RAAF), 133

No. 101 Squadron (RAAF), 133

Ostfriesland, 151

Pacific Monroe Doctrine, 14

Parkhill, Robert Archdale, 198, 203-204, 217-218, 222, 224, 233

Pearce, Sir George, 30, 32, 199

Percival, Lieutenant General, Arthur, 248

Pick, Frank, 74-75, 78, 82

Point Cook Air Field (Australia), 39, 64, 133, 150, 231, 243

Portal, Group Captain Charles, 178-179

Prince of Wales, HMS, 5, 248

QANTAS, 90, 198

Report of National Expenditure, 58

Repulse, HMS, 5, 248

Richardson, Brigadier General George S., 41

Richmond, New South Wales

Royal Australian Air Force (RAAF), 1, 3, 4, 7, 21-22, 31, 39, 40, 41, 51, 63, 64, 65, 69, 125, 126, 132, 133, 136, 142, 149, 150, 151, 156, 157, 158, 159, 166, 176, 195, 197, 198, 199, 200, 201, 204, 205, 207, 217, 219, 220, 223, 224, 225, 227, 228, 229, 230, 231, 232, 233, 238, 239, 243, 244, 245, 246, 247, 243-253

Royal Air Force (RAF), 3-7, 11, 16-19, 21, 24, 29-30, 37, 39, 44, 51—59, 61-63, 65-69, 71-74, 79-88, 90, 94-95, 99, 107, 10*-111, 119-121, 124, 126-129, 131, 134-136, 138-139, 141, 144-145, 147-149, 154-161, 164, 168, 170, 174-175, 178-179, 184-188, 195, 197, 199-201, 203-204, 206-207, 211, 214-17, 219, 223-224, 230, 232-233, 237-239, 249

Royal Australian Navy, 19, 21-22, 158, 239

Royal Flying Corps, 17, 252

Royal Naval Air Service, 17, 62, 252

Royal New Zealand Air Force (RNZAF), 3, 4, 5, 134, 196-197, 199, 201, 209, 237, 239, 245-249

Royal Navy, 2, 5, 7, 11, 13, 19, 26, 43-44, 52, 55-56, 61-63, 84, 94, 99, 110, 121, 136, 145, 160, 180, 221-222, 235, 243, 248-249, 251

Royal New Zealand Air Force (RNZAF), 3, 5, 134, 196-197, 199, 201, 209, 237, 239, 245-249

Ryujo, IJN, 179

Salmond, Air Marshal John M., 137, 149-157, 163-164, 168, 171, 176, 197-198, 209, 239, 249, 251
Salmond, Sir John William, 48
Salmond Report (Plan), 152, 156, 194, 199, 210, 220
Samoa, 14, 164, 168-169
Samson, Group Captain Charles R., 104-105
Saratoga, USS, 143
Sassoon, Sir Philip, 89, 183, 214
Savage, Prime Minister Michael J., 208, 221-222, 234-237, 241-242
Scullin, Prime Minister James, 158-159, 166, 175-176, 194
Seely, Major General John Edward Bernard, 29, 66, 97, 120 q
Shaw, Thoms, 161
Shadow Factory Scheme, 201, 214, 239
Shedden, Frederick, 229
Simon, John, 184, 186, 188-189, 192
Sinclair-Burgess, General, William, 208
Singapore, 5, 62-63, 90, 117, 122-123, 127, 129-131, 144-145, 147-148, 155, 171-172, 178-179, 192, 195, 198, 202-203, 208, 215-217, 222-224, 235, 238, 242, 247-249
Smith, Keith, 79-80
Smith, Capt. Ross, 79-80
Smuts, Prime Minister Jan, 15-16, 46-47, 192-193
Sockburn Flying School, New Zealand, 25, 29, 41
Solomon Islands, 3, 172-173, 235, 247
South Africa, 79-80, 97, 103-104, 137-138, 144, 160
Spooner, Stanley, 33, 100
Statute of Westminster, 165
Steel, Air Commodore John N., 71

Sudan, 79-80, 141, 156
Swinbourne, Squadron Leader Thomas A., 219-220
Sydney, Australia, 38-39, 65, 90, 112, 143, 150, 166, 198, 218
Sykes, Major General Sir Frederick, 20, 78, 81-83, 85, 94, 101

Tanaka, Lieutenant-General Kunishigi, 48
Ten Year Rule, 55, 179-180, 184
Thomas, James Henry, 121-122, 190
Thomson, Lord Christopher Birdwood, 109, 113-114, 161, 164-165
Thorby, Harold, 225
Treasury, Department of, 54, 99, 138, 161, 184
Trenchard, Air Marshal Sir Hugh, 6-7, 12-13, 17-19, 24-25, 27, 29, 49, 51, 57, 71-72, 76, 78, 81, 84, 86, 94-96, 107-108, 110-111, 128-132, 134-135, 145, 147-148. 159-161, 164, 235, 250

United Australia Party (UAP), 176, 234
United States Army Air Forces, 3

Versailles Conference, 14-16, 77, 173, 247
Vickers Ltd., 98, 101, 105-106, 110
Vyvyan, Vice Air Marshal Arthur V., 104-105

Wallingford, Flight Lieutenant Sidney, 167
War Office, 54, 59-60
Ward, Prime Minister Joseph, 168
Washington Naval Conference (Treaty), 47-48, 50, 52-53, 64, 118, 123-124, 130-131, 142, 149, 176

Webb, Sidney, 158-159
Weir, Lord William Douglas, 11, 17, 73, 76-77, 81, 85, 201
Whiskard, Sir Geoffrey, 218
Wigram Aerodrome, 153, 168
Wigram, Sir Henry, 25
Williams, Air Marshal Richard "Dicky", 40, 159, 204, 219, 223, 226, 229, 232-233
Williams, Commander T.A., 41
Wilson, President Woodrow, 14-15
Wilson, Field Marshal Henry, 60
World War I, 1, 7, 11, 25, 73, 142, 155, 158, 160, 167
World War II, 4, 6, 61-62, 66, 71, 123, 143, 172
Worthington-Evans, Sir Laming, 60

ABOUT THE AUTHOR

Alex M Spencer earned his PhD in modern European history from Auburn University. His research focuses on British and Commonwealth military aviation during the twentieth century. He curates two collections at the National Air and Space Museum: British and European military aircraft and flight materiel. Together they include the Supermarine Spitfire, Hawker Hurricane, de Havilland Mosquito, Messerschmitt Bf 109 and Me 262, Heinkel He 219, Arado Ar 234, and over sixteen thousand artifacts of personal items, including uniforms, flight clothing, memorabilia, ribbons, and medals. Spencer was the coeditor of *Smithsonian National Air and Space Museum: An Autobiography*.

www.ingramcontent.com/pod-product-compliance
Lightning Source LLC
Chambersburg PA
CBHW061429300426
44114CB00014B/1602